AN INTERFACE WITH STRESS: CAUSES AND PREVENTIONS

AN INTERFACE WITH STRESS:
CAUSES AND PREVENTIONS

Ambalika Sinha

TM

Prints Publications Pvt Ltd
New Delhi

Published by

Prints Publications Pvt Ltd
Viraj Tower-2, 4259/3, Ansari Road,
Darya Ganj, New Delhi-110002
Tel. : +91-11-45355555
Fax: +91-11-23275542
E-mail : contact@printspublications.com
Website : www.printspublications.com

First Edition : 2022 (Hardbound)

ISBN: 978-81-948490-5-6

Price: ₹ 1495/-

Published and Printed by Mr. Pranav Gupta (Director) on behalf of Prints Publications Pvt Ltd, New Delhi.

CONTENTS

PREFACE

It is a matter of great pleasure to present this book entitled "An Interface With Stress : Causes and Preventions" to the readers who want to comprehend the basic concepts, theories, and various coping strategies of stress management. It is an humble attempt to cover major areas of stress and it's reduction strategies.

'An Interface With Stress : Causes and Preventions' may be useful to post-graduate students, doctoral students, other readers who desire to know about various stress areas and also want to be aware of variables which lead to stress occurrences. They may also get information about various approaches to overcoming stress.

The book may also be useful for heath clinics, sports arena, as stress encountered by the patients and players are of various types and they do need some information for dealing with stress.

The book comprises of nineteen chapters. The first two chapters deal with concepts and theories related to stress. Chapters three and four deal with physiological and psychological elements in stress. Chapters five, six and seven are about family stress, social stress and children under stress.

Chapter eight is all about age related stress. Personality and its relation to stress are discussed in chapter nine. Next two chapters deal in environmental stressors and victims of stress.

Chapter twelve deals with stresses in organization. Chapter thirteen deals with health and stress emphasizing nutrition requirement in various age groups and exercises which one should perform to be free from impact of health problems.

Chapter fourteen and fifteen deal with various stress management exercises and time management with stress.

Chapter sixteen, seventeen and eighteen deal with various techniques of dealing with stress giving emphasis on common man de-stressors and the last chapter deals with death, thus concluding stress.

The salient features of this book include the following :

* The subject matter has been presented in simple language and examples are mostly from indigenous areas, all can grasp it easily, students as well as general public.

* The book may be useful in health clinics, sports institutes, as well as in homes where people suffering from many ailments exist.

* Use of diagrams, tables, boxes have been made to illustrate the important topics.

* May help professionals in the areas of stress.

I have received continuous inspirations from large number of individuals and well wishers in bringing out this book. In particular I wish to acknowledge the following persons for providing me suggestions, tips, and advice in writing this book, viz : Dr. R. K. Naidu(my guide, Retired Prof, Psychology Deptt, Allahabad University, Allahabad.), Dr. Rashmi Kumar (Prof, Psychology Deptt, Allahabad University, Allahabad.), Dr Namita Pandey, (Prof., Deptt of Psychology, Allahabad University, Allahabad.), Dr. Anjali Srivastava(Prof. Psychology Deptt, A. P. S. Univ, Rewa). I also acknowledge help provided to me from my research scholars Ms Raj Laxmi Srivastava and Mr. Tarun Dhingra.

In no small measures I am grateful to my publishers for extending all the assistance in bringing about this book. Comments from readers, viewers will be highly welcomed.

Ambalika Sinha

Chapter 1

WHAT IS STRESS ?

1.1 STRESS

Stress has become a major concern of the modern times as it can cause harm to persons' health and performance. In simple words, stress refers to pressures or tensions people feel in life. As living human makes constant demands, so it produces pressure *i.e.*, stress. Stress, is therefore, a natural and unavoidable feature of human life (Chhabra, 2001). However, stress beyond a particular level can cause psychological and physiological problems which in turn would affect the individuals' performance.

Selyes has defined stress as "the non-specific response of the body to any demand made upon it." R. S. Schuler viewed stress as a dynamic condition in which an individual is confronted with an opportunity, constraint or demand related to what he desires and for which the outcome is perceived to be both uncertain and important. Thus, when a student takes entrance test for engineering, he feels stress because he has to confront opportunities, constraints and demands. A good ranking may decide his career path, which in turn may lead to better status, earning and reward in future.

Definition of Stress

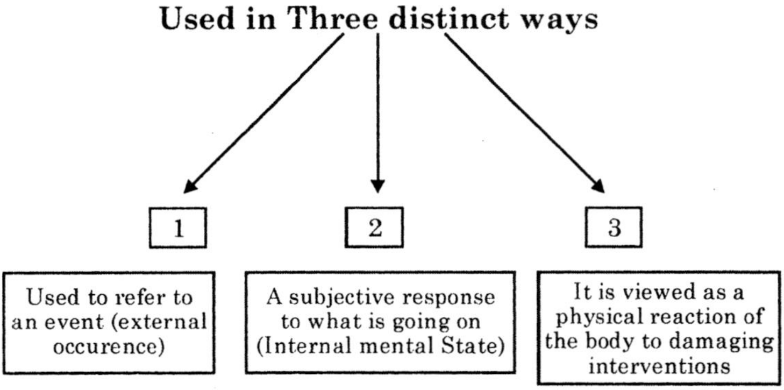

Stress : A Question : Is there a man on earth who has never encountered stress? Man lives life full, *i.e.*, he passes through happy phases, comfortable phases, sad phases and uncomfortable phases. All these are part and parcel of one's life. No one can say that he has had a full life if he has faced no ups and downs. Both are significant facts of one's life.

Stress : Life Cycles : A new born baby feels tensed up when he is hungry and yells as loud as he can, until the cause of tension is removed. This starts his life with all colours. Parents feel stressed at all steps of the development of their children. If a baby sleeps for a long time without yelling parents feel uncomfortable that why is the child not making any demand by crying. They want him to feel stress (though a minor one) before they can respond to him.

As the child grows up step by step, every step is a cause of tension for parents, if baby doesn't eat properly, drink rightly, sleep properly etc, than they feel stressed, if he doesn't walk and crawl at the right time, sit at the right time, then also it is a cause of tension. As schooling starts, stresses are felt by parents regarding his admission, his performance, his position in class, extra curricular activities, etc. As child reaches teenage, parents are stressed by whether he has the right amount of caliber for the right type of profession, they are stressed by reservation policies and their effect on their children's jobs and careers.

Once child gets fixed in some training programmes or jobs, parents start worrying about his complete future. This stress cycle does not end with parents. It becomes part of their child who also feels the tremors of life stresses. This depicts to some extent the life of stress.

For parents their child's marriage, job, children, family, old-age problems, sickness, home caring etc. all lead to stresses, some mild some strong, nevertheless they feel stressful.

1.2 STRESSFUL EVENTS FROM LOWEST TO HIGHEST MAGNITUDE AND THE COPING STRATEGIES

Stress Event 1 : There was one book in the library for which ten students raced to get hold of it. Outcome was that whoever got it, read it in the library and hid it in insignificant sections where others could not reach. This was a cause of tension for the others. Lot of antagonism developed, and they stopped interacting. The teacher intervened and tried to solve the problem and ultimately came up with the suggestion of putting the book at the photocopying section and telling all the boys to get photocopies of all the chapters which they wanted. This solved their problem and they became friendly again.

Stress Event 2 : Sharmaji bought a second hand car for Rs. 1 lakh with the help of loan from his Provident Fund. Every month Rs. 3000 were deducted from the salary for loan payment. Every month he had to spend at least Rs 2000 in maintaining the car and petrol. This created a big dent in his salary and it became difficult for him to maintain his other home affairs. He gradually became very unhappy, pensive, and started getting irritated, later his blood pressure also started showing a higher level. Gradually, he became so stressed that the sight of his car in the garage made him sick. His wife saw and understood his condition. As Sharmaji had bought the car because of his desire for it he could not even utter a word against it. Mrs. Sharma talked about his condition to his sister and brother. Brother sent a buyer to Mr. Sharma who offered him Rs. 1. 25 lakhs for the car. First he refused to sell it, but then his wife requested him to sell it, and use the money for the payment of his loan, somehow he saw a bright beam in this idea and sold his car. He appeared greatly relieved and his blood pressure also became normal.

Stress Event 3 : Mr. Murali worked in a T. V. manufacturing firm as a senior engineer. His organization was flourishing and so was Mr. Murali. Gradually, the organization's profits started declining and a time came when they had to close down the firm. Mr. Murali's son was in the second year of engineering. His daughter was in I. Sc., a crucial period for both of them. At this point Mr. Murali's income stopped coming. He was very worried, and gradually got all his money spent in children's studies. Son required about Rs 20 thousand more to complete his studies. His daughter had not yet started her professional life. Mr. Murali panicked because of the devastating situation and became extremely depressed. He tried for other jobs, but they were not paying sufficient money, hence he didn't feel like taking them. A state came when he became bankrupt, he didn't know what to do. He sold his AC, TV, fridge. It was his wife who cared for him, pacified him and prevented him from going into deep depression. Gradually, his efforts helped and he got the same level job at a firm in Delhi. He had to shift to another city, but atleast his situation became much better.

These situations reveal that stress if not cured, may have devastating impact and may also lead people to mental asylums and death beds if not removed.

Dark sides of Stress : Among the more important discoveries, a decade back is that the ill effects and poor health due to unmanaged stress can be avoided if some simple skills are learnt and minor adjustments are made in life style e.g. in stress **event 1**, if students would have discussed before hand the significance of the book and planned together about how to get equal access to it than they would not have had to fight and all would have got equal benefit from it. The perception of threat caused due to deprivation of book caused the stress which could be resolved by pre discussion among the students. In the stress **event 2**, if Mr. Sharma would have assessed beforehand the impact of buying a car, and would have resisted the temptation of buying the car then he would not have faced the stressful situation. The degree of status symbol (Buying a car), greed and frustration all made Mr. Sharma depressed and ill. This situation would not have arisen if he would have decided rationally. In stress **event 3**, Mr. Murali was a senior engineer and he must have been aware of future forecast of his organization and should have thought of shifting to another job before the organization stopped functioning. Mr. Murali's blindness to future turn of events was the cause of stress. This stress could be avoided by keeping his mental and physical eye open to unexpected occurrences.

All these events show that perceptual distortions and wrong communication influence people under condition of stress. These events reflect on the extent of loss that occurs due to unmanaged stress.

A Canadian study (1974) identified four factors for disease and death, *viz.*

(1) Inadequacies in the existing health care system.

(2) Behavioral factors or unhealthy life styles.

(3) Environmental hazards like professional, industrial or ecological.

(4) Human biological factors such as genetic defects, physical weakness etc.

Findings revealed that 50% of all deaths in the U. S can be attributed to unhealthy behavior or life stresses. Atleast 50% of premature deaths due to defective life styles can be prevented. By exchanging improper life styles for proper life styles may work as a silver lining to reduce mortality.

Recent evidences and day to day observations have revealed that many people have begun to make positive life styles, they participate in exercise programs that has improved their overall physical fitness.

Every year thousands of people seek medical or psychological help for emotional distress that exceed their ability to cope with stress. More marriages are ending in divorce. About 20 on every 100, 000 Indians commit suicide because they could not find ultimate happiness. Every year thousands of people burnout on the jobs. This results in personal crisis of shattering proportion causing stress to the whole family.

About thousands of Indians die each year from some type of occupational stress, while about thousands die from industrial injury. Industrial workers do not get adequate protection from hazardous industrial condition. There are acts of violence, including rape and murder.

The psychological effects of stress which are well recognized are insomnia, anger, irritability, inability to concentrate, self pity, reduced capacity for decision making, depression etc. Stress also harms physical health. The presence of life threatening hazards, environmental hazards, family pressures and social and psychological stress, all affect the way in which our bodies function. These result in variety of health problems.

1.3 SELYE'S GENERAL ADAPTATION SYNDROME (GAS)

Stage 1 (Alarm Reaction)

Bodily changes are subtle, hence go undetected.

Stage 2 (Mobilized Resistance)

Some disturbing malfunction, or serious physical illness

Stage 3 (Exhaustion)

Variety of ailments e.g. Cancer stroke, Heart attack, etc.

The reason for stress-health connection lies in the way brain interprets what is going on. Brain works laterally. Stress (anticipated or real), threat (perceived or real) when presented to brain, sounds the alarm and the body responds by mobilizing the defensive systems. In this way brain can induce many changes in vital life sustaining functions e.g. increased output from pituitary, elevated adrenal flow, increased blood pressure and increased heart rate. Their aim is to restore balance to the body as quickly as possible, a process called homeostasis. When threat goes on for a long time the body's defensive changes may be forced to work continuously at high speed. Then the body may start wearing down, lose it's resistance and be unable to ward off added stress. This is called **General Adaptation Syndrome (GAS)** by Hans Selye, which begins with an alarm reaction, continues with mobilized resistance and ends with exhaustion if stress is not removed or relieved. In the first stage of stress unfortunately many bodily changes are so subtle, they are not noticed. It is only when there is serious malfunctioning or some severe physical illness that a person recognizes stress occurrence. Next comes the stage of fallout, exhaustion, when the person gets a variety of ailments like cancer, stroke, accident or suicide.

Mental, Physical Stressors to Behavioral Excesses : Very often in order to overcome the mental and physical stresses people indulge in self defeating behaviors of an endless variety e.g. smoking, drug abuse, sedentary life style, overeating, improper diet, refusal to pay attention to many warning signals from the body etc. The physical impact from these actions is alarming. On the lighter side, the improper life style may result in higher blood pressure, reduced cardiovascular fitness, increased risk of coronary failure, diabetes, fatigue, lowered resistance to illness. On the extreme (severe) side are pre-mature death, deaths due to alcohol, traffic fatalities.

The cyclic relation starts with poor health leading to physical stress, body malfunctioning, injury, this information sends signals to brain that something is wrong resulting in usually extreme anxiety. If person seeks proper remedy like surgery, chemotherapy, exercise etc, then he may recover. But if counter forces work he seeks harmful remedies. Tension may be reduced by smoking, anxiety, by drinking, boredom by eating. They start easily but are difficult to stop.

The above stated facts make two main points : -

(1) Relation between stress and health is a two way street, the negative side of the coin is stress affects health and health affects the ability to deal with stress. Poor health reduces individuals' capacity for successful coping. It may be because of injury, or environmental hazards, poor lifestyle and self defeating behavior. Poor health puts more stress into the system.

The positive side of the coin show that engaging in adaptive coping and healthy behavior conserves the body's defensive resources, increases resistance to stressors, improves both mental and physical sense of well-being. The outcome is enhanced personal functioning, benefiting interpersonal, social and professional areas of life. Energy which was formerly consumed in maintaining a stressful existence is used in problem solving, creative expressions and personal relationship.

(2) Second point aims at making a balanced effort to give proper and equal weightage to both coping and wellness programmes. Efforts to maintain wellness should incorporate sound health strategies, which aim at curing both the body and mind, and aim at maintaining an equilibrium between them.

1.4 WHY CHANGE LIFE STYLE ? (A PREVENTIVE MEASURE FOR STRESS OCCURRENCE)

Many reasons have been specified to learn coping skills before hand and to maintain a healthy life style. These include likelihood of reducing physical discomfort and disease, increasing self-actualization, reducing stress and improving conflict management in interpersonal relations.

All round observations reveal such reasons as reducing loss in wages due to stress related illness, reducing the cost of health care and bypassing the shortage of good doctors. Self managed health programs are being given greater value by society and the medical community. Some traditional methods of caring for the ill, and self managed stress are also being emphasized. Since 1960s the desire to reassert control over one's personal lives and reducing dependence on outside help has acted as a powerful motive.

Forces against change : Changing lifestyle is not very easy. There are personal as well as social pressures which are hard to tackle with. Internal pressures arise because learning new skills takes time, effort, sacrifice and also some discomfort. Old habits being replaced by new habits is not very easy. External pressures also exist in the form of low positive support from family or friends and unsupportive cultural values.

Breaking Habit is almost Impossible : Deeply entrenched living routine cannot be removed easily. Living routine reflect our preferences for eating, sleeping, exercising working playing etc. This is a lifestyle, which becomes a source of solace and comfort, e.g. a habit of eating dal, rice, chapatis and vegetable for lunch is difficult to break. Lifestyle once set requires no planning, no maintenance cost. Habits are difficult to break, good or damaging, changing lifestyles requires planning and effort, thinking about personal preferences and values and making conscious attempts to make it an unconscious manner of living.

Keep on waiting : We are making efforts, conscious attempts for some purpose like feeling better, reduced emotional level, which are symbolic or intangible. The principle working against our desire for changing lifestyle is that we have a very low tolerance for delays in reward. We look for immediate rewards.

Fast food is tempting but harmful. Dal, roti, salad are bland but in the long-run are light on stomach and keep body operating system better. Problem lies in taste being felt immediately while benefit of salad, dal, roti have long term benefits and difficult to see.

Motivators for Health and Stress Management : Unexpectedness of stress. Stressful situations come uninvited, unexpectedly. They appear suddenly and require immediate attention. Doctor, personal therapist need not be available. Hence, one should develop coping skills to dear with problem when they arise.

Mrs. and Mr. Ram came to Allahabad from Mumbai to attend the marriage of their nephew. They were about to return back and planned to visit the temple at Civil Lines. Mrs. Ram met with an accident and landed in the hospital. When they were approach, they appeared to be very well adjusted and satisfied with their condition. Reason was their coping mechanism which they repeated again and again that whatever happens is for the best. They took life in their stride and after the momentary shock of the accident they become mentally prepared for the future and adapted themselves to it.

There may be several possible outcomes.

1. Irritation may increase and turn into out right anger.
2. It festers inside robbing of energy, vitality and spontaneity.
3. One may find a solution to the problem and resolve the conflict coping skills must be available to be used when needed.

Doctors in demand are few

The health practitioner works more than 51 hours per week, yet they are able to provide no more than 18 minutes of contact time for each patient. It is estimated that nearly 1.5-2 million men and woman suffering from serious psychological problems are being overlooked. One reason for this is shortage of trained practitioners and paraprofessionals. Society cannot possibly afford the size of professional work force that would be necessary to solve problems of this scope and magnitude. This suggests that taking responsibility for personal health is a practical necessity. It is personally desirable in view of the potential for developing an over all higher quality of life

Being Sick is Expensive

Failure to develop coping and health skills can lead to increased illness. Cost of being ill adds up in four ways. It is costly for each person in two ways

(1) It costs financially from lost wages.

(2) It costs physically in terms of physical discomfort, and increased toll on body reserves.

(3) It costs great loss when it interferes with work e.g. through increased absenteeism and risk of injury.

(4) Government suffers loss when subsidies are involved either in health agencies or by paying for sickness or accident patients.

1.5 PRESENT-FUTURE SCENARIO OF STRESS IF MOTIVATORS INFLUENCE

Are motivators working, are they propelling people to change their life styles.

A good example in this scenario is the sight of morning walkers. Every morning a number of people, age ranging from five years to ninety years are engaged in morning walking. Some also engaged in jogging and exercises. This gives a good view of changing life style, the awareness of the negative aspects of stress and the preventive methods in order to ward off stress as much as possible.

A brief survey of about 100 breakfast tables, tea tables have also revealed a change of life style. Previously, deep fried pakoras, samosas, halwas were a common sight on these tables, people use to eat these eatables with relish, forgetting the calories that they add. Now people usually have bread, soaked grams, porridge idlies, rotis etc. for breakfast. On majority of tea tables, puffed rice and roasted grams with tea or bhelpuri, churmura are a sight. People are changing, very old persons are still highly rigid about old fooding system but their health forces them to eat light food, while younger groups have themselves become aware of the risks of foul eating habits and changed themselves to a great extent. These are two reasons why longivity of people has increased, one finds healthy people moving about even at the age of 90.

The third area are the gyms. Most of the gyms are full during the early morning hours, apart from this people pour in these gyms whenever they want to do the workouts to remain slim and trim.

All these changes show a bright impact of the motivators to prevent stress from entering ones life as much as possible.

Many people who can't go to gyms practice yoga, meditation, other exercises to ward off various problems. People are also turning towards acupressure and reikie to prevent situations from becoming so drastic that they may have to turn towards doctors and paraprofessionals.

A very important trait required for being influenced by these motivation is patience. These motivators do not affect person overnight. They have to practice these activities like walking, jogging, exercises in a regular manner for days before they can see its outcomes, together with this trait they require a positive thinking on the part of the people with regards to the positive effects of these motivators. A very big lacuna in the effectiveness of these motivations is temptations. Person may bend to the weakness of sleeping when he should go out for a walk, he may be tempted to eat one more chapatti if curry is very tasty, temptation to do some thing more interesting than going to gym may woo people away. All these temptations prevent people from adopting the various motivators for prevention of stress in their lives.

Moreover, they start thinking in term of dealing with stressful situations when they come up rather than trying to prevent their occurrences.

References

Chhabra, T. N. (2001) Human Resource Management, Dhanpat Rai & Co. Delhi. P. 638.

Selyes, Hans. (1974). Stress Without Distress, Signet Books, Philadelphia.

Schuler, R. S. (1980). Definition and Conceptualization of Stress in Organizations. Organizational Behavior and Human Performance, April, p. 189.

CHAPTER 2

STRESS : CONCEPTS AND THEORIES

2.1 RELATED TERMS

Related terms which are used in discussing stress are many, *viz.* Anxiety, Conflict, Frustration, Hassles, Tension etc. Brief explanations for these terms are given here.

Anxiety and Tension : Anxiety is "a specific, unpleasurable state of tension that indicates the presence of some hazard to the organism". Clinically defined anxiety reactions are "sudden onset of intense apprehension, fear or terror," often associated with feelings of impending doom. Anxiety as distinguished from fear is a general state of apprehension, while fear has a specific object. Anxiety is not related to any particular thing while fear is towards something like fear of cat, dog, snake, etc. Very often anxiety and stress are perceived as undistinguishable. If a person feels anxious then his body acquires a stressed, strained expression and internal bodily changes found under stress are observed like perspiration, increased heart beat, palpitation, adrenal secretion etc.

Conflict : Conflict arises when there are more than one goal, and a person has to select only one of them.

Conflict types are basically three, *viz.* : Approach-Approach, Avoidance-Avoidance and Approach-Avoidance.

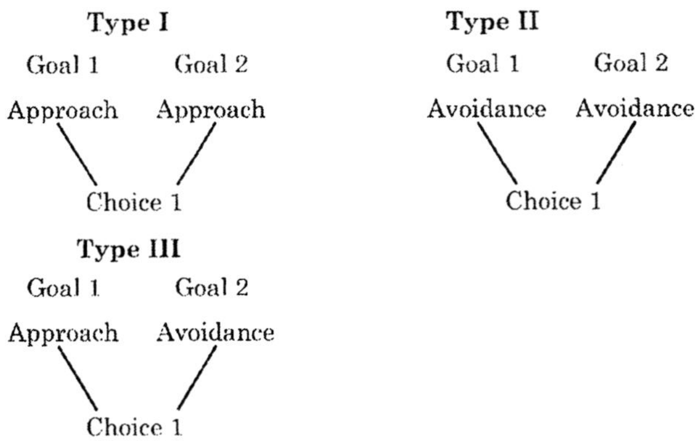

Approach-Approach Conflict : It occurs when two equally attractive goals compete and only one goal can be obtained. A twelfth pass student faces conflict of whether he should choose institute no. 1 or institute no. 2, both have equal attraction but he cannot chose both of them. He has to select one.

Avoidance-Avoidance Conflict : It occurs when two goals have equally unattractive values. Mr. Shiv can take a promotional post at Lucknow, or stay at his home town at the same post with no further benefits. This situation leads to conflict in Mr. Shiv.

Approach-Avoidance Conflict : It exists when the same goal has both positive and negative features. Heading the institution leads to more status, more fame, more significance, more worthiness but the negative side is no relaxation. Too much responsibilities, jealousy, enmity etc. It poses a conflict for a would be head, as to whether he should take it or not. All our daily activities are probably of this variety, there are some good aspects and some bad aspects of the same situation and one has to choose from them.

Frustration : Encountering of barriers in attainment of goals leads to frustration.

Person → Barrier → Goal

Frustration

The person who wants to start a business project cannot do so because of government interference or a person tries to woo a girl, but always finds someone with her, hence he cannot do so.

Outcome of frustration will show itself in aggression or irritation. Person starting the business may indulge in corrupt means to reach his goal or the person trying to woo the girl may smash the other person who comes in his way.

Frustrated persons, if they do not find an outlet will face enduring stress and may later, if no solutions for their problems are found, indulge in physical wildness and harm others, may also later become mental cases. Hamilton believes that greater the load from these stressors (Conflict, frustration and anxiety) greater the chances of crossing the limit of stress tolerance.

Hassles : Getting late for bus, reaching office unpunctually, unexpected problem occurrence at home, all these are day to day happenings which cause minor stresses to persons. They go on piling, one adapts to them as much as possible, but a stage comes when they are difficult to adjust to, people suffer from headaches, stomach aches, backaches, burning eyes etc, and a time comes when they are at a breaking point, because of these hassles people take holidays, break from work to relax their muscles and get away from daily hassles.

Hassles are the irritating, frustrating, distressing demands that in some degree characterize everyday transactions with the environment. Lazarus research work demonstrated a higher relationship between hassles and illness than between life changes and illness.

2.2 THEORETICAL EXPLANATIONS FOR A STRESS

Theories help in predicting occurrence of behavior under specific conditions. There are Psychological theories, Social theories and Holistic theories. If these theories are grasped, undesirable outcomes may be prevented in the future through some preventive actions or measures.

Psychological Theories

Psychological theories try to interpret personality, expectations, interpretations, etc, picking them up from personal and social situations and using them to assess situations of stress.

The major psychological theories include the psychodynamic, learning and cognitive transactional models.

The Psychodynamic Model : Sigmund Freud's Psychodynamic theory has set standards which are accepted world wide. He elaborated on two kinds of anxiety.

(1) Signal anxiety which occurs when the organism receives signals from external dangers corresponding to stressor-strain (danger-anxiety) relationship.

(2) Traumatic anxiety refers to instinctual, traumatic, or internally generated anxiety. If a person's sexual urge is not satisfied he shows anxiety. His psychic functioning is strained which can be observed from various psycho pathological behaviors in everyday living. This is a dominant form of anxiety according to Freud.

The Learning Theory Model : Learning theory is based on two types of conditioning, *viz.* classical conditioning model pioneered by I. P. Pavlov (the Russian Nobel Laureate in Physiology). The second is the operant conditioning, model proposed by B. F. Skinner (an American psychologist).

Classical condition is illustrated in a famous experiment conducted by John Watson, father of Behavioral Psychology. He showed 11 month old Albert a pet rat. Initially, there was no fear of the animal. Later, Albert was shown the rat together with a very loud noise. He responded with fear because of the loud noise. This condition was repeated seven times, after this Albert became afraid of rat even when there was no noise made. He also showed fear to other similar objects like rabbit, santa claus mask, etc.

In classical conditioning, loud noise was the unconditional stimulus (U. S), they are powerful biological unlearned signals and response to them is unconditional response (UCR), such as fear. Stimulus of rat was conditional stimuli (CS), a simple neutral stimuli paired with a powerful UCS loud noise. Later, the rat (CS) was responded to by fear (UCR) even when loud noise was not presented, *i.e.*, Albert learnt to respond to rat, this learnt response is conditional response.

Two aspects of the conditioning process are important for stress theory.

1. Emotional responses such as fear and anger are complex including elements like behavioral, psychological

and physiological. Escape and avoidance behaviors are practiced by a person to keep far away from stressful stimuli. Psychologically, he experiences internal tension when the feared object is seen. Finally, bodily changes occur like increased blood pressure, heart rate, body temperature which reveal physiological arousal.

2. Anxiety may become anticipatory after the original conditioning has occurred, *i.e.*, anxiety may be felt just by thinking or talking about it.

Operant condition proposes that behavior changes because the behavior produces either good or bad outcomes. That behavior which leads to reward is increased, and behavior that leads to punishment, unpleasant outcomes is reduced. Avoidance behavior is viewed as an operant behavior engaged to reduce learned fear or anxiety for example, for Albert, association of rat with loud noise created a condition of fear for the rat. Fear is an unpleasant emotion which increases internal tensions, hence people avoid fear creating situations.

This model is useful in understanding why difficulty is faced in certain types of interpersonal relations. e.g. teacher and student. If teacher scolds a child a number of times the child avoids meeting the teacher as much as possible.

The Cognitive Transactional Model : The central point of the transactional model is that stress is "neither an environmental stimulus, a characteristic of the person, nor a response but a relationship between demands and the power to deal with them without unreasonable or destructive costs. Some important implications are :

1. The same environmental event may be interpreted as stressful by one person but not by another. What makes the event stressful or not depends on some cognitive appraisal by the person.

2. The same person may interpret an event as stressful on one occasion but not so on another. This may be due to changes in physical conditions or changes in psychological states. At one time person may take the event as lightly because he is physically relaxed, at another time he may take it seriously because he is tired or tensed up. Emotional and motivational states can also differ from time to time.

Biological Stress Theories

The General Adaptation Syndrome

Selye's observation that laboratory animals subjected to stress (learning difficult task, practicing avoidance behavior) reacted with suffering from acute traumatic ulcers. He proposed a three stage process called General Adaptation Syndrome (GAS).

(1) **Alarm reaction** : It occurs at the first appearance of a stressor. For a brief moment the body has a lower than normal level of resistance, but adjusts very fast and marshals defensive resources.

(2) **Stage of resistance** : If stress continues because of factors beyond organism control the body will call for full scale metabolic adjustment. Here body has to expand more resources to fight the stress. Gradually resistance reduces, many serious symptoms such as ulcers may develop, and person reaches the third stage.

(3) **Stage of exhaustion** : If stressors stay for a long period the body's reserves of energy are further depleted, resistance breaks down and shortly person may die.

Genetic Constitutional Theory : The ability to resist stress may be related to individual's genetic history. These factor are called predisposing factors.

Genetic constitutional research attempts to develop a link between genetic make up and some physiological characteristics that lower person's ability to resist stress. Genetic make up is responsible for autonomic nervous system balance which deals with emergency situations. General temperament is also genetically determined to some extent. Most important role in stress resistance is played by kidney, cardiovascular system, digestive system and nervous system.

Social Stress Theories

Here, the focus is on tensions that are part of the society. They are called conflict theories. One source of tension is demand by society to adhere to social norms which include stability of social relations, opportunity for individual growth, services adopted for society, welfare distribution of interpersonal power personal control. Stress is associated with poverty, unstable social relationships, partialities etc. These stresses can be overcome if people accept the fact that social change is part of society and they should not fight it.

The Holistic Health Model : This approach is based on humanistic philosophy with antiscientific sentiments which goes against medical establishment themes. The term encompasses every type of health practice like herbal medicine, acupuncture, acupressure, yogic meditation, biofeedback, etc. Western medicine is seen as devaluing the role of mental processes in health and healing. The Holistic Health Model is seen as a synthesizing movement trying to regain a sense of humane medical treatment and respect for the whole person. It is visible in eastern medical tradition.

This overview has provided varying concepts relate to stress and discussed some stress models and theories in summary.

References

Freud, S. The psychopathology of everyday life (A Tyson Trans.) New York : Vintage Books.

Rice, P. L. (19) Stress and Health. Brooks/Cole Publishing Company, Monterey, California.

Selyes, H. (1980). The Stress concept today. In Kutash, Schlesinger, & Associates, Handbook on stress, Chapter 7, p. 129.

Skinner, B. F. (1974) About Behaviorism. New York : Vintage Books.

Watson, J. B. (1924), New York, Norton.

Chapter 3

THE HUMAN PHYSIOLOGY AND STRESS

The body is beautiful and should be allowed to function as it is intended to function. Six systems are linked with stress, *viz.* nervous, respiratory, endocrine, immune, cardiovascular and digestive systems. These systems are central to defensive reactions of the body under stress, they are often abused through misbehavior and can be influenced through modest behavioral and attitudinal life style changes. This chapter is providing the basics necessary to understanding stress and health physiology.

3.1 THE BRAIN IN STRESS AND HEALTH

Brain refers to the mass of neural tissues housed in the skull. It is a physical organ but the way in which it behaves makes it unique. This uniqueness is conveyed by terms like mind and mental process. Mind includes what is going on when we remember, make decisions, solve problems, reason, reflect and observe. Mental system refers to the interconnected operations of the mind like perceiving, evaluating, reflecting on and responding to external stimuli.

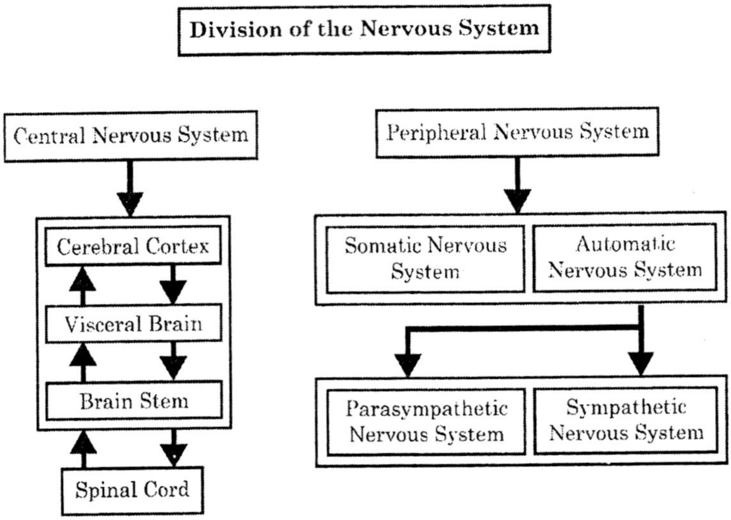

Fig. 3.1 : Division of the Nervous System

Brain holds more mysteries than all others. Learning how the brain works is a Zigsaw Puzzle in which when one feels he has reached the end, he finds himself still in the confusion. Since decades, this confusion has not been removed. In order to understand the functioning of the brain first lets look at the nervous system (Fig : 3.1). The nervous system includes two parts, *viz.* : the central nervous system (CNS) and the peripheral nervous system (PNS). The central nervous system is made up of brain and spinal cord. The peripheral nervous system is made up of the autonomic nervous system and the somatic nervous system. The autonomic nervous system includes two major parts, *viz.* : parasympathetic and the autonomic system. The brain and the autonomic systems play a significant role in body's reaction to stress. Neuroautonomists have recognized several layers of tissue in the brain, they include brain stem, visceral brain (include many different parts) and the new brain or cerebral cortex.

The Brain Stem

The brain stem is a bulb like outgrowth at the top of the spinal column, and it keeps the vital life functions (e.g. breathing, heart activity) going. The brain stem includes structures like medulla and reticular activating system. Under normal conditions there is even rate of breathing (12 breath per minute). However, stress occurring in every day living can alter this valance, like public speaking stress may cause breathlessness, sudden loud noise, sudden light in front of your eyes may make you catch your breath.

Extreme Stress Situation : Under extreme stress situation a condition called anxiety hyperventilation occurs. Under this condition, the person feels dizzy and faces a blackout. Heart may start pounding and one may feel shortness of breath. He may experience a numb sensation in various parts of the body, *i.e.*, experience parathesia. This causes heightened anxiety leading to an uncomfortable experience of encountering heart attack symptoms, creating anticipatory fright. Hyper ventilation comes from psychological, social traits and circumstances, rather than physical pathology. Two ways have been suggested for getting relief in this situation : 1) Breathe voluntarily at a measured slow pace, or hold breath for short periods. 2) Breathe into a paper bag and rebreathe the same air.

The Reticular Activating System (RAS)

The reticular activating system (RAS) is a bundle of fibers that run like a great rope through the middle of the brain stem upward into the hypothalamus and thalamus. It works in three ways, 1. two way communication between brain and body, 2. selection of sensory information processing by the cortex, and 3. vigilance or arousal.

Brain-body Communication : The primary two way streets for communication between the brain and the rest of the body are served by the Reticular Activating System. RAS is divided into descending reticular pathway and ascending reticular pathway.

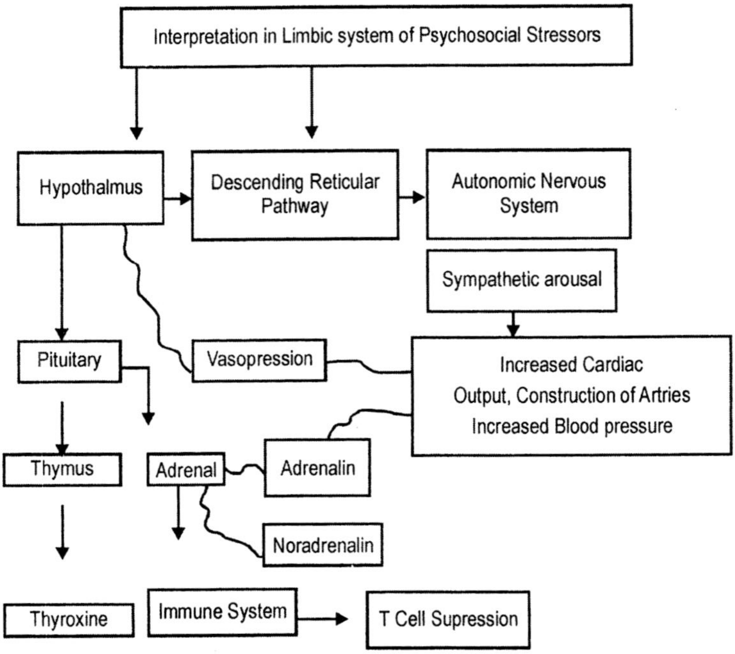

Fig 3.2 : Effects of prolonged stress in the Hypothalmus-Pituitary-Adrenal complex and autonomic systems.

Psychosocial stressors are communicated to the body *via* the descending pathway and the hypothalamic pituitary pathway (Fig 3.2). They initiate major changes in physical systems like cardiovascular, glandular, and immune systems. Undesirable effects may be produced under enduring stress.

On the contrary, physical stressors are communicated to the brain through the ascending RAS. These stressors include extreme temperature, body injury etc. These stressors may produce various kinds of emotional states leading to discomfort and tension. Because of negative emotions one's sensitivity to pain increases. This occurs because of the role of reticular and thalamic centers. But at the same time normal healing processes are also stimulated to reduce level of pain experienced. Body also produces analgesic like substances for this purpose.

Gating : The RAS receives inputs from all sensory organs. It can have effect receptors and relay stations for any of the senses (eye, ear). But it processes only those informations which is important. Otherwise, a lot of noise will occur causing too much confusion. The RAS only serves really important informations and sees that its reaches where it is required.

One issue coming up from this is, how does the RAS know the significance of the information. A general answer given is that the RAS has inputs from virtually every part of the brain including centers for motivation, emotion, attention, associative processes, etc. Changes in any of these internal states may be communicated to the RAS e.g. a student has his final exam the next day. He receives a lot of stimulation from various external stimuli like T. V. is running his favourite movies, loud speaker playing his favourite song, train whistling away on the railway track near his house, a hooting scooter near by and the exam matter in front of him. He is able to block out all other noises excepting his course material because he is highly motivated to do well in the next day exam.

Vigilance and Arousal : The RAS's third function is vigilance or arousal. It is very important for the functioning of higher brain centers. RAS is always on the lookout for important information reaching the senses. On receiving such information it provides alert signals to higher centers of the brain, warning that something important is coming.

Limbic System

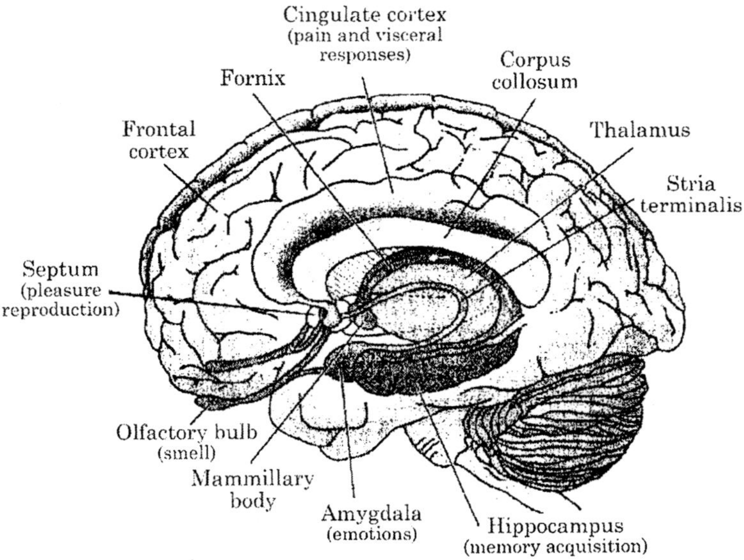

Fig 3.3 : Cross section of the cerebral cortex showing the major limbic system nuclei for control of emotions.

The Visceral Brain

The visceral brain is a complex set of structures lying virtually in the center of brain, its most important structures are the thalamus, the hypothalamus, the hypothalamus pituitary complex and centers associated with limbic system.

The Thalamus : The thalamus is the major relay center for every sensory system except smell. It evaluates the emotional contents from information provided by the senses. The clinical observation to support this view was patients with physical damage to the thalamus, overeact to emotional stimuli. The thalamus plays an important role in perception of pain as depicted by pain researches. They have identified three types of pain *viz.* prickly pain (from needle or sharp object), burning pain and aching pain (muscle or bone pain). All these pain pathways terminate in the thalamus. Some promising measures are being used to provide people with some relief when suffering from chronic pain. Some stimulation techniques have been developed to control pain of nominally ill patients without using drugs.

The Limbic System : It is the part of brain concerned with survival. It includes the thalamus, the hypothalamus, amygdale, hippocampus and septum. Functions associated with limbic system are anger, aggression, punishment, reward, sexual arousal and pain.

Here are some incidents of damage to various parts of limbic system and their effects.

Damaged structure		***Effect***
1. Amygdala	→	Increased Appetite
2. Septum	→	Overall increase in emotionality. Extreme irritability, rage response may occur
3. Hippocampus	→	Deficit in long term memory and slows down various learning processes dealing with avoidance and discrimination

Two points to be stated here are that amygdala and septum serve to balance aggressive tendencies, the amygdala starting and the septum moderating aggressive tendencies.

The Hypothalamus : It is situated above the root of the mouth, towards the back, is directly connected to pituitary gland, the master gland of the body. It has a very powerful effect on nearly every visceral system in the body. It can respond directly to psychological and emotional stumuli, cognitive stressors originated in the cortex. Sexual behavior originates in the limbic region but is controlled by hypothalamus. Sleep is also partially controlled by hypothalamus. The hypothalamus is richly supplied with blood so that it can, monitor blood nutrients, body fluid volume and concentration of hormones in various parts of the body. Hypothalamus has two centers that regulate the stress response.

(1) anterior lateral, that slows down sympathetic activity and inhibits production of pituitary stress hormones.

(2) posterior medial, that stimulates the sympathetic system and produces pituitary stress hormones.

The Autonomic Nervous System (ANS) : It is the primary control system for three different types of tissues *i.e.*, cardiac muscle, most of the glands and all smooth muscles. It controls heart activity, blood pressure, digestion, urinary and bowel elimination and some other body functions. The ANS is controlled by brain stem hypothalamus and spinal cord.

It has two parts : -

(1) The Parasympathetic System, which controls when one is relaxed, quiet. Most reconstructive processes occur during this time. Blood concentrates on other important activities like digestion and storing energy reserves. Breathing balance is slow under its control.

(2) The Sympathetic System is in control under emergency situations, in situations of increased emotionality. This stress response originates from the hypothalamus. When emergency is over the hypothalamus activates the parasympathetic system. This system is responsible for increased blood pressure, increased blood flow to active muscles and decreased blood flow to less active organs, increased energy consumption, increased blood glucose concentration, increased muscle strength. (Guyton)

Pituitary Gland. It is called the master gland, it secretes six important hormones, several less important hormones from the anterior region and two from its posterior region. Virtually, all the secretions are under the direct control of the hypothalamus, which produces its own hormones to accomplish this like ACTH (Adreno corticotrophin hormone), CRF (Corticotrophin-releasing factor). Almost any kind of stress (physical or psychological) leads to immediate increase in level of ACTH. Other hormones are cortical, Hydrocortisone epinephrine and Norepinephrine.

Cortical provides energy to body through conversion of glucose stored in body. Researches have revealed that it suppresses the immune system, thus reducing resistance to infection, disease and may play a possible role in cancer development in the body.

Epinephrine has a very powerful effect on the heart, it increases its rate and strength of contractions, it increases blood pressure and also leads to increased secretion of ACTH and other hormones. It has greater effect on visceral system, may have powerful effect under stressful condition.

Researches suggested that epinephrine is more important when mental stress occurs, like solving mathematics, continuous vigilance and public speaking. On the other hand, norepinephrine is associated with physical stressors like being immobile encountering isometric stress etc.

This was disproved by standard researchers who took blood samples to check this. This solved the puzzle of the relationship. Epinephrine moves very fast in blood while norepinephrine moves slowly, when mental, physical tasks are mixed in testing procedures and mental tasks are given later, it appeared that norepinephrine was relate to mental work, but the reason was that it moved slowly hence was found in test samples.

Vasopressin (ADH) is another major hormone released by the posterior section of pituitary gland, it is produced in the hypothalamus. It influences heart activity, blood pressure and fluid loss through urinary system. If volume and pressure of heart are low than vasopressin is increased and if they increase then vasopressin is reduced, thus the output of heart is regulated. When blood pressure is low then vasopressin causes increase in blood pressure through constriction of arteries. In case of an accident, when blood loss occurs, than ADH increases to preserve pressure and restore volume. In periods of severe stress vasopressin may help in elevating already high blood pressure caused by other neural and hormonal processes.

3.2 THE THYROID GLANDS AND THYROXIN

The rate of metabolism is effected by physical and psychological stress. Such changes influence mood, energy, nervous irritability and mental alertness. The hypothalamus regulates these changes through the pituitary and through the thyroid where the hormone thyroxin is released. The regulation is done through three steps. First, when a demand is placed on the system like strenuous exercise or some psychosocial stress, the hypothalamus releases neural hormone called Thyrotropin Releasing Factor (TRF). This release stimulates pituitary gland which tells thyroid to release thyroxin. As feedback loop is built, when demand increases, TRF also increases, thus increasing metabolic rate. When demand is over, the output of TRF is reduced to make metabolism normal.

A side effect of this is that as the level of thyroxin increases the system becomes more responsive to adrenaline. This leads to amplification effect. A picture that appears is that adrenaline is a short term stress hormone while thyroxin serves as a long term stress hormone.

Behavioral effects stemming from high level of thyroxin are as follows. Mental activities are aroused, one feels more nervous and anxious, person may feel tiredness but feels sleepless. Blood flow increase leads to high blood pressure. Gastric juice production increases, causing diarrhea, all these are symptoms occurring during stress.

3.3 NATURAL DEFENSES OR IMMUNE SYSTEM

Immunity is defined as the power of an individual to resist or overcome the effects of a particular disease or other harmful agent. Body may be invaded by germs, toxic substances, then body produces antibodies to attack and destroy the invaders. Robert Ader has argued that "the immune system is integrated with other physiological systems and, like all such systems operating in the interest of homeostasis, is sensitive to regulation or modulation by the brain. A body of research has suggested that stress alters the way in which the immune system operates. Effect of stress is lowering of body's resistance to disease by suppressing a number of disease fighting cells available. This results in increased frequency of afflictions, lowering down recovery chance from existing disease. Plaut and Friedman revealed that the risk for contracting infectious diseases, allergic reactions and auto immune disease is released through life stress of humans.

Researches have also shown that prenatal exposure to alcohol can be toxic to the immune system. The implication of this research is better education of pregnant women and improved prenatal care techniques to reduce potential harm.

The Brain's role in Immune System

One major neural hormonal system has a central role in influencing the immune system *i.e.*, the Hypothalamic Pituitary–Adrenal. (HPA) system. When stress occurs HRA system activates the adrenal glands. Output from adrenal glands stimulates the immune system. This has the desired effect of initiating defensive reactions, increasing resistance and speeding recovery.

How does the body fight with itself ?

When external agent attack the body then antibodies come up to fight with them. Thus, allergies occur. The fight results in rupture of two different white blood cells and release of toxic material into the blood stream.

Hives and Hay Fever

The most common allergies are hay fever, asthma, urticaria and anaphylaxis. Hay fever occurs when the allergic reaction occurs in the naval area, leading to increased capillary pressure and rapid fluid flow into the nose. Hive is a type of anaphylaxis localized in the skin causing inflammation and swelling. Another term for it is urticaria. Remedy is antihistamines since histamine is the primary cause of these difficulties. Psychological stress may also cause this problem.

Asthma

Asthma is defined as intermittent, variable and reversible obstruction of bronchial airway. Asthma afflicts high number of people. Psychosocial origin is behind it, like family stress or personality problem. Lifestyle intensifies the symptoms and defeats medical treatment.

Acquired Immune Deficiency Syndrome (AIDS)

AIDS seems to attack male homosexuals, intravenous drug abusers and people requiring blood transfusion. AIDS is caused by a virus HIV–III/LAV Virus. Because, it has created public fear, people run away from persons having AIDS fearing that they may get infected. They become more stressed.

Stress and Heart

Heart is the most significant part of the body, if it stops functioning the life goes out. Apart from physical origin for heart failure, psychological factors and life style forces also cause cardiovascular problems.

Hypertension is an elevation in blood pressure above the normal level, cause may be any. It is usually diagnosed when systolic blood pressure exceed 160 and diastolic exceed 120, serious danger exists when systolic pressure reaches 200.

Atheroscierosis is a disease of the large arteries in which yellowish patches of fat are deposited forming plaques that decrease the size of the opening. Causes are genetic risk, diet, lack of exercise, stress. Rosenman and Friedman noted the relation between the stressful events and the appearance of cholesterol. Another effect is tendency of blood to coagulate. Plaques may also break the boundaries of arteries. Body does try to repair this breakdown. Further when calcium deposits occur it hardens the cell walls and narrows the passage. Heart then works harder to produce blood flow. This gradually leads to deterioration of heart and coronary problems.

Ulcers

A number of observations support the contention that psychological factors play an important role in the origin of ulcer e.g. urban population suffer more from ulcer than rural population, at war time ulcer occurrence increases. Certain occupational groups which have more responsibilities suffer more from ulcer like traffic controllers. There are types of ulcers, two most prominent are peptic ulcer and gastric ulcer. Peptic ulcer occur when gastric juices used for digesting food are produced at a very high rate and the neutralizing secretions are absent, these juices attack the lining of the stomach wall itself causing irritation, bleeding in severe cases. Peptic ulcer may be acute or chronic.

Acute Ulcer is Stress Ulcer

Gastric ulcers are deeper erosions in the stomach lining usually occurring on the bottom surface of the stomach. They are caused by too much use of aspirin and alcohol. They are also linked with chronic anxiety and depression.

This chapter briefly discusses the role of brain in helping persons to deal with stress, through natural defense mechanisms it also talks about damage. The physical damage caused by stress may have damaging impact on the body, if exposed for a long time.

References

Guyton, A. C. (1977) Basic Human Physiology, Normal functions and mechanisms of disease. Philadelphia, Saunders, p. 399.

Rosenman, R. H & Friedman, M. (1974). Neurogenic factors in pathogenesis of coronary heart disease. Medical Clinics of North America, 58, 269-279.

CHAPTER 4

PSYCHOLOGICAL ELEMENTS IN STRESS SYSTEM

Premature Presumptions : If a doctor tells a patient with pain in the abdomen region that he will have to do some test to find out what is wrong with him, at once the patient comes to the conclusion that he might be suffering from cancer, or stone or something extremely severe.

If the boss calls his junior through intercom, at once fear enters in the mind that may be he is calling me for some negative purpose like scolding, or giving some warning etc.

Our mind always thinks of the worst situation possible, why ? Because most of these events have lot of uncertainty attached to it. This leads to very personalized thinking which in turn influences transactions within people and leads to distress reaction or positive impact. People basically fill in gaps and make guesses. The presumption is that one must be calling because of some negative aim. The real reason may be positive but only negative thing comes to mind.

Anticipatory Reactions : If a person is told that you he has a stone in the abdomen region and has to be operated for cure, at once he feel tensed. The blood pressure increases, heart rate increases, sleep is lost, what is the reason? The reason is not the pain but the fear of the pain and suffering which one may have to encounter due to the future surgery, also there is uncertainty regarding complete cure. All these anticipations are responsible for the despair and fear.

4.1 THE MIND'S SUSPENSE AND PSYCHE

Observations and various real life experiences have revealed that thoughts, labels and expectations have impact on stress reaction and health. Stress does not occur because of physical circumstance like heat, humidity etc. but it occurs because of cognitive processes, processes which make the mind work in thought processes and evaluation. The way in which one bears the stress and the way in which one copes with stress depends upon one's ability to think about ways of coping with it. Now more emphasis is being given to understanding the cognitions of person under stress and in developing cognitive approaches for treatment and for making people seek help for themselves. Mind is an information processing system.

4.2 COGNITION

Cognition is defined as all the ways of knowing, thinking, reasoning and deciding. It includes processes of attention, perception, memory, problem solving and creativity.

Cognitive model, *i.e.*, information processing model is adopted from three separate fields of computers, communication and language. Here input, throughput, output are the three stages of its functioning together with feedback. Eyes and ears serve as inputs channel for all information, other cognitive processes like attention, memory, reasoning, planning, problem-solving etc. are regarded as throughput. They have to depend on internal organization. Speaking, acting are outputs. The cognitive scientist helps in understanding all these functions. Two theoretical notions are been advanced to reveal how mind works. One comes from George Kelly from the area of personality theory and the other comes from work of Jean Piaget from area of developmental area. They are personal construct and schemata. Kelly says that constructs are predictive guesses imposed on reality, and if they are tested than this construct may be changed e.g. view of boss may be bad or good, friendly or hostile. These constructs may also refer to one's self. People become mentally prepared for up coming event based on their construct about it.

In Piaget's theory a schemata means assimilation, *i.e.*, when some new information about something becomes available, changes occur to fit it into available schemata. We have a schemata for everything, like food, party, office, professional behavior, etc. They contain the rules about how one should behave in various situations.

Interpretation of senses : Perception A person receives information from it's various sense organs like eyes, ears, skin, tongue, but it is through perception that he understands the various sensations and interprets them according to his personal constructs and schemata. Perception may be defined as the interpretation and organization of all information provided to the brain by the senses. Interpretation means one gives meaning to what one sees or hears, attaches weight to it, this may be positive, negative, pleasant or unpleasant. Organisation means one connects something new with something already existing in one's mind, stored in long-term memory. The new information is clubbed with old information, this is placed in some category, e.g. something moving on four wheels is clubbed together with car, or a new sweet tasting like round natural thing may be considered similar to fruits. We have sets ready in our minds which help us in understanding new sensations. Sometimes interpretations given by persons may not match with reality, one may indulge in erroneous judgement, e.g. seeing black thick moving cords may be erroneously interpreted as snake. Two of the most familiar perceptual distortions are delusions and hallucinations. Delusions are mistaken beliefs like 'I am the object of ridicule for everyone' or 'I am very beautiful'. Hallucinations are seeing or hearing something which is not there, e.g. hearing crying sound from next room when actually nothing occurs. There may be less extreme cases, like fear that teacher may fail me.

All these are misperceptions and may very often cause stress.

Role of Attention in Stress

Attention is the process by which a person chooses what to attend to. This choosing may be involuntary or voluntary, impulsive or deliberate, automatic or selective.

A sudden shaking of all objects and furnitures in the houses made people automatically run out of their houses, a sudden sound of bomb made people run here and there for protection. Surprise, novelty may lead to involuntary attention.

Selective attention is a process which helps person to select only significant information from too much information, thus preventing information overload. When this process is followed deliberately, using means like concentration and control then one practices perceptual vigilance. This process is very handy in various types of jobs like medical field, Indian traffic police, army etc.

Enduring attention may create various types of problems, e.g. one can be highly vigilant in just 15 to 30 minutes, but gradually as time passes his alertness subsides. Carelessness occurs and chances of accidents may be very high. Hyper vigilance may hinder one from taking the right decision.

Defensive Approach to Perception

Perceptual Defense : Sinha (1986) studied fear of death, in an experiment. Some neutral sights and some death sights were shown to subjects and it was observed that the subjects responded very fast to death sights as compared to neutral sights, which proved that they wanted to avoid such sights so that the fear of death may not be aroused in them. This finding was contradicted by Postman who observed that people were much slow to respond to bad or obscene words than to neutral or good words.

Sinha's study revealed that people usually avoid or turn away from frightful sights in order to avoid them. *i.e.*, they practice perceptual defense.

Perceptual Deprivation and Perceptual Overload

Imagine if someone is locked in a very small room, his limbs are tied, he is not allowed to speak or hear any external sound, then how he will feel. A person cannot tolerate such a situation for very long. This was proved by a study at Mc Gill University by Beston *et. al* (1954). Volunteers were paid $20 per day to lie in bed and sleep. They could quitted whenever they could, result revealed that most of the volunteers quit in the first 24-36 hours. After so many hours the number of volunteers who left, faced hallucination problems, and deterioration of intelligence. This revealed that some amount of input is essential to keep the cognitive system in smooth order.

Too much stimulation also causes psychological overload, when too much starts happening in one's life one faces a stressful situation. Simple solution would be running away, being alone. If these don't work then person requires some cognitive coping methods and some problem solving therapies.

Secondary Perception

Some time people don't face any problem but still they feel the danger in it. One's schemata and constructs make a person interpret situations on the basis of his way of thinking and imaginations, these are called secondary or derived perception. They develop their own personal norms, stereotype ways for interpreting various situations. Three more important derived perceptions are self perception, person perception and situation perception.

Self Perception

It is an image one makes of oneself on one's own mind, a person may see himself in a positive light like more intelligent, more capable or may evaluate oneself in negative light like less intelligent, less careful. A person with a positive self image will look at all situations, however threatening or challenging they are, from a positive angle, on the other hand, a person with negative interpre-tation about himself will respond to neutral as well as threatening situations in a stressful light. Leonard Pearlin and Carmi Schooler of National Institute of Mental Health observed that three psychological traits helped persons against stress, *viz.* self esteem, self denignation and mastery. In various types of stress situations like marital stress, parenting stress, family financial stress or work stress, self denignation is the most influencing element.

Self concept and stress relate to one another in either of two ways, a person with low self concept may view situation stressful, or a person facing a very stressful situation may make one's self regard weak, e.g. If an accident occurs on the street, the way one decide, will influence one's self perception. Persons with high self-esteem can take a better decision as compared to persons with low self-esteem. They are able to face failures and cope with them more easily. They can defend themselves against events with negative implications or consequences, (Freud).

In order to make accurate self portraits Carl Roger has devised an exercise (Self Study Exercise). This exercise consists of three steps, in the first step a person is asked to write things which most describes him. In the second step the person is asked to describe how other people see him. Next, the list is then compared with the person the list given in the first step with descriptions given by others in the second step. If differences are found how the person will go about correcting them. The last step involves writing all traits which he feels are his ideal self, how he would like to be. The ideal self should be realistic and attainable. Once this ideal picture is created try to match it with real self, if differences are observed then how would he go about coming closer to his ideal self.

Perception of Others : Perception of others play an important role in stress transactions. Two aspects influence one's perception of other *viz.* implicit personality theories and attribution.

Implicit Personality Theories : When someone interact with others, their behavior, appearance is clicked into ones mind as memory. In this way, schemata for various people are built. They are implicit theories, these are subjective and vary from person to person. This is in contrast to formally stated theory. The implicit theory is built on the link between emotional, behavior and intellectual traits. When new persons are encountered having traits seen previously then persons are clubbed in that schemata, same label is applied to future happening. The schemata helps to predict, to some extent, what the other person will do and to adjust our own behavior accordingly.

Problems are created when predictions are made very quickly, without giving thought to reasons for that behavior or rationalizing it. The first look at a person, his action and one tries to match with a schema that matches it and give ones judgement to him. Here, chances of error are quite high because first impressions are based on very limited information for example, if two doctors are talking in the corridor of the hospital and one says that he will not operate if he will not be paid the full fees, at once the third person jumps to the conclusion that the doctor is inhumane without analyzing why he said so.

The first impressions tend to leave a halo effect *i.e.*, the previous encounter with that person influences one's impression about him at present and future. Once the first impression is made, it becomes difficult to eliminate them.

All these are person perception based on implicit personality theories and hasty judgement that create stressful situations.

Attribution

Attribution means assigning causes or blame for outcome of behavior. When we are made responsible for some outcome we have a tendency to put the blame on external forces, e.g. if I fail, it is because teacher did not mark correctly. This is external attribution. But if someone else is responsible for some outcome then we attribute it to something inside that person, his character, his ability, etc. This is internal attribution.

Stress occurs when we perceive ourselves as helpless when we really can control the situation. Only when persons make realistic attribution, then only one can prevent tensions from occurring.

Situation perception : Event scripts are mental rules about what actions are right in a specific situation, this is called schemata for situation. In every situation the behavior demand are different e.g. in office, in temple, in art gallery. When unexpected behavior occur in situation then tension may occur, e.g. shouting in library may alert everyone sitting as there may be fire.

Faulty Memory : 'I don't remember the time for reaching the place of appointment' : 'I can't remember the receipe for black forest cake'. 'I don't remember the names of my colleagues'. All these are daily heard statements which reveal that one can forget, it is very difficult to keep everything in mind and to remember everything hundred percent. Human mind is not so strong that it may remember everything. Often it is proclaimed that memory is very powerful, and whatever is placed in memory is very powerful, and whatever placed in memory becomes very permanent. In memory, usually a number of forces work that can selectively discard, suppress or recreate memory to fit personal motives and needs.

Two important memory processes are Reintegration and Reconstruction. Reintegration means that some bits of information are recalled when some item is being recalled e.g. if a person meets his school time pal after 20 years and he tells him that we were together in 7th class, we played a cricket match in which you got hurt and I took you to the infirmary, at once this incident may remind his friend of many other happenings of childhood together. But sometimes information recalled are guesses or inferences with very little truth. This becomes a problem, one may use logical fabrication to fill gaps to make the picture complete. In reconstruction a memory is shaped to fit the persons expectations, beliefs, knowledge or schemata, for example a murder story is narrated to a lawyer, a professor, a doctor and a writer. Each of them were then asked to recall the story, it was observed that each of these professionals added bits and pieces of information according to their profession, to colour the story. The details they gave were reflections of their professions. This reveals that memory can change selectively to fit a person's personal schemata.

4.3 FACTORS LEADING TO STRESSFUL APPRAISALS

Lazarus proposed that there are three appraisals that provide meaning and influence the course of coping when a situation is appraised as stressful. They are primary, secondary and re-appraisal. Primary appraisal provides the initial evaluation of the type of situation. Secondary appraisal considers the match between coping styles and situational demands. Re-appraisal is base on feedback from transactions that occur after the first two appraisals.

Now the question relates to determiners of stress appraisal. *i.e.*, which situations are stressful and which are not. Three factors influence the appraisal process, *viz.* emotionality attached to the event, uncertainty occurring because of lack of complete information, meaning attached to stressful situation.

Emotionality : Lazarus has considered cognition and emotion as linked in an ongoing negotiations with environment. Emotions influence coping in four ways.

1. Emotions give signal to show that something is wrong. They usually relate to survival. If emotional transactions lead to positive outcome, then every similar situations are perceive positively. But if outcomes have negative outcome then negative memories will remain in the mind and when similar events occur they will be judged negatively as well.

2. Emotions are attention getters. They redirect attention to something that is more significant because of threat attached to it.

3. Emotions prevent person from thinking rationally, many cognitive tasks are disrupted, tasks which have emotionally occurred become more important. Concentration on other mental tasks becomes very difficult.

4. Emotion can act as motivators. In the case of unpleasant emotions one will try to avoid them, on the other hand, if emotions are pleasant one will engage in a variety of behaviors to maintain such emotions.

Thus, emotions may aim at increasing those behaviors that are aimed at controlling, eliminating or reducing tensions.

Uncertainty : Uncertainty may lead to judging a situation as stressful. Uncertainty means providing inadequate information about a situation, creating confusion. Mishel observed among medical patients that when they were not given full information about their situation, there was greater stress perceived in such situations.

Two factors determining uncertainty are : 1) Tolerance for ambiguity, 2) Information seeking skills. Ambiguity means having unclear meaning or having many confusing interpretations. Tolerance means how much a person can endure. Whether the situation is judged as stressful or not depends upon one's ability to endure an unclear situation. Under such condition one searches for more information and clears the situation. This involves information seeking behavior, that much time of uncertainty in which a person engages in information seeking is tolerated by the person.

The ability to predict future depends on availability of relevant information.

Changed meaning of stressful situations : As situation unfolds, new meaning can be created by various new informations entering into the scene, and this may change perception, schema thus changing the definition of the situation.

Self Efficacy : It refers to the person's perception that he is capable, that he possesses skills, performance ability that will enable him to act rightly and successfully in situations which arise. According to Bandura, a person behaving in various ways faces positive and negative outcomes for each behavior, hence he learns to anticipate which behaviors are most likely to lead to which outcome and thus outcome expectations build up.

Efficacy outcome means that the person is confident that if he makes a particular behavior then he will achieve the outcome which he expects from that behavior. Only when one feels that he has low efficacy, then the situation becomes stressful.

Coping with stressful events during reappraisal

Three ways are used by people to deal with stressful events during reappraisal, *viz.* rationalizing, changing the meaning of the event and reducing significance of event. In rationalization, a personally desirable meaning is attached to the event whether it is appropriate or not. If new information becomes available then one can change the meaning of the event. Third is reducing the meaning of the event. If situation becomes very painful, one should divert himself, should engage in something else and develop interest in it, thus giving less weightage to the stressful event.

Summary

This write up has concentrated on psychological framework of various people under stress, and has tried to elaborate on various cognitive elements related to stress and coping like perception, attention, memory etc.

References

Beston, W. H., Herson, W. & Scott, T. H. (1954). Effects of decreased variation in the sensitive environment, Canadian Journal of Psychology, 8, 70-76.

Kelly, G. A. (1955) The Psychology of Personal Constructs. Vol 1 & 2, New York, Norton.

Lazarus, R. S. & Launier, P. (1978). Stress related transactions between person and environment. In L. A. Pervin & M. Lewis (Eds) Perspectives in interactional Psychology, New York : Plenium Press.

Pearlin, L. I. & Schooler, C. (1978). The structure of coping. Journal of Health and Social Behavior, 19, 2-21.

Piaget, J. (1965) The moral judgement of the child. New York, Free Press.

Rogers, C. R. (1980). A way of being. Boston : Houghton. Mefflin.

Sinha, A. (1986). A study of certain determiners of perception of threat, Doctoral. Thesis.

CHAPTER 5

FAMILY UNDER STRESS : VARIOUS PROBLEMS AND COPING STYLES

Ravi pushed his younger brother from the terrace causing a fatal accident, reason was jealousy. Shyam killed his father because he use to beat his mother very often making her cry. Ramu slapped his wife, seeing this, his ten year old daughter picked up a stone and hit her father on the head.

All these are family problems leading to stress and tension in the family. Another way in which stress occur in family are, problem of one person causing stress to other family members. If a teenaged son fails in twelfth class, his whole family gets concerned about his future and are stressed. If the supervisor gets a shout from his boss, he becomes unhappy and this inturn influences his behavior with his family members and all suffer from stress. Family itself may cause stress, like marital adjustment, family planning, child bearing and retirement each of these events may create joy, sorrow, harmony or stress.

5.1 CHAIN FOR FAMILY STRESS

Economic problem → emotional load → social problem → psychological problem → personal failure → coping styles required

This chain portrays how money problem lead to disruption of family life and if some coping measures are not applied there may be utter pain and suffering for the whole family. If economic problems occur, the greatest sufferers who are completely innocent, are the children. They become victims of family disturbance and face various problematic states like depression, poor school work and sometimes even attempts of suicide may occur. Very often some unique resistance power is found in family members which provides social insulation against the storms and stresses of daily life. This can occur only if family interaction is positive, they communicate well and are skilled in problem-solving.

Differentiation between personal and family stress

If accident occurs and the family losses a member in it, then the sufferers left, are other family members, their grief is highly personal, as they are in the same boat, but they suffer in singles. On the other hand, family stress may be different. Reason is that family is a system with connecting elements. It is a unique cluster of people who enjoy a special relationship, which occur due to love, mutual dependence, marriage, procreation, etc. Stress in the family leads to malfunctioning of most of its elements. Management of family resources is reduced *i.e.*, the difference between family stress and personal stress is basically based on qualitative aspect; Personal stress causes emotional stress, while family stress disruptes connection, compatability. In brief, person stress is degrading for the bio-psychological system while family stress is an insult to a social system. Stressors causing malfunctioning of family include life events like death of a parent, long term hospitalization of a family member, lack of income or imprisonment of a family member. Family's response to such crisis of distress depend on how the family interprets the situation and the types of resources and problem solving skills they have to manage the stress.

5.2 THE ABCX MODEL OF FAMILY STRESS

R. Hill (1940) proposed the ABCX Model of family stress. Klien called it the stress-crises-copying theories. This model states that some events (A), interacts with the family's resources for meeting crisis (B), the family definition of the event (C), to produce a crisis (X). This model is similar to Lazarus's cognitive transactional model of personal stress. This model means that a stress only occur when the family appraises the event as threatening and the family resources are inadequate to meet the demands. The ABCX Model give emphasis to two concepts, *i.e.*, (1) amount of change induced by the stress event (2) the family's vulnerability to stress. Examples of the first concept are death of wage earner, divorce, taking up a new project. Examples of the second concept are lack of money resources, lack of skill, ability etc. Below are described some components of family stress, based on Hills's model.

Family vulnerability

This is a complex factor in family stress. There may be a stress event with lot of threat, and then regardless of vulnerability, the family is facing crisis. On the other hand, the family may lack resources, may be highly vulnerable, whether the stress is threatening or not may cause family stress. Sometimes, one event may be so intensely threatening that it may wear off the family. On the other hand, stressor events may occur one after the other, adding up and creating a situation when the family losses its power of copying and becomes highly vulnerable, hence vulnerability of family and power of stressor are related.

Family appraisal

The way the family defines a stressful situation, assesses it, also matters. If the situation is valued by each family member and also valued by all family members jointly, then the stress may be perceived as highly serious. The appraisal is also influenced by family's strength to deal with the stressful situation. If they perceive themselves to be strong in dealing with stress they will not appraise the stressful situation as threatening.

Family resources

How vulnerable the family is to stress depends upon the personal resources of family members and combined resources of the family system. Personal resources include financial status, physical status, personality variable and education level.

Family decision making and problem solving

The family's pattern of decision making is a very important family resource which is dependent on other family resources like health, education, money etc. Karl Weick has identified eleven aspects of family problem solving which make them different from other problem solving groups.

1. Families sit together to solve problems in the morning or evening when they lack the proper energy to take various actions.

2. Family members give authority for decision making to person possessing legitimate power rather than person possessing expertise.

3. More informed members are given more weight even though the quality of decision they take may not be so superior.

4. Affection among family members very often prevent decision making based on intelligence and cognitive abilities.

5. Usually during decision making sessions, family should not take problem independently, moreover they ooze out their emotional turmoil through the problem which they narrate. Rational thinking is very often prevented.

6. As family members are biologically and physiologically linked, they should open up in both ways, but usually they suppress their psychi and thus cause greater harm in decision making.

7. Family problem solving does not occur in a separate session, rather than it is solved while other matters are being tackled.

8. Family problem solving does not include external factors hence they may often be rigid, baised and narrow in their thinking.

9. Many family problems are left untreated thinking that they will be solved by themselves.

10. Consensus of various family members may be missing, hence a problem may result in more tensions and problems.

11. The ecology of families is relatively disordered and body cues are cryptic at best.

5.3 COPING WITH FAMILY STRESS : STAGES

McCubbin has identified four general assumptions about how family coping actions work to protect the family from stress,

First assumption is that coping behavior will reduce vulnerability of the family e.g. if a family member seeking independent decision, threatens to leave the home then the family will have to gather energy and give himself time to deal with his stressful situation.

Second assumption is that coping may bring the family together and closeness may increase.

Third assumption is that coping may help in removing stress events.

Fourth assumption is that coping may make the environment change so that person's family feels less stressed.

Sometimes, coping may do more harm than good to the family, like coping may suggest unrealistic strategies. A person while coping may find the situation tough and may go for suicide or may indulge in refusal or denial behavior. Coping during terminal illness in the family may include refusing to accept the condition realistically and making down to earth coping strategies.

During war times very often father (male member) of the family went missing from their home for long period. McCubbin observed, how families adjusted to this situation. He came up with three stages in the family adjustment, *viz.* Resistance, Restructuring and Consolidation. Resistance means denying to accept reality that was in front of the family. Next, restructuring occurs when gradually the family start accepting the reality and are able to reorganize themselves in new roles, e.g. mother (family members) becoming the bread earner, giving orders to others. Mother also become more independent. Finally, consolidation occurred where, everyone accepted the new reality, accepted their new roles and made the new interactional relationship more stable. They accepted the reality and adopted the newly structured life style, thus giving a new meaning to it.

Separation and Divorce

Who wants to separate from ones spouse, no one, but some happenings occur which create tensions between couples, aggravate them to a point where it becomes difficult to adjust with eachother. Finally, they opt for separation and divorce. The basic cause of fights between couples are money matters, extra-marital affairs or children. Money matters can be solved easily, but only when, there is consensus between the couples. Usually they quarrel on small matters and when devastating matters come up like money matter or children then they fight so badly, that a situation comes when one walks out of the home and opts for divorce or separation. Death of a spouse may also lead to separation. In India arranged marriages are the trend and the couples try their best to adjust to one another but still divorces are on the increase. Here, attempts are being made to pinpoint the causes of divorce and reduce the devastating impact of divorces.

Personal characteristic of divorced person

A team of community psychologists from the University of Colorado did a comprehensive review of stress and marital conflict and reported that psychiatric problems were more among divorced and seperated people as compared to marital people. The National Centre for Health Statistics reported that divorced, separated or widowed persons had higher rates of illness and disability than married and unmarried persons. Higher rate of alchoholism is also observed among separate and divorced persons. Very often these problems may be present during marriage period and may be the cause of breakup.

Attacks and threats

Suzanne Steinmetz did a study which revealed four approaches to conflict in marriage. Screamers are couples who make verbal and physical attacks on each other. The silent attackers avoid fight to a great extent but when matters aggravate they make physical assault. Threateners are persons who attack each other verbally and threaten to use physical means but do not do so. Fourth group consists of adaptors who resolved their marriage conflicts without use of verbal or physical beatings.

They are more prone to accidents and death rates due to accidents are higher among them as compared to normally married people.

One legged family : The single parent

Divorce or separation lead to problem of custody of children. Schlesinger observed that 90% single parents were women. The types of problems they encounted were financial difficulties, lack of sexual expression, feeling of isolation, Nancy Colleta compared low income families with average income families and observed that major problem were encountered in low income families, both for mother and children. Single parent family is more disorganized. Divorced parents showed greater anxiety, anger, rejection and depression. Parent who left the house face many problem because they had to start somewhere else from the very beginning.

Impact on children

As single parents encounter stress caused by the changing pattern of life, similarly children also face stress. Avis Brennet observed that children from such family were made to feel more mature, with more responsibilities, their play age becomes their work age. They are also creators of greater stress in the family. Sons become problematic for their mothers and daughters becomes problematic for theirs fathers. As most of the times mothers retain their children, and if the children are sons, they escalate the problem for their parents. Children dream of a future when their parents will be together again. Parents have to make persistent efforts to make their children accept the reality and to adjust to it. This often leads to remarriage, with a new parent added, thus shattering all hopes of the children for reconciliation among parent.

Post divorce Interactions : Many settlements force parents to interact even after divorce like moving to new home, financial settlement. Five different patterns that mark post divorce conflict are as follows :

(1) **Hostility regarding parenting** : One difference has been observed between parenting styles of father and mother. Father gives more time to his child, plays more with him, while mother resumes the same life styles for dealing with the child. This

difference may be because father has to prove that he can look after his child as well as the mother does.

(2) **Hostility may continue** : Causes for divorce may be remembered causing anger and feeling of unfairness and unjust behavior.

(3) **Interactional pressures** : Children force parents to maintain some contact among each other hoping that one day they may come together permanently.

(4) **Children used to harm one another** : Parents use their children as pawns to cause more pain and suffering to the other parent. This procedure causes greatest hurt to the children. Children will be normal and alright only when their parents maintain friendly relationship.

(5) **Extended families stress** : Many members of the family like grand-mothers and grand-fathers feel that their dreams are shattered if their children go for divorce. They feel that to some extent they themselves are responsible for the divorce of their children, they also feel shame in talking about it to others. They also have personal interest in their grandchildren, making arrangement for seeking themselves from time to time becomes very stressful.

Violence in the family

Spouse beating, beating of children, causing physical harm to family members is the cause of highest percent of stress. These sufferers suffer not only from physical harm but also from damaged self image, emotionally battered, mentally unsound, poor family relationship, lack of confidence in themselves. Sheer frequency of violence reveals that it is a normal occurrence. About 20% of homicides occur due to family violence.

Child maltreatment : The National Center on Child Abuse and Neglect has defined child abuse as marked inattention to child's basic needs, behavior of guardians which cause avoidable injury or impairment to a child. The types of maltreatment found was physical assault, emotional abuse of being killed. Factors contributing to abuse and neglect are as follows :

Parents who maltreat their children have had a developmental history that predisposed them to do so. An example is a student who narrated that if he performed any fault, his mother use to take him in the kitchen and burn his finger, the reason narrated was that because she was treated like this by her mother hence she applied it to her child.

Another factor is observation of aggression which influenced the people who practiced child and spouse abuse. Bandura observed that if children saw their parents fighting among themselves, and also if they were rewarded for performing aggressive acts then they were motivated to adapt these aggressive methods.

Last factor is ignorance on the part of the parents about how to treat their young ones. Another likely factors of stress within the family that precedes is the abuse. Under strain and tension one sometimes unexpectedly indulges in abusive behavior and then later feels sorry about it, but the harm is already felt. If abuse is performed then it becomes the cause of greater strain and stress in the family.

Life changes such as death of a spouse, divorce, loss of a job or economic hardships are highly influential in causing child abuse and neglect. Once abusing starts in the family, it becomes a part of life causing a chain of unhappiness and emotional disruption.

Another powerful stressor in the family is marital conflict. When marital conflict exceeds bearable bonds then abuses of children and family members occurs. Steinmetz observed that husbands and wives who used physical and verbal aggression in resolving marital conflicts also uses similar tactics when dealing with their children. Sometime, parents are not prepared for taking the responsibility of the child hence when the child comes into their lives, they become inbalanced and start abusing their child.

Sometimes, conflicts among parents are because of the child, if child cries or is unwell then father taunts the mother that her skills for looking after the child is not sufficient, thus shaking her confidence in her ability, if this taunting continues, then a stage will come when mother may turn towards the child and indulge in child abuse. Children are often responsibile for parents' fights. Fights over studies of their children, academic time of their children, marriage of their children are very common.

It has been observed that maltreated children are usually premature, they are slow in developing social responsiveness. This causes irritation, and when this continues for a long time, a feeling of rejection may build that makes one feel that one is incompetent. This leads to frustration, anger and ultimately to aggression. Elder children often do not cooperate with their parents. If they are punished they become more coercive thus leading to more deteriorating situation. All these occurrences may end in more powerful adult physical attacks. Sibling abuse is also a common sight in families, this may occur because of sibling rivalry. If one child is treated comparatively better than the others fights may occur. Often these are ignored by parents which aggravates sibling abuse.

Spouse maltreatment

Many factors causing child maltreatment may also be responsible for spouse abuse. It has been observed that men who beat their wives and battered wives come from families where violence is common. Woman attacked from childhood by parents is inclined to indulge in aggressive inter-relationship. They can leave their spouse if battered, but they don't do so. They can walk out from the relationship with their partners but they stay together inspite of the risk of facing trauma again and again. Don Dutton and Susan Painter explained this paradox through traumatic bonding. It is a complex process in which personal, familial and social forces operate to consort and to maintain the women into the abusive relationship. Periods of quarrelling are alternated with almost equally passionate attempts to make amends. This makes them feel that abuse was exceptional and now they will have better relation.

Another factor involved in traumatic bonding is power imbalance between the abuser and the abused. Abuser demands submission from the abused, and abuser wants some sense of power from the abused, hence they stick to one another.

Sexual abuse

Sexual abuse is the greatest crime as it breaks the trust between child and parent. In 1981 there were 17, 880 cases of sexual abuse of children under 12 years, more than 2000 of these childern were below 5 years.

Usually, incidences of sexual abuse occur within the family. The abusers usually are stepfathers, father, uncles or other members of the extended family, or acquaintances of family. Usually, abusers vent their sadistic rage to exercise power. Physical and psychological impact on sexually abused child are sleeplessness, nightmares, eating problems, restlessness, digestive problems, genital irritation, painful discharge of urine etc. Brenner elaborated on psychological effects like poor self concept, poor social skills, depression, maladjustment with family, suicidal tendency, etc. Some types of behavior may occur in children only after sexual abuse like fear of being alone, of being in the dark, trying to be with mother always, not going to the favourite place, showing changes in emotionality like irritability, worry about staying clean, crying, being away from parties, etc. or showing adult like behavior like sexuality or seductive talks. The perpetrator buys the child's loyality by giving gifts, money, clothes, etc.

The most important and easily detected signs are those associated with physical injury, such as irritation, bruises, swelling, bleeding in the gential region, or signs of veneral disease. Effect on the family are straining of family relations, natural family roles may change. The abused daughter may feel that she has the power because if she gets the abuser caught she may harm him, hence he tries to buy her silence by bribery or threats. He play upon her by the ignorance of cognitive understanding. He makes the child feel that whatever is happening is not wrong. But later she feels shame and guilt for what is happening. These problems lead to the sexually abused child not being able to lead a healthy life with her husband.

Coping Strategies of the family

Family is a social system, a variety of close contacts and supports are provided by it to its members. As a Social Supporter Pearlin defines social support as the access to and use of individuals, groups or organizations in dealing with life's vicissitudes.

Within a family social support works in two ways, First family is a social support network for family members. Second, family is part of the community, which tries to pass down its social norms through the family to all its member.

According to Cobb, social support serves three purposes, first, a person feels close to the family and feels secure in it. Second, person is valued on the basis of the family to which he belongs to. His status, esteem in community depends upon his position in the family. Third, give-take interaction is strengthened in the family, members learn mutual communication pattern.

There are other social systems also, which give support to a person like his peer group, work associates, community leaders. They work at different levels of life e.g. in teenage, peer group is helpful in job work, associates are significant helpers, in older age community, leaders may help. But family as a support system is most significant. It acts as a support system for the children the day they are born and do so in all events, whether it is learning to walk, talk, eat, study, facing stresses like hospitalization, surgery, illness or social problems.

Social support from family minimize the impact from various stressors and may also moderate the effects of hypertensions, increase chance of survival in cardiac and cancer patients.

In brief family stressors occur, which require solution from the family itself, plus family may act as a buffer between sufferer and stressors and thus reduce the impact of stress and problems.

References

Bandura, A. (1973). Aggression : A social learning analysis. Englewood Cliffs. NJ. Prentice-Hall

Brennet, A. (1984). Helping children cope with stress, Lesington, M. A : Lesington Books, p. 26.

Cobbs, S. (1976). Social support as a moderator of life stress. Psychosomatic Medicine. 38, 300-314.

Colleta, N. D. (1983). Stressful lives. The situation of divorced mothers and their children, Jounal of divorce, 6, 18-31.

Dutton, D. & Painter, S. L. (1981). Traumatic bonding : battered women and other relationships of intermittent abuse. Victimology : An International Journal 6, 139-155.

Klien, D. M. & Hill, R. (1979). Determinants of family problem solving effectiveness. In W. R. Burn, R. Hill, E. L. Nije & L. Reiss. Contemporary theories about the family, Vol. 1, pp. 493-548. New York. Free Press.

Mc Cubbin, H. I. *et.al.* (1980). Family stress and coping : A decade review. Journal of Marriage and the Family, 42, 855-871.

Pearlin, L. I. & Schooles, C. (1978) The structure of coping : Journal of Health and Social Behavior, 19, 2-21.

Schlesinger, B. (1969). The one parent family in perspective. In B. Schlesinger (Eds) The one parent family : Perspectives and annotated bibliography. Toronto : University of Toronoto Press.

Steinmetz, S. K. (1977). The use of force for resolving family conflict: The training ground of abuse. The Family Coordinator, 26, 19-26.

Chapter 6

SOCIAL FACTORS AND STRESS

The phenomenon rate of social and technical changes has a great impact on people's lifestyles. Although, medical science has increased the life spans of people and has eradicated or reduced the threat of many diseases, the pace of modern living has increased stress and decreased personal wellness. The concept of wellness has been defined as "a harmonious and productive balance of physical, mental and social well-being brought about by the acceptance of one's personal responsibility for developing and adhering to health promotion program (Krietner, 1982). Because people get caught in the urbanized and crowded of today, their wellness in general has deteriorated and the potential for stress has increased.

Life changes may be slow or sudden, like getting older, or death of a spouse. These changes have a dramatic effect on people. They found a definite relationship between the degree of life changes and the subsequent health of the person. Faye Crosby, reports that divorce interferes with work more than any other trauma in a person's life. During the first three months after a spouse walks out, the other spouse-male or female usually is incapable in focusing on work.

Sociological variables such as race, sex, and class can also become stressors. Minorities may experience more stressors than majority groups. When gender difference on stress was studied it was observed that (Marlocchio & Leary, 1989) women perceived more job demands than men in both male dominated and female dominated occupations. For professional women, the particular sources of stress have been identified as discrimination, stereotyping, the marriage/ work interface and social isolation (Nelson & Quick, 1985). In a recent study by Capowisky (1993) a significant number of working women reported feeling of personal or family stress which inturn leads to job stress. In particular, dual family and work roles frequently result in job stress. People in middle and upper classes may have particular or common stressors.

There are stressors about which people may be oblivious or may deny their existence, for example people who don't know what sunami or katrina means may be oblivious to their devastating effects. A person may also employ stress reducing strategy to deal with changes, their speed, which are beyond his understanding. They may be living in society but not as part of society. Thus, changes can exact heavy penalties from those unprepared or unwilling to meet the challenges of change.

6.1 SOCIAL THEORY OF STRESS

Sociologists, psychologists have conducted studies which suggested that crime, mental illness, and poor health increase in direct proportion to the degree of (i) financial stress, (ii) urban crowding and (iii) lower socio-economic status. The logic behind human misbehavior is that social pressures are at the root of psychological stress and physical illness altogether.

Dodge and Martin, two social theorists made explicit statement about relationship between social pressures and personal stress. Their theory was based on frequency of illness. It stated that both chronic (long term) and acute (short term) illnesses have social factors contributing, but the social factors differ for each type of illness.

Aubrey Kagan, a life change researcher, pointed to the dramatic increase in ill health associated with the Industrial Revolution, a period associated with a virtual explosion of technology and tremendous pressures on social structures. Kagan saw a greater danger in it. The method dealing with danger was, and still is, to recognize them, usually after a large measure of damage and to apply rational connections. This method is called planning from crisis to crisis, and is perceived to be too slow and dangerous with the rate of change that exists today. Hence, there is impelling motivation to understand the effects of social stressors in contemporary society.

Critical assessment of early Social Theories

Most early theories, whether sociological or psychological were one tracked. They emphasis at the causes of stress in social structure (Sociogenic causes) or within the person (psychogenic causes). The idea of rational analysis did not occur. Another glaring weak point of these early theories was that they did not study poverty stricken or inhumane conditions which had immuned them toward stress. They also did not study people who were deserted the impact of stress.

A Review of Social Stressors

A review of literature on stress has revealed few important sources of stress in our society. A major governmental study entitled 'Healthy People ' identified some major sources contributing to stress and poor health.

(1) Up-rooting or the effect of dislocation and frequent relocations.

(2) Dehumanizing of societal institutions by impersonal and mechanical delivery of human service.

(3) The spread of technology.

(4) Obstacles to the efficient and effective delivery of human services.

Apart from these, there are several other causes of stress like dual career causing family and social problems. Reservation policies which have caused upheaval in the services sectors, women fighting for equal rights has made both men and women stressed and has led many to courts. These major social stressors may be summarized as (i) sociological and technical changes, (ii) dehumanizing and victimizing forces, and (iii) environmental stressors including overcrowding, pollution, etc.

Social-Change Stress Interface

The first dramatic change was presented in the classic book, titled "Future Shock" by Alvin Toffler. Toffler talked about the information overload that comes from too much changes in too short period of time. Future shock is a disease which is characteristic of highly developed technological societies. It is premature arrival of the future. It occurs when the pace of change is so rapid that it exceeds our ability to integrate change.

The speed of sociological and technological change is very fast. Technological changes have drastically affected the way in which people work, learn and spend their leisure time. Technology changes the environment, which in turn changes jobs. Education changes the outlook of people, which creates more awareness of their rights and duties. Science has changed the amount and range of information, which is available to them. This pace will increase further in future. It has been observed that scientific and technical information increases at the rate of 13% per year. At this rate of production the volume doubles every 5. 5 years. It has been projected that the rate of growth will reach 40% in the near future. In this exciting, challenging and fast moving world, what might come next no one can predict.

Social changes are reflected in life style changing. Changes in family have challenged old values and religious traditions, like gays, liberation, abortion, lesbians, adoption of orphans. They have provoked families, communities, cities and governments for arguments. Religious traditions have been revised. World is no longer what it was before.

Toffler wrote another book entitled 'The Third Wave'. It described the end of the second wave civilization, which was founded on industrialisms, religious idealism and centralized democracy. This second wave included society of the past 300 years, and some part of moving present. He suggested that the changes now occurring are revolutionary, in pace and impact. This change also includes changing life-style which is based on diversified, renewable energy source on new production method, the radically changed schools, corporations and electronic cottages.

The old society with all of its values and traditions is being torn down to make way for a new society with a new set of values and traditions which are standing on the rubbles of the old society. It may excite the young adventurous but may be disheartening for old and inadventurous.

Many people may take up these new changes only after fighting expensive psychological warfare, which is fought privately by individuals for getting personal meaning of the new changes. Later it may be fought at an open arenas in the form of interpersonal conflicts, such as marriage, nuclear family and the community.

6.2 IMPACT OF SOCIAL CHANGES ON PERSONAL STABILITY

The psychological impact of the revolution is highly visible. There is rise in confusion, anxiety. One's self identity reduces as many relationships which provide security, are moving continuously. Anomie (Durkheim) increases. It is a sense of aloneness, loss in impersonal social setups. This may make the person turn towards structures of the past, or may approach some cults of religious fervor. These cults are financially supported by fast fragmenting population. Various religious ashrams, temples, churches take up these opportunities to brainwash human beings and give solutions for their various problems, providing them solace. They provide definitive conceptions of private individual identity which can be strongly internalized and which are usually backed up by psycho-social support structure. There is a gap between one's expectations and fulfillments. The gap between one's dream and what one gets in the form of unemployment, victimization, discrimination, yields frustration and quiet desperation. It is the gap between one's reach and one's grasp that translates social stressors into the personal stressors.

Social Readjustment

Social readjustment was defined as "the intensity and lengths of time necessary to accommodate to a life event, regardless of desirability of this event. Holmes and Rahe (1967) formulated a Social Readjustment Rating Scale (SRRS) (Table 6.1). It ranked life change events with association of the stressor. After collecting responses to this questionnaire Holmes and Rahe computed the average severity of life change produced by the stressors and ranked the items from most intense to least intense. The original rating was done with an arbitrary value of 500. When the final mean ratings were computed, the investigators assigned the most severe stressor the value of 100. All other means were then adjusted to the standard, so that the relative intensity of each item was still reflected accurately. The three items ranked as most stressful by this sample were death of spouse, divorce and separation. All involve life changes in marital situation. Moreover, eight of the top stressors were either family or work related. There are a relatively large number of low to moderate severity stressors. Very few items are high severity stressors.

Table 6.1 : Rank of Life Change Events with Associated Life Change Units (LCU) as an index of the Disruptiveness of the Stressors.

Rank	*Life Events*	*LCU*
1.	Death of Spouse	100
2.	Divorce	73
3.	Marital Separation	65
4.	Jail Term	63
5.	Death of close family member	63
6.	Personal injury or illness	53
7.	Marriage	50
8.	Fired at work	47
9.	Marital reconciliation	45
10.	Retirement	45
11.	Change in health of family member	44
12.	Pregnancy	40
13.	Sexual Difficulties	39
14.	Gain of new family member	39
15.	Business readjustment	38
16.	Change in financial state	37
17.	Death of close friend	36
18.	Change to different line of work	35
19.	Change in number of arguments with spouse	35
20.	Mortgage over $10, 000	31
21.	Foreclosure of mortgage or loan	30
22.	Change in responsibilities of work	29

23.	Son or daughter leaving home	29
24.	Trouble with in-laws	29
25.	Outstanding personal achievement	28
26.	Wife begins or stops work	26
27.	Begin or end school	26
28.	Change in living conditions	25
29.	Revision of personal habits	24
30.	Trouble with boss	23
31.	Change in work hours or conditions	20
32.	Change in residence	20
33.	Change in schools	20
34.	Change in recreation	19
35.	Change in church activities	19
36.	Change in social activities	18
37.	Mortgage or loan less than $10, 000	17
38.	Change in sleeping habits	16
39.	Change in number of family get-together	15
40.	Change in eating habits	13
41.	Vacation	13
42.	Christmas	12
43.	Minor violations of law	11

Note from "The Social Readjustment Scale" by T. H. Holmes and R. H. Rahe, 1962. Psychosomatic Medicine, 11.

It was also observed that a large number of events are obviously pleasant rather than negative. They produce some stress, examples are marriage, pregnancy, vacation, festivals, outstanding achievement. Some produce more stress than others. As defined by Selyes, the body does not distinguish positive and negative stressors. The excitement of pregnancy is as nerve touching as grief suffered due to loss of a close member of the family. Subjects were asked to respond to the scale. Circle the number of the event that have occurred in the past six months, next locate the score of that event, sum all of the scores. After obtaining these ratings Holmes and Rahe interpreted the findings to determine if life changes influence one's personal health and adjustment. There is some deteriorating effect on health. Three lines of evidence contributed to this finding. First comes from a wide variety of laboratory and clinical research programs based on the work of Selyes. The second line of evidence comes from observations of the reactions of people to natural disasters, such as earthquakes, floods, observations of individuals under conditions of abnormal stress, such as soldiers in combat. The third line of evidence represents the concerted efforts of many investigators working over nearly two decades. They tried to determine the relationship between the amount of stress and the amount of illness occurring in populations in the natural environment. These researches suggested that stressful life changes could precipitate a variety of detrimental effects, including psychological disturbance and physical illness.

6.3 PROFESSIONALS AND LIFE CRISIS

Physicians : Holmes and Rahe asked a group of 200 resident physicians to list all the major health changes they had experienced in the previous ten years and to fill out the SRRS. Of the 96 major health changes reported, 89 were associated with total Life Range Unit (LCU) scores over 150. When the LCU score was under 150, the majority of the physicians also reported good health in the succeeding year. But when the LCU score was over 300, over 70% of the physicians reported illness in the following year. The value of 150 was then used for a preliminary definition of a life crisis. Holmes and Rahe further analysed and established more precise categories for life crisis.

150-199	Mild Life Crisis
200-299	Moderate Life Crisis
Over 300	Major Crisis

They made the assumption that as more life crises accumulate, the more likely the persons will incur some illness within a short period following the crisis. Holmes and Masuda found a number of supporting evidence. They have found increased life change associated with myocardial infection, fractures, diabetes, tuberculosis, leukemia, etc. Another study on academic environment revealed that as life change increased among college frehmen, their grade point averages went down. These findings were repeated in other countries like Sweden, Wales, Norway, Denmark, France.

Telephone Operators, Carrier Pilots : Using a random sampling technique, Hinkle and his colleagues took a sample of 226 employees who had 20 years or more of services with the company. A review of the medical history of the group revealed a phenomenal difference in the amount of sickness. Some employees had no sickness disability at all during the 20 years. Many had just 5 days total absence due to sickness and only 1 or 2 episodes of illness-related leave each year. The third group of employees revealed some startling facts. Many members of this group had mixed up to a total of 1000 work days during this 20 years period. Some had suffered nearly 100 episodes of disabling illness during the same 20 years.

Next, Hinkle and his associates wanted to determine if a particular biological or psychological pattern might provide some explanation for the major differences between healthy and the sick group. There was a strong evidence of a consistently different psycho-social pattern between the two groups. It was observed that healthy telephone operators liked their work, found it easy and satisfying, liked their families and associates, and were generally content with their lot in life. While the frequently ill telephone operators were working at their jobs out of necessity, they found it binding and boring. They were unhappy with their family and life.

Hinkle also studied two other groups. One was a group of Chinese born graduate students, technicians and professionals living in New York. Other was a group of Hungarian refugees who had escaped from United States following 1956 Russian invasion of Hungary. Both groups had gone through severe dislocation, separation from families and long standing social support groups and extreme cultural shock. Chinese showed little evidence of illness at all. Hungarians showed the same distribution of illness as telephone operators. They were not happy in Hungarian regime, they felt insecure and frustrated. However, during the revolution and flight and inspite of severe disruption in their lives they actually showed an improvement in overall health. General excitement and the anticipation of making a fresh start in a new country served as a type of inoculation against sickness. Hinkle concluded from these studies that the effect of dramatic social change on a person's health could not be determined solely from the nature of the change itself. Other factors like psychological factors are also significant.

A very interesting study on a real world environment was carried out on aircraft carrier pilot trainees. The type of situation encountered by these trainees appears similar in many respects to that arranged by Brady in his famous executive monkey study, (Rubin, 1974). The physical reaction observed was also very similar.

Rubin described the training situation and aircraft. In the aircraft F-4B Phantom jet fighter-bomber, two persons are required to operate it, one is the pilot in the front cockpit, having complete flight control, while the other is a Radar Intercept Officer (RIO) in the rear cockpit, he monitors radar and other instruments but has no flight control. In an emergency both the persons can eject from their air craft, but RIO must depend completely on the pilot's skill for his own personal safety. Measurement of physical response of both the persons showed an interesting finding, *i.e.*, there was higher level of subjective anxiety among RIO as compared to the front cockpit pilots.

Another observation made on sailors revealed that men found ill were those in menial jobs, in hazardous or uncomfortable jobs (Rubin). Another label attached to persons facing physical impact was immaturity among people which prevented them from maintaining their health.

Hinkle studied telephone company employees. Study was done on 226 employees with 20 years of service with the company. The review of their medical histories revealed a clear cut difference between the healthy and the unhealthy employees. The healthy telephone operators liked their works, found it easy and satisfying, liked their families and associates, were content with their lives. The often ill telephone operators did not like their work, worked due to necessity, found the work boring, were unhappy in their lot, with their families, their associates and the community. This study has implication for personality types. Persons with positive view of life could adjust in all situations and found something nice in every thing hence were more happy, however, persons with negative view of life could not adjust anywhere, were always dissatisfied with life, whether it was home life or office life. It is these personality types who pass down their natural endowments to their future generations and see that this cycle goes on always.

The criticisms coming up regarding life changes causing illness are the methodological weakness of research design used to establish the relationship between them. Such designs may have many difficulties like subjective biases, fallibility of memory as intervening variables, all these may affect subject's report of what actually was happening. Another criticism is always linking illness to some psychological problem, this attribution may not be right. David Schroeder and Paul Costa reported a study on a group of people, their preliminary medical examination was made before the start of stress year, and after the year they were asked to report on life change using a "56 item checklist by Home Rahe, plus a medical examination was done, to see if any new disease had erupted. They found no connection between life change in the 12 months and incidence of illness. These findings may be the result of moderator variables. Sarason, Levine pointed some moderators like locus of control, psychological hardiness, prior experience that influence how a person responds to stress.

6.4 COPING WITH LIFE CHANGES

Social change is the most permanent phenomenon, it is global, pervasive and constant. One should be prepared for the future. This is possible only by being alert, keeping eyes open to all that is happening in ones life, one should prepare oneself for the future through self education, self discipline and self control. Person who is well educated, socially alert, culturally aware will be mentally prepared for new innovations, will adopt better with new technologies, will always be prepared for confronting new life styles without feeling much stress. One cannot stop stress but one can learn to accept it, respond positively to it and will adjust better to it. Stress inoculation techniques may help. This approach focuses on imagining some of the very worst situations, which may induce very high stress, like computer banking, test tube babies, becoming bankrupt, being alone. Considering oneself in any of stress producing situations, and seeing how one will respond to it. Trying to anticipate how it will influence his/her life makes the person to act according to the situation. If one works on some of these worst possible anticipated fears one may find it easier to deal with such situation when they really turn up.

Another approach is value classification. This is a cognitive coping strategy which enables a person to determine how much value one attach to the stressful situation, once the amount of value attach to various stress situations are identified then one can take information related to them more comfortably and can respond better.

Some ways of coping with stress include belonging to a group, having acceptable substitute acitivities available, be ready to take advice, have someone for giving outlet to frustrations, etc.

Summary

Changes put person in many stressful situations, some changes may be within your controlling power, some may be uncontrollable. One should search for coping methods for dealing with such stressful situations.

References

B. P. (1982) Some issues in research on stressful events in T. Millon, C. Green, & R. Meagher (Eds). Handbook of Clinical Health Psychology, New York, Plenum Press.

Durkheim. E. (1951) Suicide, New York : Free Press.

Hinkle, L. E. (1974). The effects of exposure to culture change, social change and changes in interpersonal relationships on health. In Dohrenwend & Dohrenwend Stressful Life Events.

Holmes, T. H. & Rahe, R. H. (1967). The Social Readjustment Rating Scale. Psychosomatic Medicines, 11, 213-218. Dohrenwend, P. & Dohrenwend.

Rubin, R. T. (1974) Biochemical and neuroendocrine responses to severe Psychological stress. In Gunderson & Rahe, Life Stress and Illness.

Schroeeder, D. H & Costa, P. (1984) Do stressful life events influence objectively measured health?A prospective evaluation. Paper presented at the Mid Western Psychological Association Annual Conference, Chicago.

Toffler, A. (1970). Future Shock. New York : Bantan Books.

CHAPTER 7

CHILDREN UNDER STRESS

Traditionally, stress has been defined in terms of its source (e.g., internal and external) (Marion, 2003). Internal sources of stress include hunger, pain, sensitivity to noise, temperature change and crowding (social density), fatique and over or under stimulation from ones immediate physical environment. External stressors include separation from family. Change in family composition, exposure to arguing and interpersonal conflict, exposure to violence, experiencing the aggression of others (bullying), loss of important personal property or a pet, exposure to excessions expectations for accomplishment, "hurrying" and disorganization in one's daily life events (Bullock, 2002). Although the research literature tends to focus on the impact of single-variable stressors on children's development, in real-life situations, children experience stress from multiple sources. Researchers note that multiple stressors interact with the another and can have cumulative effects (Stansbury & Harris, 2000).

Are children stressed in the present period ? The answer is 'yes'. Children lead a busy life in their school, at playgrounds, cyber points and homes.

In schools, they go with a burden of books on their back. During school hours they are taught numerous subjects, they are made to retain these variety of subjects in their tiny brain. They also listen to the yells of their teachers, seniors, etc. All these affect them. Than in the playgrounds, they play competitive games which imbibe in them competitive win-lose spirit which again causes tension. Children cannot skip the stresses of their lives. They have to bear their stresses and try to cope with them. Just as adults, they face adjustive demands which may be classified as frustrations, conflicts and pressures.

Frustration

Frustration occurs when one's strivings are thwarted, either by obstacles that block progress towards a desired goal, (book deprivation, opportunity deprivation) or by absence of an appropriate goal (too difficult target, too easy goal).

A wide range of obstacles, both environmental and internal, can lead to frustration. Group prejudice, discrimination, death of loved ones are common frustrations coming from the environment. Physical handicaps, lack of needed competencies, inadequate self control are sources of frustration that can result from our own personal limitations. Often barriers arise out of psychological factors in the form of moral restraints. College students cannot speak their minds in front of their elders because their moral values make such behavior inacceptable, plus there are faulty value assumptions like if we do badly in our studies our parents will face disgrace. The frustrations one faces depends heavily on such factors as age and other personal characteristics, our specific life situations and the society in which we live.

Conflict

In many instances stress results from the necessity of choosing between two needs or goals. Usually the choice of one alternative means frustration with regard to the other, e.g. choosing one of the two friends for a specific purpose, or choosing one course of study instead of the other (art vs. science vs. commerce). The key element in conflict is often the frustration that arise when we must choose one alternative and give up the other. The necessity of making a choice commonly involves "cognitive strain". It is often difficult to make up one's mind, especially when each alternative offers values that the other does not. Conflict is conveniently classified as approach avoidance, double approach, and double avoidance type.

Approach avoidance conflict : Conflict involves strong tendencies both to approach and to avoid the same goal. A student may want to opt for science in his higher classes but may fear the amount of time and effort which he may have to put into it. Similarly. other desires may conflict with inner reality or ethical restraints or with fear of failure, for example a student has literary tastes but because of higher status involved in joining the scientific stream he may be forced to join it.

Double approach conflict : Conflicts involve competition between two or more desirable goals e.g. a student may have to decide about whether he should prepare for cricket match in summer vacation or go for an excursion. Such simple "plus plus" conflicts result from the inevitable limitations in one's time, space, energy and personal and financial resources. More complex cases may be such as when an individual is torn between two good career opportunities or between present satisfactions and future ones, decision making must be difficult and stressful.

Double avoidance conflict : This occur when a person is caught between "the devil and the deep blue sea" e.g. he has to choose between finishing a project assigned to him which is very difficult or quitting it and being called a failure.

Pressure

Stress may stem from pressures to achieve particular goals or to behave in particular ways. Such pressures may originate from external or internal sources. A college student may feel under severe pressure to make good grades because his parents demanded it, or she may submit herself to such pressure because she wants to gain admission to graduate college. Pressure may force a person to speed up, intensify or change the direction of goal oriented behavior. In some instances pressures seriously tax our adjustive resources, and if they become excessive they may lead to a break down of organized behavior.

Children are affected by stress, just as are adults, but tile mechanisms or the effects art; not necessarily the same. Children, for example, may be subject to stress from the family directly, and clearly, children may experience work-related stress through its effects on the family, but they themselves cannot directly experience the stresses generated in the workplace. For them, however, there will undoubtedly be stress from the school they attend. Children's coping strategies are likely to be less sophisticated than adults, due to a lack of experience of the world. The effects of stress on children is a topic which as yet is relatively unexplored and is worthy of a carefully considered approach, as current explanations of perceived pupil misbehavior tend to focus on events in the child itself and not externally defined criteria which may bring about such changes.

We will look at the effects of stress on children developmentally, *i.e.*, from birth through to adolescence and to make some form of assessment as to how childrens stress may be reduced.

Some form of stress may affect the baby before it is even born. The expectant mother may have high stress in a number of cases. These can include such things as an unplanned, unwanted baby, insufficient income for the baby, a lack of physical space for the baby, other very young children, poor nutrition, poor prenatal care, physical complications (things like nausea, swelling, high blood pressure etc.), a fear of the birth, a fear that a baby will bring about a loss of freedom and a fear or knowledge that the baby will be deformed or diseased. One study has shown that there can be a relationship between mother's stress level and baby's temperament at birth. On the other hand, other research has found it very difficult to measure a link between the woman's psychological state and the baby's emotional state at birth and concluded that nervous, worried women may not digest food well and smoke more than those who were more confident and these factors could affect the unborn child more than the adrenaline or other physiological factors associated directly with stress. It would appear that a relaxed and safe pregnancy is good for baby and mother and so it would make sense that as many of the conditions outlined previously are avoided.

The birth of a baby is an event that will bring change to all members of the family, and as such may be a stress-inducing factor. In fact on the Holmes and Rahe (1967) Life Change Index pregnancy is rated as 40 stress points, which in isolation may not be much, but as stress is cumulative, it is easy to see it as a major contributory determinant. It is common for a mother to begin to overreact to what once were considered minor annoyances, begin crying for no apparent reason and even begin to resent the new member of the family. This condition is known as post-natal depression or post-partum depression and according to some research affects the majority of new mothers. Some of the sharpest effects of this post-partum depression will manifest themselves in, what is currently termed, abuse, on the new-born infant. Emotional deprivation, too, cannot be overlooked as a contributory factor as inducing stress in the child. Some research has concluded that any breakdown in the mother-child relationship could cause severe emotional, intellectual and social consequences. The idea of an infant's and a young child's need for unconditional love and concern is further advanced by the Newsons (1976) when they say '...the developing personality needs to know that to someone it matters more than other children; that someone will go to unreasonable lengths... for its sake'. Perhaps, this is more in line with the current psychological view that mothers need not be the sole care-givers, but as long as there are not too many and that each gives the child the love and care and stimulation, the stresses imposed on the baby or infant will be minimal.

When a new baby is born, there may be stress placed on any young children at home. They may feel a sense of loss as this could be the first time that the mother has been away from home for any length of time. Where a child is made aware that mother has gone into hospital this may bring on feelings of fear and anxiety, especially in cases where the child associates hospitals with death and disease. There may be emotional scenes when mother and new baby do come home; older children may feel threatened and therefore placed in potentially stressful situations by the attention parents may devote to siblings. When the focus of attention has become the new baby it is not unknown for sibling rivalry to manifest itself in the form of aggressive behavior towards the intruder, with, for example, bites being substituted for kisses and objects that could harm being placed near the - rival. In some instances, the method of coping with the stress is that of regression, a term used to describe a condition where an individual who is under stress reverts temporarily to a more immature state. In the young child, this is typically shown by a reversion to babyish behavior, talking baby talk, crawling or bed-wetting for the first time in months. Psychologists do not consider this to be harmful as a coping mechanism as long as children return to age-appropriate behavior when they have adjusted to the stress. It has been suggested that some emotional envy and jealousy is inevitable when a new baby is born as far as older siblings are concerned. The nature of this stress can be minimised by parents taking the older brother or sister to visit their new baby in hospital and be present at gift-givings and be encouraged to become involved in the upbringing of the new child.

In their early development, children will have several reasons for being distressed; they will cry when hungry, cold, tired, in pain or when support to which they have become accustomed is withdrawn. On the other side of the coin they will display pleasure, laughter and smiles when they are content. This can be brought about by being securely wrapped and cuddled, seeing potentially interesting sights, and hearing soothing noises such as a regular heart beat. Thumb sucking is used by babies as a way of relieving tension, especially when going to sleep, when anxiety seems to be at its greatest. Smiling is well documented, and is a response to such things as a full stomach, a pleasant noise or a social response to a face. By 4 or 5 months, a baby will smile quite broadly and laugh, as opposed to grinning, at exciting stimuli.

During the age of around 6 to 12 months, crying in babies usually lessens as the stressful effects due-to the developing digestive system reduces, since digestion becomes more stable, and curiosity of the world around acts as a destructor to minor problems of the self. The baby will undoubtedly respond to the stresses in the home, and may become the subject of rough handling where parental tensions, for whatever reason, are high. Too much stimulation and constant bouncing around, even with the best of intentions, can cause the baby stress and will result in crying intending to send signals that the infant wants to be left alone. Opposite to this is the case, where the baby begins to smile and laugh in anticipation of a pleasurable experience rather than during something that is eliciting pleasure.

From around 12 months of age, the baby is likely to show signs of stress when it is forced to do things it does not want to, such as going to bed when not tired, or having something taken away from it. Typical signs of this frustration will be loud cries that sound more than anger rather than pain or sadness. Smiling and laughter are likely to continue as before, but may be inhibited by something the child perceives as fearful. Fears and hence anxiety and hence stress have been observed to increase from age 6 months to about 18 months. Two researchers subjected babies to potentially fear inducing stimuli : a visual cliff, a strange adult, a jack-in-a-box, a small moving dog, a mask, and a loud noise. They found that babies up to 7 months rarely showed fear, those above 7 months became wary of the stimuli and those age 11 to 18 months were most likely to be frightened by all six stimuli. From 18 months, it was noticed that the fear declined. Clearly there are important implications for early child-rearing practices in order to minimalise stress during these early years. What appears to be necessary, is a secure, loving home environment, where stimulation that does not induce fear is used.

The developing child in its early childhood may have feelings of fear, or anxiety by virtue of the fact that it is now able to recognise that it is physically small in relation to the adult world in which its carers exist. In some homes this may be compounded by adults who continually make the child aware of its size and limitations by 'standing tall' when speaking to the child, or by hectoring when the child makes mistakes. When toys become broken, this too can cause stress in the child, and this is especially the case where they cannot be repaired, as it emphasises to the child its own imperfectness in a world where adults and older siblings do not seem to have these problems. The child may have fears, in the home where disapproval, and possibly punishment are the order of the day when things get broken. It has been established that fears of such occurrences go beyond the fears of earlier years mentioned earlier, and reach a peak at around 3 years of age. This again reinforces the view that young children need stability and a home where love, cuddles and reassurance are much in evidence.

For the four or five year old, starting school can be a traumatic experience and as such produce stress feelings. In some cases, there will be a difficulty in adjustment, from what may have been a quiet, ordered environment with few, if any, other children, to one of apparent confusion,, bustle and noise. Frequently, 'new starters' suffer separation anxieties and may have real fears about being hurt or bullied by older children and even little things such as being allowed to go to the toilet. In order to ease such a child into a new situation, a sympathetic teacher is required. This is perhaps less easy today, now that schools have responsibility for a finite budget, and in order to balance the books, frequently have to go for the cheapest teachers, who are usually the least experienced and adept at handling situations. The problem of easing the less than confident child into school may also be compounded by increasingly large early years' class sizes.

Middle childhood, roughly from age five to ten or eleven, is a period where children who develop normally and are not developmentally delayed, appear to suffer from potential stressors and begin to make their own coping strategies. Some of the fears from early childhood may remain and as such prove stressful; typical examples are fear of being left alone, and fierce animals. Fear of the dark and of ghosts and strange creatures can also persist. These fears gradually fade at around age ten and so stress from such matters is reduced. During the middle childhood, children can be subject to pressures from within their family, which can cause them stress. Where they fear the death of a parent, or a parent leaving home this can lead to stress for them. Where there are arguments in the family, this can lead to feelings of anxiety in case one parent leaves or physically harms the other. Unstable relationships can be unsettling for a child at any age, but it would appear they are particularly vulnerable during this period of middle childhood. One body of research, describing a case of twin boys, has demonstrated that compensation can be effective. The boys in this study were placed in a children's home after the death of their natural mother. Then from the ages of one and a half to seven years they were subject to extremely harsh treatment by their father and stepmother. They were kept in almost total isolation, lived in a small unheated closet and were not allowed in the tidy areas of the flat. They had to sleep on polythene sheets and were often locked in the cellar and cruelly beaten. The twins were also denied adequate access to food, fresh air and exercise. Whilst neighbours were aware of some of the happenings, they were unwilling to interfere as they did not want to enter into a confrontation situation with the step-mother, as they knew her to be an aggressive person. Eventually, at the age of seven, the boys were placed in an institution where they received special education. It had been envisaged by a number of professionals that these children had an extremely low chance of ever becoming 'normal'. On entry to the institution, the boys' mental age was assessed as being about three years of age'. By chronological age nine, after two years in the institution, they were considered to be able to integrate into an ordinary school and be placed with foster parents. During the first year with the foster family and whilst attending the ordinary school, the boys showed an improvement in their IQ of around 10 points, as measured an IQ test. The intellectual development continued; by the age of 12, the twins' IQs were within two points of 100, the average level. Psychological reports also seemed to indicate normal emotional development. It was noted that there was a great bond between foster mother and with each other on the part of the twins. School relationships were also good. Clearly, it is not possible to know how well the boys would have developed given an upbringing like this from birth. What it does show, however, is the importance of a stable family, where there is care and love, if stress on children is to be minimalised.

The period of adolescence, usually from age 12 to 18, has been seen as particularly stressful for children, who are now growing into young adults. It was believed that this period is characterised by emotional and psychological stress due to the young person trying to cope with physical and sexual development, coupled with problems of self-identity and independence. At the turn of the century, it was the commonly held view that erratic growth spurts were coincident with erratic emotional and moral development. As long ago as 1904 it was said that it is perfectly normal for adolescents to pass through phases of 'passionate cruelty, laziness, lying and thievery.' This is a view mirrored by some psychoanalysts, who believe it should be of greater concern to parents where their children do not show emotional upset during adolescence than where they do. Consequently, this was a view that prevailed for many years and is probably still the easy classical solution to describe adolescent behavior today.

From the 1960's onwards, psychological research began to show that the previous descriptions regarding adolescent reactions to the stress factors described, which whilst valid in a number of cases, were in fact over- generalisations. They were the pictures painted by the media and by parents who in some way were legitimising their behavior towards their offspring.

In short, these were adult ways of coping to the stresses that their children were placing on them at this time. Studies concentrated on examining the behavior of 'ordinary' adolescents and found that adolescents are not in turmoil, not deeply disturbed, not at the mercy of their impulses, not resistant to parental values, not politically active and not rebellious.'

It is our belief, that a stable family, where there is love, care and concern is of paramount importance in the alleviation of child stress. Further weight is added to this argument 'based on a research study in 1975 which looked at a group of boys through adolescence and into early adulthood. This placed 80% into one of three categories 22% fell into the group which had many crises; 23% showed a smooth transmission and had mutual respect, trust and love with their parents; the remaining 35% fell midway between the other groups, coping quite well, but with recourse to displays of anger and regression before moving towards a more mature method of coping with the demands that body and cultural changes forced upon them. In summary it would appear that the research tells us that there is no hard and fast rule for adjustment to the stresses of adolescence. As with the adult, the individual must establish his or her own method of coping or succumb to the pressure.

There is some evidence to suggest that the rate of maturation, and when it occurs can have an effect on the self-esteem of the individual. Physical size, shape and appearance can be stressful to the adolescent. It has been found that characteristics, in order, boys looked for in girls were : good looks, good body, friendliness, intelligence; girls looked for in boys : intelligence, good looks, good body, good conversationalist. This reinforces the adolescent's concerns for physical attractiveness and goes some way to explaining why they spend so much time in front of mirrors and large amounts of money on clothes and cosmetics in attempts to make themselves more attractive. One researcher observed that early maturing girls were more likely to be respected and liked as they were perceived as attractive to older boys and were able to offer advice to less mature girls. Boys who matured later than their contemporaries appear to suffer from stress in that it can affect their self-esteem through their lives. One study found that late maturing boys were inclined to be less poised, less relaxed and more talkative than those who matured early. They were also less likely to be chosen as leaders. Follow up studies were conducted on the same late maturing individuals when they were 33 years old and again when they were aged 38. Most of the subjects had reached at least average height but a number of earlier personality characteristics remained as did feelings of social inferiority. They were also found to have less responsible positions at work and had feelings of inferiority and rejection. Thus, in order to counteract the feelings of stress, brought on by very early and very late maturers, it would seem to be important that teachers and parents deal positively with the special emotional needs of such individuals in order to minimise long lasting feelings of inferiority and rejection.

Schools are institutions where a child or young person can experience stress. Anxiety that may befall a child on starting school. There are some children who are known as 'school phobics' and seem to experience severe emotional and possibly physical problems at the thought of going to school. Whatever the underlying cause of the refusal to attend school, it is clear that there is a situation which is causing the child severe stress that goes beyond the child-mother separation on first starting school. This is the child's way of coping with an immediate problem. In such cases, expert medical opinion needs to be sought and acted upon. Bullying is of great concern to a number of children at school. It is of concern to parents that their child is not popular and is subject to bullying in one of its forms. Most of the bullying in school takes the form of exclusion from groups, or verbal abuse rather than physical attacks, which many regard as the only form of bullying. It seems that children loath to inform on bullies as this will indicate, particularly in the case of boys, who are frequently told that they should 'stand on their own two feet', that this is an admission that they are weaker than their peers. Children who are bullied are frequently distressed and this stress may show itself in a dropping off in academic performance, arriving home from school later than normal. Taking different routes to and from school or showing general stress and unhappiness. It is not unknown for bullied children to ask for different packed lunches or increased pocket money to 'pay off those who are doing the bullying. Children who are bullied need help. What form this takes will depend on the nature of the child and the nature of the bullying. Simply drawing attention of any incident to the school may suffice, particularly where the school has an adequate support system in place. Counselling may also help some children. Intervention is necessary as it has been found that in some cases, there has been a permanent lowering of self-esteem in the recipient of the bullying which has affected their adult relationships. It may be necessary for staff to re-examine their own attitudes towards bullying in order to change the school and children's perceptions of bullying and this involves a mutual respect for each other. It appears much can be done in anti-bullying by changing the ethos of the school, organising awareness programmes, and taking action immediately when any form of bullying is noticed.

Children may experience stress at school due to academic pressures which stem from their parents. Parents can place children under pressure to do well. With the result that children who did not come top in every examination and test, feel they are failing their parents. Such stress can make the children ill and it is not uncommon for children placed in these circumstances to suffer from conditions such as eczema and/or asthama. In order to counteract this, parents need to become less demanding and reduce their expectations. It has been observed that once parental pressure has lessened, the physical signs of stress in the child also diminish and can eventually disappear.

Perhaps, one of the most disturbing aspects of chronic stress in adolescents is that the pressures may seem so great at times that they feel they are totally unable to cope and end up by committing suicide. A study done in the United States of America, it was estimated that there was a growing trend of adolescent suicides of 237% between 1960 and. 1980.

There is good reason to be concerned at this staggering increase, a fact borne out in 1968, where suicide was the second most common cause of death among North American teenagers and the most common amongst teenagers in Japan. The table of what are called : 'frequent participants and events preceding adolescent suicidal behavior' looks like this:

1. Arguments between parents
2. Arguments with parents
3. Loss of parent
4. Divorce of parents
5. Break-up of close relationship
6. Failing grades
7. Loss of interest in usual activities
8. Complaints of boredom

All of this again reinforces the argument about the necessity for a stable home, where love, care and mutual respect is the norm.

Near the beginning of this answer we made reference to events outside the child. Clearly from the work listed above these have an obvious bearing on stress in children and adolescents, and are events that by and large are outside their locus of control. One such event is bereavement, which can strike at any age. A baby will have no conception of death, but will become anxious if it has become to a main carer, who is suddenly no longer there. A pre-school child might target blame onto themselves, working on the principle that the parent has gone away due to their behavior, especially in a household where they may have been told that a parent will not come back until they improve their behavior. These children can show their stress by becoming fretful and not sleeping properly and may resort to more immature behavior. It has been noted that children tend to fall ill after a death, an indicator that they are suffering from stress. Holmes and Rahe, on their Life Change Index rate a bereavement at 100 for a spouse and 63 for a close relative, and whilst there is no scale available for children. It must be assumed that they would score at least the maximum on the adult scale. Hence, it is easy to see they tend to fall ill. It appears that children are beginning to recognise the permanency of death from around the age of five or six. Where one parent has died, it is common for the child to transfer all their affection onto the survivor, and to become very protective. There will be extreme cases where one parent will have suffered a violent death at the hands of the other; an event that may have been witnessed by the child. Such an occurrence must surely be most stressful and it is likely that the child will suffer from post traumatic stress disorder. It is believed to be important that the child should be interviewed a few days after the event and encouraged to recall as much as detail as possible by drawing, playing and talking about the incident. The intention here is to make the child feel that the event is outside them and in some way allows them to grieve normally instead of internalising any blame. Any trauma, such as the events in Dunblane in Scotland, and in the USA where very young children witnessed the shootings of adults and teachers, is certain to have an effect on those present and their families, which may last throughout their lives. Hence any method which can reduce stress at the time and later, is worthy of consideration. It may be useful in the attempted alleviation of stress for the child to be introduced to picture books and stories where characters have undergone similar trauma and 'emerged unscathed. This aspect of didacticism in children's literature can be important in the construction or redefinition of reality in the child's world. One study showed how important it is in reduction of stress in the case of a childs mother having died, for the school to be sensitive to the grief shown by the child. It is perhaps best in cases of a parent having died, for the child to have stress reduced gradually until the pain of the death becomes a distant, but not forgotten memory.

Children are susceptible to stress when parents decide to divorce. It is self-evident that the situation leading up to the decision may also be stressful. The child can be subject to many internal tensions : which parent is right and which is wrong or wronged? is one example. Whatever the age of the child at the time of the separation, there will be a number of emotional experiences with which the child will have to try to cope. The child will feel saddened by the parting and loss of one parent, in a similar way to bereavement. There will no longer be as easy an access to one parent, or even other loved members of the family, as there once was. A child may undergo stress through an inner anger which results from feelings about an event being outside their control. This will be especially difficult where a child has always been used to being the focus of attention and getting their own way. The child may have feelings of anxiety over the situation. It may worry about the consequences of the divorce and in some way feel some responsibility for what has happened and for what the child perceives will happen. The child can feel confused as to the reasons for the divorce and may suffer from stress associated with divided loyalties between the parents. For children in middle-childhood, there can be adverse effects on school performance when parents divorce, as a result of feelings for parents being uppermost in their minds. For some, it may have little or no effect on attitudes and work in school, as they are able to treat school and home as mutually exclusive entities. They may feel a desire to prove to themselves and others that they can succeed and feel comfortable and reassured in an atmosphere where there is now a distinct routine and order. For them, school has become their focus of stability. Child behavior in the breakdown of a marriage is unpredictable; there may be a rejection of the parent-carer, or there may be over-protectiveness. This may cause the parent who has remained with the child(ren) to become stressed, which in turn can increase the stress on the child. Where there is more than one child in the family, the eldest child may assume the role of the parent who has left, a factor which can increase the pressures, and eventual stress, on itself, both physically and emotionally. A study of the impact of divorce on children, conducted in the United States of America, attempted to explore the feelings of 131 children and assess the effect of divorce on them after five years. They found that the initial phase was very stressful, with the effects reduced by the end of the first year, with boys being more affected than girls. This particularly affected boys between six and eight years of age when the father left home. This would appear to be consistent with role identification theory, in that there would no longer be a role model for boys at this crucial phase in their development. After the first year had elapsed, it seemed that the boys and girls entered a plateau, or transitional phase, in which there was a degree of acceptance that the parents had divorced. This phase was observed for two to three years. Following this, some, but by no means all, the families, had succeeded in making a happy home.

Adolescents may undergo stress during and after a parental divorce as they have now developed a moral code of their own. They may have to face up to questions such as 'Who is right and who is wrong?' 'Which parent ought I, or do I, want to live with?' They may also have definite views on their parents morals and cannot come to terms with a succession of 'boyfriends' or 'girl friends', or even one, who may become their stepparent. Step-parents can pose problems at any age, because, however willing the stepparent, may be to become a member of the family, he, or she, can never be the biological parent. It has been noted that there are no cases of little girls wanting to be step-mothers when they grow up, unless possibly, they have been brought up by one.

There will be problems for the child in a situation where there is a step-parent and then new step-siblings come along. This will be very evident in family where children from the new marriage appear to be given preferential treatment, or the child perceives that they are given better toys. Parents and step-parents need to exercise extreme caution in their dealings with the children in the new family, if stress is not to be raised to an unacceptable level.

Problems over child access can cause the child stress. Most children, from a divorce are in the custody of their mother. Some mothers will want father to have no further contact with children, perhaps because there has been a history of violence towards her and the children prior to the divorce, or for reasons, that she may simply want to begin again on her own. Where a father no longer has his own home, problems over contact can upset children. There can be problems over where to go and what to do during the contact time. There can be problems over being seen as too generous, by the other parent, if many trips take place, or many gifts are given at the contact time. There can be problems for the child over parental attitudes towards each other. It is not unknown for either parent to interrogate the child about the behavior of the other, or to be very critical of whatever the other is doing. This can upset the child in that it has decisions to make over how to behave and what to say so as not to appear disloyal to either parent. It has been suggested that during contact visits, activities ought to be age-appropriate and reflect the children's current interests. This researcher also hold the view that children should not be placed in a situation where they have to have their loyalties strained or continually hear parental criticism. He goes on to say that where a child does behave badly, that parents need to understand this is a stress response to the situation and that the child's changing attitudes are related to developing maturity.

It seems to be the perceived wisdom, certainly from the adult perspective, that where a marital relationship has broken down, that to reduce stress all round, the solution is that the parents get a divorce. The corollary from this is that it is best for the child to be brought up by one parent in a non-stressful home, as opposed to being brought up by two parents who are continually arguing. American and British research indicate that children preferred a non-divorcing family and were prepared to accept a situation where the marriage was unhappy, as their perception was they were no worse off than families around them. It is likely that children who are brought up in such an environment, where aggressive in their behavior, overt violent and possible excessive drinking and substance abuse became the norm, displaying conduct disorders. In these situations, the conventional wisdom of divorce for the sake of all may be an appropriate choice to make. It has been shown that boys in a family who miss their father can become defiant and difficult, following the divorce, but show an improvement after about two years.

It is clear that children are subject to stresses throughout their lives, and as with adults it is those who are unable to develop appropriate coping strategies who will fall ill. The Sunday Telegraph, 01.12.96, states that some 40% of children have mental health disorders. The breakdown of the family is cited as a cause together with inner city deprivation, lengthy time waiting for psychological assessments and rapid changes in fostering arrangements when placements break down. Other factors mentioned are family related problems, including marriage break-down and poverty. The British Psychological Society refer to effects of trauma, social relationships in the play, and the Witnessing of physical or emotional violence. Valerie Riches of Family and Youth Concern has said : 'Why are so many children disturbed? Because the family is crashing down, they are confused, they do not have the enduring love that they must have to become responsible adults.

7.1 FACTORS INFLUENCING THE SEVERITY OF STRESS

The severity of stress is gauged by the degree of disruption in the human system that will occur if the individual fails to cope with the adjusted demand.

The actual degree of disruption that occurs depends partly on the characteristics of the adjustive demands, partly on the individual and partly on cultural and situational context in which the stress occurs.

Characteristics of the Adjustive Demand. Several objective factors influence stress severity which are independent of the individual involved or situational context in which the demand occurs.

(a) **Importance, duration and multiplicity of demands** : It has been observed that certain stresses such as death of a loved one, divorce and serious personal illness, tend to be highly stressful for most people (Holmes and Rahe 1967). Ordinarily, the longer a stress operates, the more severe, it becomes. Prolonged exhaustion imposes a more intense stress than does temporary fatigue. Often stress has a cumulative effect, small fights between parents, irritates the child. These fights go on increasing causing prolonged stress in the child and later explodes leading to the child becoming a drug addict or a psychological case.

Encountering a number of stresses at the same time makes a difference too, e.g. for a child, home fights, school fights, poor scores in class, loosing in game, all at the same time result in stress more severe than if these events occur separately.

(b) **Strength and Equality of Conflicting Forces** : Conflict between weak motives or between motives with little self investment involves minimal stress, for neither of the alternative would cause a serious loss. On the other hand, conflicts between strong motives such as one requiring a choice between self esteem and social approval are likely to subject the individual to considerable stress. In addition, the more nearly equal the strength of the opposing motives, the greater the stress.

(c) **Imminence of Anticipated Stress** : As the anticipated stress approaches near, the severity of stress increases. Mechanic (1962) observing graduate students found that although the students thought about their examinations from time to time and experienced some anxiety during the prior three months, anxiety did not become intense until the examinations were nearly upon them. For individuals who repeatedly subject themselves to a regular stress situation as in the sports of sky, a somewhat different pattern of severity may be involved. For novice jumpers, the peak of anxiety or avoidance does not come at the period of greatest danger-the free fall-but at the ready signal, when they can choose to go ahead or to cancel the jump. On the contrary, for experienced jumper the anxiety peaks up during the morning of the scheduled jump, and once they have decided to jump that day, their fear usually decreases.

(d) **Unfamiliarity or Suddenness of the Problem**: Often new adjustive demands that have not been anticipated and for which no readymade coping patterns are available will place an individual under severe stress. All one's knowledge, skill seems to be totally inadequate and irrelevant to the task at hand. By contrast, if a stressful event, even a potentially catastrophic one, if known, can be prepared for, it thus, loses its severity, e.g. fire fighters, policemen, soldiers.

Characteristics of the individual : The persons perception of the problem, the degree of threat it entails and available resources for meeting it, all influence the severity of stressful situations.

(a) **Perception of the Problem** : An individual's evaluation of the stress situation determines to some extent the severity of the stress. Individual always react not simply to the situation but to the situation as evaluated him, especially in relation to his ability to cope with it. For example, if a person lost his calculator in the class, he will react depending upon how he evaluate it. If he feel highly deprived he will complain to the teacher and make him take action for findings his calculator, or he may wait for the lunch time to come and then he will talk to his friends and take their help in getting his calculator, therefore, the approach he will use is based on his evaluation of the situation.

(b) **Degree of Threat** : Threat is the anticipation of harm. Stress situations that are perceived as potentially damaging or threatening to survival such as having a limb amputed or being given a diagnosis of cancer carry a high degree of threat. Similarly, stress situations that threaten the adequacy and worth of the self such as loss of social status or failure in one's chosen line of study, or occupation, or desires incompatible with one's self concept and self ideal involve a strong element of threat. Persons also likely to be threatened in situations that place demands on them which they see as important but beyond their power to meet *i.e.*, if we doubt our general adequacy and worth we are much more likely to experience threat than if we feel generally confident and secure.

(c) **Stress Tolerance of the Individual** : The severity of a given stress depends on resources for withstanding stress in general and that stress in particular. If a person is marginally adjusted the slightest frustration or pressure may be, highly stressful. Stress tolerance refers to one's ability to withstanding stress without having integrated functioning seriously impaired. Both biologically and psychologically people vary greatly in general vulnerability to stress as well as in the types to which they are most vulnerable. Emergencies, disappointments, etc. that one person can take in stride may prove incapacitating to another. Sometimes it is earliest traumatic experiences that leave the individual vulnerable.

(d) **External Resources and Supports** : Lack of external supports either personal or material makes a given stress sever and weakens an individual's capacity to cope with it. A divorce or death of one's mate is more stressful if one is left feeling alone and unloved than if one is still surrounded by people one cares about and feels close to. Pressures to violate one's principles or beliefs are less stressful and more easily withstood when one has an ally than when one is alone.

Studies have revealed a tendency for individuals exposed to highly stressful situations to turn to others for support and reassurance.

Often culture provides for specific rituals or other courses of actions that give support as the individual attempts to deal with certain types of stress. Religions provide rituals that help the bereaved through their ordeal, and in some faiths, confessions and atonement help people deal with stresses related to guilt and self-recrimination.

7.2 TYPICAL STEPS IN COPING WITH ADJUSTIVE DEMANDS

Present day computer simulation studies support the notion that human brain is a centre for elaborate communications, problem-solving and decision making, here incoming information is continuously evaluated, alternative responses are formulated and weighed, decisions are made and implemented, and feedback is checked with a view to correcting possible error.

(1) **Appraising the stress situation** : When a new adjustive demand is perceived, it is quickly assigned to a particular category of problem based on its similarities and differences from previous demands. At the same time, the degree of danger or threat posed by the adjustive demand is assessed. If the stress is evaluated as a serious threat, it is likely to elicit anxiety and lead to interruption in ongoing activities in order to cope with it.

(2) **Problem solving and decision making** : After the situation has been appraised, alternative courses of action are formulated which in turn,

provide possible ways of dealing with such stress situations, because these categorisations were used in the past in similar situations. Next, the individual must assess the relative merits of alternative solutions and make a choice. This choice will be based on probability of success, the degree of satisfaction he is willing to accept, and the cost he is willing to pay, in short he must balance probability, desirability and cost.

(3) **Taking action and using feedback** : Once a decision has been made, the next step is to implement it. Once the course of action has been embarked upon, the individual can keep checking on whatever feedback information is available to see if corrections in ongoing actions are indicated and feasible. This may include two steps, termination of one course of action and the formulation and implementation of another that appears more effective.

But human brain is subject to error. It may make faulty assumptions, time pressure emotional involvement, and many others factors that may lead to wrong answers. Such errors may lead to seriously maladjusted behavior.

These adjustive demands, severity of stress, coping strategies may apply to people of all ages. But childhood is the phase of learning and if pressures, conflicts and frustrations are experience by them in a disrupting manner then they will spoil their whole lives. They will not be able to develop themselves in a balanced way and their adolescences, adulthood, old age all will be negatively influenced, which will be very harmful.

Looking at these harmful outcomes of stress, it is imperative on the part of parents, family members, teachers to provide a healthy environment to the children, environment provided should inspire in them healthy competition, friendliness, we feeling, team spirit, helpfulness etc. and prevent them from developing jealous, derogatory behavior, ill treatment of others, etc.

References

Coleman, J. C. (1982) Abnormal Psychology and Modern Life. D. B. Taraporevala Sons & Co. Private Limited, Bombay.

Holmes, T. H. & Rahe, R. H. (1967) The social readjustment rating scale. J. Psychosom. Res., aril, 1 (2), 213-218.

Mechanic, D. (1962) Students Under Stress. New York, Free Press.

Chapter 8

AGE RELATED STRESS

'Old is Gold'. This phrase means old age is the most glorious period of one's life, one is free of responsibilities, free from work, cocooned in his habitat with his children who care for them.

Old age starts after retirement, *i.e.*, 60–62 years old of life. The person starts getting pension. His children are usually settled down, *i.e.*, he/she is free of all responsibilities, now one can relax with no worry of getting up in the morning rushing up daily routine works and going to workplace for the whole day, coming back home at the sunset, completely exhausted. In this age there should not be any stress, any conflict, any frustration, any pressure. But is it so ? No.

In any Indian household, an old, moaning, unwell individual is present in most of the homes. And asking about their health, they answer that they are suffering from one disease or the other. This shows the stresses which they have encountered and they were bearing their impact.

In order to highlight old age stress lets scan through the physical changes that occur as a person passes through the aging process.

As a person moves up the ladder of life he encounters various stimuli in his environment. They bring changes in his physical, emotional or mental state. Causes of aging are presented in the two major headings : Stochastic Theories and Programmed Theories (Baron 2004).

8.1 STOCHASTIC THEORIES

"Growing old is the result of living". Other term used is "wear and tear" theories of aging. They suggest that we grow old because of cumulative damage to our bodies from both external and internal sources. Because such damage is not completely repaired, we simply "wear out" over time. Damages cumulates overtime, thus producing declines associated with aging. Indirect evidence for wear and tear theories of aging is provided by individuals who repeatedly expose their bodies to harmful conditions or substances for instance large doses of alcohol, various drugs, or harsh environments. Such persons often show premature signs of aging, presumably because they have overloaded their bodies' capacity for internal repairs.

8.2 PROGRAMMED THEORIES

According to the programmed theories of aging, every living organism contains a kind of built in biological clock that regulates the aging process. Next, the immune system seems to wind down over time and the endocrine system and the neural areas that control it, declines with increasing age. These systems regulate many basic processes (e.g. our metabolism) so as they decline our vitality drops too.

Support for programmed theories are provided by several observations.

(1) All species have their characteristics for maximum life span; this suggests that length of life is somewhat built into different species genetic codes.

(2) Longevity appears to be an inherited trait, one rough indicator of how long you will live is the life span of your parents and grandparents.

(3) Age related changes in our bodies show a regularity that can be explained with reference to genetic factors.

(4) Findings suggest that certain cells do indeed divide only a set number of time before dying. No environmental conditions seem capable of altering this set number.

Selyes has used two separate terms to distinguish between the positive and negative effects of stress on the individual, even through bodily reactions to the two forms of stress are similar. Eustress is positive stress that accompanies achievement and exhilaration. It is the stress of meeting challenges as found in interesting high level jobs. Distress occurs when we feel insecure, inadequate, helpless or desperate as a result of too much, or too little, pressure or tension.

Depending on the type of stress experienced by retiring people they will face frustrations, tensions, pressures, satisfactions in their old age.

Stress is additive. It builds up. Each new and persistent stressor adds to an individual's stress level. A single stressor, in and of itself, may seem relatively unimportant, but if it is added to already high level of stress, it can be "the straw that breaks the camel's back". To appraise the total amount of stress an individual is under, his opportunity stress, constraint stress and demand stress are to be sumed up.

Retirement usually is a meaningful change in a person's personal or work situation. Holmes and Rahe reasoned that major changes in a person's life can lead to stress and eventually to disease, several incidents may occur in a persons life and may be reflected on the individual. At one extreme is spouse death (most traumatic), at the other extreme minor violations of law. Apart from these, there are other events which influence an individual. They include divorce, death of close family member, change in health of family member, sexual difficulties, change in financial state, children leaving home, change in living conditions, change in residence, illness, or some chronic illness like diabetes, arthritis, blood pressure, etc. Holmes and Rahe research suggested that stressful life changes could precipitate a variety of detrimental affects, including physiological disturbance and physical illness.

If a person has encountered eustress more than distress after retirement, he will feel a sense of fulfillment, satisfaction, self actualization and achievement. He will possibly not be physiologically disturbed, hence he may not also be physically ill. For e.g. our ministers Sri Atal Bihari Bajpai, Sri Advani, our president Sri Abdul Kalam, all are shinning figures. They have held significant political positions and are still holding them, they have fulfilled their need for self actualization, achievement, satisfaction, *i.e.*, all the events they have encountered were eustresses. On the contrary are persons who encounter stresses which have overburdened them with physiological disturbance and physically illnesses, and they face mental problem, heart diseases, chronic disease etc.

8.3 PHYSICAL CHANGES DURING ADULT YEARS

Physical changes are very revealing if one looks through a family photo album, one that spans several decades. Grandparents, aunts, uncles, stare back with youthful eyes. A comparison between their present looks and past looks provides the scope of physical changes that occur during one's adult years.

Physical changes occur during early adulthood. It is a period which is faced after teenages, here physical growth is usually complete. But some parts of the body shows aging, like eyes. Eyes become weak and person wear spectacles from very young age of 5-6 years. Teeths of some people have weakend. Aging is a continuous process that starts very early in life muscular strength, reaction time, sensory activity and heart action are all near their peak through the mid-twenties and then decline-slowly-through the mid thirties. Physical changes occur that very slowly.

8.4 PHYSICAL CHANGES DURING MID-LIFE

By the time people are in their forties, most people are aware of the age related changes occurring in their bodies. Cardiac output, the amount of blood pumped by the heart, decreases noticeably and the walls of the large arteries lose some degree of flexibility, hence less oxygen can be delivered to working muscles within a given period of time and people usually become aware of some decline. They simply can't do quite as much as they could. Other changes are readily visible when middle aged people look into the mirror and see thinning and graying hairs, bulge and wrinkles.

Among most dramatic changes occurring during middle adulthood is the climacteric-a period of several years during which the functioning of the reproductive system and various aspects of sexual activity change greatly. Among women, menopauses is experienced, cessation of the menstrual cycle in their later forties or early fifties was previously perceived as a stressful period but in the present circumstances most women do not find menopause as disturbing or anxiety provoking event. (Datan, Antonovsky and Moaz 1984).

Among men, the climacteric involves reduced recreation of testosterone and reduced functioning of the prostrate gland, they get enlarged, this may interfere in sexual functioning and urination.

Strength, beauty, vigor, all decline during this period in adults, the magnitude and the rate of such decline is dependent on the individual's life styles. Growing evidence suggests that one can achieve successful aging by applying the following factors, *i.e.*, physical exercises, personal nutrition, effective stress management.

8.5 PHYSICAL CHANGES IN LATER LIFE

Average age is currently rising at a steady pace. In the United States, the proportion of population *i.e.*, 65 or older has risen from about 4 or 5% in 1900 to about 12 or 13% now. Similar trends are occurring in many other developed countries, e.g. in Sweden they have risen from 17% in 1900 to 24% in 2005, in United Kingdom, from 16% in 1900 to 21% in 2005. Stereotypes suggest that people in their sixties, seventies and eighties are generally frail, in poor health and unable to take care of themselves. Now this has become untrue. In the United States, a very large proportion of people in these age groups report good health. The picture of older people that emerges in developed countries is quite encouraging.

A point to be noted is that many physical changes in older people occur due to primary aging changes caused by the passage of time and perhaps genetic factors, while some physical change occur due to secondary aging changes due to disease, disuse, or abuse of our bodies. As people age, they experience decline with respect to vision, hearing, smell, tastes and other senses, however, there are large individual differences.

8.6 CONSEQUENCE OF STRESS

Stress is the spice of life. Complete freedom from stress can only be experienced in death. Stress becomes distress when one begin to sense a loss of one's feelings of security and adequacy. This phase becomes more prominent for old people. They face many physical, behavioral and psychological consequences.

Physical Consequences

The physical or medical consequences of stress affect a person's physical well-being. Heart disease and stroke, among other illnesses, have been linked to stress. Other common medical problems resulting from too much stress include headaches, backaches, ulcers and related stomach and intestinal disorders and skin conditions. These physical consequences become more pronounced in old age. About 70% of old people face blood pressures, diabetes and heart problems. Out of one thousand people, one person may be found free of all these problems.

Behavioral Consequences

The behavioral consequences of stress may harm the person under stress or others. One such behavior is smoking. Research has clearly documented that people who smoke tend to smoke more when they experience stress, alcoholism and drugging also is linked with stress. Other possible behavioral consequences are accident proneness, violence and appetite disorders. Some of these consequences are quite prominent in old people like appetite disorder, alcoholism, drugging.

Psychological Consequences

The psychological consequences of stress may be relate to a person's mental health and well-being. When people experience too much stress in home or outside life then they face depression, they find themselves sleeping too much or not enough. Stress may lead to family problems and sexual difficulties. All these consequences get aging lighted when people grow older.

8.7 FIVE GOLDEN PRINCIPLES TO A STRESS FREE LIFE

Proper Exercise : This is done by following yoga posture or asanas, which work systematically on all parts of body-stretching and toning the muscles and ligaments, keeping the spine and joint flexible and improving the circulation.

Proper Relaxation : By practicing yoga one releases one's tension in the muscles and relaxes the whole system, leaving as refreshed as after a good night sleep. It carries over into all activities and teaches to conserve energy and let go off all worries or fears.

Proper Breathing : This principle involves breathing fully and rhythmically, making use of the whole and not just a part of your lungs, to increase your intake of oxygen. Yogic breathing exercises of Pranayam teaches how to recharge body and control mental state by regulating the flow of *prana*- the life force.

Positive Thinking and Proper Mediation : By following this principle one removes his negative thoughts and stable the mind.

A Proper Diet : A proper diet is one that is nourishing and well balanced, based on natural foods. It keeps the body light and supple and the mind calm increasing resistance to disease.

If these golden rules are followed seriously old age may be a period of quietness, relaxation and unproblematic.

References

Baron, R. A. (2004), Psychology. Pearson Education.

Datan, N. Antonovsky, A. & Moas, B. (1984). Love, War and Life Cycle of the Family. In K. A. McChuskey & H. W. Reese (Eds.). Life Span Development Psychology. Historical and Generational Effects, pp. 143-159). New York : Academic Press.

Holmes, T. H. & Rahe, R. H. (1967) The Social Readjustment Rating Scale. Journal of Psychosomatic Researches, 11, 213-218.

Selyes, H. (1976) The Stress of Life. (2nd ed.) New York. McGraw Hills.

CHAPTER 9

PERSONA AND STRESS

Recent interviews with doctors have revealed that personality does correlate with both the types and the intensity of the stress reactions in human beings. In the West the notion that personality is somewhat related to coping and health is ingrained. Personality types have some relation with types of health problems. Personality may also be related with variety of sickness behavior which in turn has affected their recovery process.

Before discussing more about personality–stress relationship, it is essential to understand what personality means. The term 'personality' has been derived from the Latin term 'persona' which means to 'speak through'. The term denotes the masks worn by actors in ancient Greece and Rome. Common usage of the word 'personality' signifies the role which the person displays to the public. Personality of a person is unique, personal and a major determinant of his behavior.

According to Allport "Personality is the dynamic organization within the individual of those psychological systems that determine his unique adjustment to his environment". According to Ruch 'Personality includes external appearance and behavior, inner awareness of self as a permanent organizing force and the particular pattern or organization of measureable traits, both inner and outer'. How a person effects others depends upon his physical appearance (such as, height, weight, facial features, colors, etc.) and behavior (such as, courteous, friendly expressive, cooperative, etc.). Personality is the essence of the person behind the mask, *i.e.*, persona has come to mean some characteristics within a person. Personality is also stable and enduring, providing a private reference point in the midst of constant flux and change. Most definitions share common theme, such as, uniqueness, organization and style of adopting or coping. The perceptions, thoughts, feelings and behaviors of each individual are organized in different pattern which in turn make them unique, different from other persona and determines their styles of responding.

Theodore Millon was highly concerned about personality in relationship to stress and health. His view, like Psycho dynamic view holds that personality summarize the person's style of dealing against interpersonal stress, anxiety and psychological conflict. Uniqueness of his view is his statement that personality acquired by a person is his coping style to deal with stressful occurrences.

9.1 THEORETICAL PERSPECTIVE ON PERSONALITY

Several personality theories have come up from time to time. These include (1) the Psychoanalytical Theory (2) The

Dispositional Theory, (3) The Phenomenological Theory and (4) The Behavioral–Cognitive Theory. The various theories are described in relevance to stress and health.

Psychoanalytic Theory in Stress and Health

Sigmund Freud propounded psychoanalytic theory which is based on the notion that man is motivated by unseen forces more than by conscious or rational thoughts. This clinical finding led him to conclude that major motivating forces in man is unconscious framework. This framework contains three aspects, though interrelated but often conflicting, these are id, ego and superego. Their brief description are as follows :

The Id: The id is the source of psychic energy and seeks immediate gratification for biological or instinctual needs. Freud believed that instincts could be classified under life instincts and death-instincts. Life instincts are hunger, thirst and sex; the energy involved in these is the libido. The id would proceed unchecked to satisfy motives, particularly the sexual relations and pleasures, were it not for the challenging activity into acceptable ways by the ego. As an individual matures, he learns to control id.. But even then, it remains a driving force throughout life and an important source of thinking and behavior.

The Ego: The ego is the conscious and logical part of the human personality and is associated with the reality principle. While it represents the unconscious part, ego is conscious about the realities of the external environment. The ego keeps the id in check through intellectual and reasoning.

The Super Ego: The super ego represents societal and personal norms and serves as ethical constraint on behavior. It can best be described as the conscience. The super ego provides norms to ego to determine what is wrong or right. However a person is not aware of the working of the super ego and conscious is developed by absorption of cultural values and norms of the society.

Freud theorized that there are five universal stages of psycho-sexual development which are decisive in the formation of personality. These stages are: oral, anal, phallic, latent and genital. The first three stages of development extend from birth to five years and are called pregenital stages since the genital zones of the body have not attained a dominant role in personality development.

(1) **The Oral Stage:** It extends throughout the first year of life. The mouth is the body zone through which biological drives are sought to be satisfied, e.g., thumb sucking by an infant or biting when teeth erupt.

(2) **The Anal Stage:** During the second and the third years of life, the focus of libidal energy shifts from mouth to the anal region. In other words, the anal becomes the body zone for sexual gratification. Young children derive considerable pleasure from both retention and expulsion of faces. Toilet training given to the child by its parents will have its influence on adulthood. If the mother is too harsh or repressive, the child withholds faces, and if this becomes excessive, the child develops an anal-retentive personality. When grown up, such personality exhibits traits of obstinacy, stinginess, orderliness, punctuality and extreme cleanliness or extreme messiness. Alternatively if the mother pleads with her child to have regular bowel movements and showers him

with praise when he does, the child will develop an anal-aggressive structure. A child reprimanded at this level would show traits of cruelty, destructiveness, disorderliness and hostility.

(3) **The Phallic Stage:** At about four years of age, focus on sexual gratification shifts to another erogenous body zone, the sex organs. During this stage children can be observed obtaining gratification by examining and finding their genitalia, masturbating and expressing interest in matters of birth and sex.

(4) **The Latency Stage:** Between the ages of six or seven and the onset of adolescence, there is the latency period. During this period, the child loses interest in sexual matters and seeks gratification of the libido from the external world, curiosity, knowledge and so on. It is a period of social development under which the child acquires knowledge and skills to get along with the world.

(5) **The Genital Stage:** The genital stage occurs during adolescence to adulthood. There is a revival of sexual and aggressive impulses coupled with an increased awareness of an interest in the opposite sex. The individual experiences satisfaction from heterosexual love. Discharge of libido through mature sexual relations with an opposite sex partner paves the way for genuine concern for one's fellow.

Freud believed that in order for people to attain the ideal genital character, they must relinquish the passivity of early childhood days when love, security, and physical comfort indeed all gratifications-were freely given and nothing was expected in return. They must learn to work, postpone gratification, become responsible, and above all, assume a more active role in dealing with life's problem.

During the popularity of psychoanalysis many attempts were made to interpret stress responses and health problems in terms of psychoanalytic theory. Most of these attempts were linked with psychosomatic disorders. A psychosomatic disorder is one in which a real physical ailment (such as, ulcers, asthma, colitis or cardiac arrbythnia) is caused by or influenced by a psychological process, such as, ongoing stress or anxiety.

For example, according to Franz Alexander, prominent psycho analyst, the asthamic person is a victim of three correlated events : -

(1) A genetically weakened organ in the body which may break down when stress occurs.

(2) There is a specific conflict that weaken the persons defence system, if and when, stress occurs.

(3) There is some threatening situation.

Presumably, life stress arouses the unresolved conflict and the person is not able to defend against it. As a result the weakest link in the body, the lung express the stress in asthamatic attacks. There is little evidence to support the psychological origin of asthma.

Dispositional Theories

Dispositional Theories generally propose that there are 'enduring, stable, personality differences which reside within the person. The two most commonly encountered dispositional theories are typological approach and the trait approach.

Typology Approach : This approach was proposed by Carl Jung. According to Jung there are two types of people, the introverts and extroverts. The introvert is described as socially withdrawn, reflective, not given to display of emotions and somewhat closed off from the external world. The extrovert is characterized as outgoing, socially active, free in expression of emotions and rather open.

Biotypes : Certain personality traits are related to particular diseases. The chain goes on as follows. Genetic mechanisms determine constitution, temperament and intellect in each person. The interplay of these factors in turn leads to the emergence of a unique personality, it's strength will depend on genetic endowment, which may make it strong or weak. If personality is weak then there are risks of stress and health related problems. One personality type may be more prone to ulcers, etc. based on this type of reasoning a number of investigations now suggest that there are particular personality characteristics that can be associated with cancer, heart attacks, ulcers, arthritis and headaches, etc. Problems like depression, alcoholism and smoking are linked with personality. Type A behavior pattern is the most commonly encountered syndromes or biotypes. Now the question that arises, is which comes first, does health problem lead to changed in personality, or personality disorders contribute to health problems. Another misperception is that personality types are irreversible. This notion is not correct because personality is defined as influenced by biological, psychological or social factors. Thus, genetic factors may be shifted in different directions by the various forces that start influencing after birth. This indicate that changes in personality may occur throughout life, e.g. Type A person can gradually be converted in their working style to adopt less risky approaches thus reducing coronary problems.

Traits Versus Types

Focus of trait theorists is on the number of characteristics and avoid approaches of type theories which give global views. According to trait theorists, an individual have all traits present in him/her but in different amounts. It is the unique combination of traits which create individuals high on some traits, average on others and low on still other traits.

Trait Anxiety versus State Anxiety

Charles Spielberger believes that there is a basic difference between trait anxiety and state anxiety. Trait anxiety tends to be relatively stable across time and space. People high on trait anxiety tend to be relatively more anxious whatever the situation and are relatively more anxious all the time compared to those low in trait anxiety. Such people require only slight external stimulations to start stress reactions. On the other hand people with low trait anxiety are more relaxed all the times and require higher levels of stressful stimulation for starting an anxiety reaction in them.

State anxiety on the other side, is specific to a situation. Situation may be such that they provoke stress in people, for example, interviews, driving tests, solo music performances, examination, etc. In a person, anxiety may vary from situation to situation for example, a person caught in an accident may handle the situation very calmly but when confronted with a robber may experience an extreme degree of state anxiety.

Many people experience a type of state anxiety called test anxiety. People in various professions have to pass periodic exams for promotions, career growth, etc. A person showing high trait anxiety plus high test anxiety would probably panic in test like situations. A person with low trait anxiety plus low test anxiety would be able to handle this situation easily.

Persons with chronic stress may be high on trait anxiety, but recognition of illness comes in the arena of state anxiety, this is based on seriousness of the symptoms. For example, recognition of the presence of a serious heart problem is mostly related to state anxiety, but observing a strict life style of exercise, diet medication, check ups is mostly because of trait anxiety.

Special Dispositions and Type A Behavior

Can personality be linked with heart disease, depressions, cancer ? Are unhealthy behavioral patterns like alcoholism, drug dependency, smoking linked with special dispositions ? If yes, what are the special traits that make people vulnerable to their special illness ? What behavior pattern ? Can such risks be tackled with ? The next few pages discuss these problems.

Type A Personality/Coronary–Prone Personality : Two doctors Meyer Friedman and Ray Rosenman narrated an observation made by their tailor, who came to their office to repair upholstery of their furniture. He said that it appears that many worried, tensed patient come to your clinics. They asked him about how he made this observation. In reply he pointed out the wearing off on the edges of their furniture. This indicated that their patients sat mostly at the edges of their chairs. This lead to innumerable researches which revealed the connection between Type A behavior and coronary thrombosis attacks. The basic characteristics of Type A person are : —

(a) One who is time driven

(b) Impatient

(c) Insecure of status

(d) High competitive

(e) Aggressive

(f) Hostile

(g) Incapable of relaxing

Time urgency is very prominent in this list of symptoms. Their internal clock is faster compared to other people, they work more rapidly, pushing themselves to complete work at a faster pace than other people do.

This pattern is referred to as hurry sickness (Rosenman & Friedman). Thirteen most significant characteristics of Type A behavior include hurried speech, rapid walking, moving, eating, irritation if things don't move fast, doing more than one things at a time, talking about your own interest only, sense of guilt at relaxation, fail to see new things in the environment, acquiring rather than becoming, schedule more work in less time, high competitiveness, express loudly when conversing, feel the necessity of fast pace for success and measure success in numbers. These characteristics have been measured in a questionnaire (Table 9.1). Answering these questions on the basis of your first impression of how you know you behave most of the time may reveal you as Type A or Type B personality. If you answer yes to all questions you will be labeled as Type A personality, if half of the questions are answered in affirmative then you may be termed as moderate on Type A.

Type A person is set aside very clearly from Type B person based on personality traits. Type B person will respond no to most of the questions given (Table 9.1). Type B persons have two very significant positive traits, *viz.*, ability to relax without guilt and the ability to have fun for the sake of having fun not to win or loose.

Type A Type B Continuum

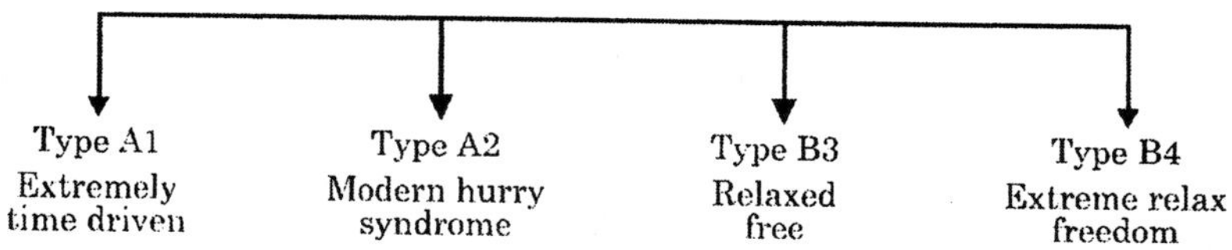

Table 9.1 : Criteria used to identify Type A Behavior Pattern

1.	Do you overemphasize some words in speech and hurry the last words in your sentences?	Yes	No ....
2.	Do you always move, eat and walk rapidly?	Yes	No ....
3.	Are you generally impatient and get irritated when things do not move fast enough for you?	Yes	No ....
4.	Do you frequently try to do more than one thing at a time?	Yes	No ....
5.	Do you generally try to move the topic of conversation to you own interests?	Yes	No ....

6. Do you feel some sense of guilt when you are relaxing? Yes .... No ....
7. Do you frequently fall to take note of new things in your environment? Yes .... No ....
8. Are you more concerned with getting than becoming? Yes .... No ....
9. Do you constantly try to schedule more activities in less time? Yes .... No ....
10. Do you find yourself competing with other people who are also time-driven? Yes .... No ....
11. Do you engage in expressive gestures, clenching a fist or pounding the table to emphasize a point while engaged in conversation? Yes .... No ....
12. Do you believe that your fast pace is essential to your success? Yes .... No ....
13. Do you score success in life in terms of numbers, numbers of sales cars and so on? Yes .... No ....

Note : Adapted form Type A Behavior and Your Heart by M. Friedman and R.H. Rosenman, 1974, New York: Knopf.

Factors associated with high risk for coronary are termed as 'Risk Factors' (David Glass). These include (1) age, (2) sex, (3) high cholesterol levels, (4) hypertension, (5) smoking, (6) inactivity, (7) diabetes, (8) parental history of heart disease, and (9) obesity. David Glass pointed that Type A behavior pattern is comparatively better predictor of coronary disease than risky factor. This relationship was established in a classic project called the Western Collaborative Group Study, which started in 1965. It ran for almost eight years and involved about 3500 subjects. Other studies have also revealed that the most important trait in the coronary–prone person is the existence of the Type A pattern, especially the impatience and over activity traits. Another two traits include depression and high levels of anxiety which indicate an over reactive sympathetic nervous system. Victims of coronary attacks and other healthy subjects experience the same degree of stressful events.

Type A persons translate their emotional upsets into bodily symptoms more frequently. Hence, they suffer more from digestion and sleep disorders, which add up to their problems. This sympathetic reactivity in Type A persons also increases risk due to a variety of stress–related illnesses apart from coronary disease. For example, in the Western Collaborative Group Study more people died from non coronary causes than due to coronary causes.

Type A people reveal both physical and behavioral traits besides the hurry syndrome that set them apart from Type B counterparts. Type A people show greater sympathetic arousal, more clotting of blood, higher cholesterol level and increased triglyceride levels under stress. While Type A people do have higher risk of coronary disease they do not necessarily have hypertension. But Rosenman and Friedman reported three to seven time more hypertension in Type A Women (34. 8%) as compared to Type B persons (4. 5%).

Type A people do report more stress symptoms than Type B people. They appear to set higher performance standards for themselves. Type A as compared to Type B people are more dominant in interactive relationship. They are impatient in competitive situation. They smoke more, exercise less. These characteristics lead to high risk factor leading to coronary attacks. An interesting finding is that

Type A behavior tends to increase with socio–economic status. First, Type A behavior was thought of as male pattern. But this thinking has been disproved. It can be found both in men and women and depends upon such variables as age, employment, marital status. Waldran, *et al* (1977) in a study observed that there were more men than women with Type A behavior, their age ranged from 18–25 years. Women revealed high Type A scores in the better educated, working 25–39 years old group. These were working women with dual roles of service women and family rearers.

Changing Type A Behavior

Attempts have been made by Rosenman and Friedman to re-educate Type A persons, they also planned detailed behavior management programs which have focused on very narrowly defined aspects of Type A behavior.

Many individuals identified as Type A have been able to change their life styles dramatically in the direction of a more temperate approach to life but this change was observed in people who had already experienced the trauma of a coronary attack, because of this threatening experience they changed, not because of treatment. They may change if they have motivation and information for change.

9.2 HYPERTENSIVE PERSONALITY–A VIEW

Franz Alexender, a psychiatrist came up with the notion of hypertensive personality which is closely related to Type A personality. According to Alexender, hypertensive patients fight an internal conflict between two incompatible feelings, on one hand, the person feels passive, dependent and on the other hand there are very aggressive and hostile impulses. Feeling of hostility is very threatening, a person fights constantly to keep it under control. This conflict produces long term autonomic arousal, constriction of blood vessels, increased blood pressure, this leads gradually to permanent arterial changes and result in hypertension. This theory is speculative, based on clinical observation of patients, no study was performed. But when attempts were made to identify common pattern of traits for hypertensive, results were not consistent. Some described them as neurotic, emotionally immature, guilt prone, tense. But as control groups were not used in the study, samples of hypertensiveness was also small, there is no support for Alexenders speculations.

Depression

Depression is a disturbance in mood, a prolonged emotional state that affects all mental processes. It is also referred to as common cold of mental illness (Rosenham, *et al* 1984). It afflicts literally hundreds of thousands of people. For some this affliction is barely noticeable, for others it is unhappiness with self and all that life has to offer and it affects their whole life, for others it is the beginning of the end, a well of sorrow and despair, people in this condition may attempt suicide, may require hospitalization.

According to the above description depression runs on a continuum of severity. The most severe form of depression is present in not more than 5–10% of the cases of depression. It is genetically determined, while the other forms of depressions result from the pressures of one's daily life. It is more than an emotional state. It includes conditions, which are highly pervasive and change virtually all the activities normally considered as a part of daily life.

There is feeling of hopelessness linked with helplessness. One looses pleasure of eating, looses weight. There are sleep disturbances frequently. Family routines are disturbed. Depression also makes a person feel worthless. There is sluggish thinking, low concentration, suicidal thinking may also occur, delusions of serious illness may also occur.

Several observations have linked depression with study of stress and health.

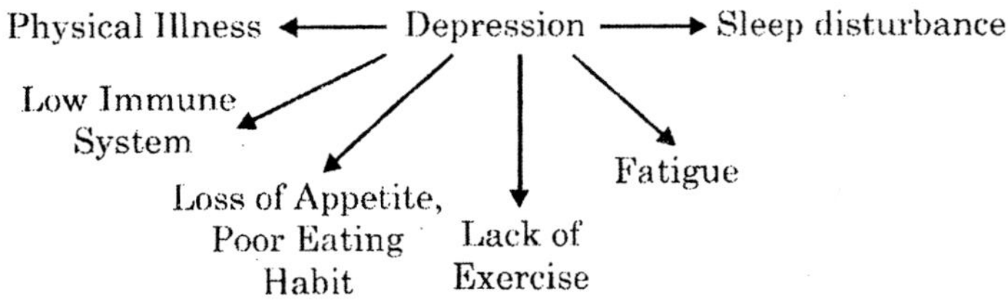

Fig. 9.1 : Depression, Stress and Health

Physical illness may occur because of depression. This occurs because the immune system becomes weak. The accumulated effect of the various problems is felt in loss of appetite, poor eating habits, lack of exercise, fatigue and sleep disturbances. Many illnesses lead to depression as a means for coping with them. For example, chronic problems like back pains continuing for long periods, say more than one year, may result in helplessness which in turn may lead to depression. Depression may also occur if a person is not able to cope with crisis. Depression may also result due to a number of stressors like loss of work, loss of savings, investments, divorce or separation. Finally, it may be expressed that depressed people experience more stress in their daily lives, but have fewer personal resources and social supports to deal with stress.

Richard Sword has described depression–prone person as generally pleasant, although inwardly sad. He is hard working, responsible, consensus, ambitious. There is a strong sense of duty he sets high standards for others as well as for himself.

Stress–Depression-Suicide Link

Potential for committing suicide is high in depressed persons but they usually commit suicide when their mental processes are alert enough to plan and execute the act and also they have physical strength to indulge in suicide. The most dangerous period is when he moves back, from depression to normal life. Family faces extreme trauma in such cases.

According to United States Department of Commerce, Bureau of the Census (1979), suicide is more prevalent in young people. In 1980, one out of every five suicide involved 15–24 year old males. Stress and suicidal thoughts move together. Higher stress leads to higher suicide level, self destruction.

9.3 THE CANCEROUS PERSONALITY

Cancer is one of the most terrifying diseases of this time. Approximately, one in four people are diagnosed with cancer sometime in their lives, two out of three families have to deal with sufferings caused by cancer. Attempts are being made to search for cure in all directions, like, medicines, surgery, radiation therapy, vitamins, diet, etc. People try all methods to beat this dreaded disease.

Now attempts are being made to eliminate cancer. Elimination of cancer is only possible if causes of cancer is detected, which becomes highly problematic as cancer is of 100 different types. Many studies have been carried out in various areas like genetic, bio–chemical, physiological and environmental to understand about growth of cancerous cells. The real reasons for cancer are still largely unknown.

In recent times, more emphasis has been given to psychosocial stressors behind cancer. The psychosocial processes linked with cancer are described below.

Personality characteristics most often leading to cancer are internalized anger and aggression. Cancer patients have higher levels of depression, anxiety, anger, hostility, denial and repressed emotionally. They occur because of some childhood trauma, unhappy childhood, family maladjustments. Family histories of cancer patients reveal wounds due to unsatisfactory home lives, neglect during childhood, etc. But the studies conducted did not experiment with control groups hence suffered from one or more inadequacies. Better controlled studies did show some interesting findings. One group of experimenters found more repression and less self reported depression among experimental group relative to control group. Another study showed that breast cancer among women occurred because of suppressed anger and abnormal release of emotions. A model has been proposed by Barfosky (Fig. 9.2), which showed a link between emotional tension release and physical changes which later got translated into cancer. The psychological conflict to tumor production pathway most frequently involves elevated adreno cortical production due to stress occurrence. This in turn produces suppression in the immune surveillance system, which controls the production of Killer–T cells involved in the detection of cancer cells. Due to this suppression, tumors form. This tumor presents a threat that is medically diagnosed and treated. Diagnosis of cancer, it's treatment add to stress. In addition conflict, anger, hostility, denial, depression occur. Their occurrence is dependent on personal coping resources. But in all cases some harm occurs as information about their uncertain future is assimilated. But usually diagnosed patients are studied, hence various psychological characteristics which lead to it cannot be separated.

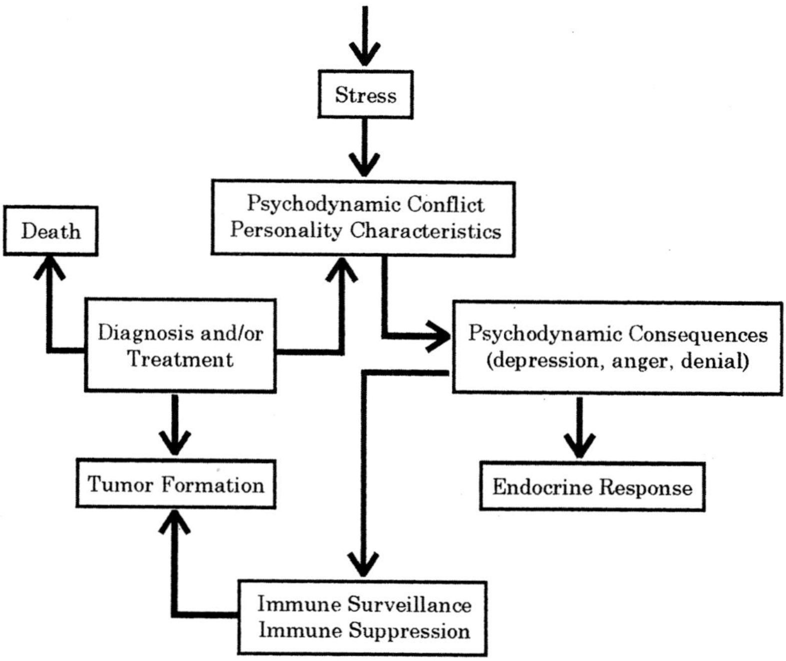

Fig. 9.2 : A theoretical model of how psychosocial stress and personality may influence the production of tumors.

Katz and his colleagues noted that patients defensive coping reactions influenced the course of a disease process. This insight was provided by a study conducted on a group of women hospitalized for breast biopsy. They concluded that being in a stress situation alone does not lead to arousal. Both emotional defenses and physical arousal of adrenal system depend on how stress is perceived, interpreted and reacted to. High adrenal reactivity was associated with apprehension, worry, fear, dejection, despair. Low adrenal reactivity was associated with hopes, faith in God, fate and ability to handle life–threatening situations. Katz observed that chronic worry, fear, hopelessness and despair generally hasten the destructive disease process. On the other hand, hope faith in supreme power, personal courage all operated to prepare best body defenses available.

9.4 PERSONALITY, STRESS, INFERTILITY LINK

Infertility due to physiological causes are cured through medical solutions, but when psychological stress occurs and leads to infertility then it is a matter of great concern. Heightened emotionality, stress, depression can lead to infertility, although, evidences are lacking. One team of researchers measured autonomic reactions, such as, pulse volume, heart rate, skin resistance and muscle tension. The reason behind this measure was that emotional stress produces some power effects through the hypothalamic–pituitary–adrenal complex. This complex controls the production of follicle stimulating hormones (FSH) and luteinizing hormone (LH) in women, both these hormones are critical for development of the ovaries and thus fertility and ovulation. Stress inhibits the production of these hormone. They also studied pattern of reactivity in the autonomic system as it and adrenal system mimic each other. Three groups of women were used from a hospital infertility clinic. One group included functionally infertile subjects, next was organically infertile while a third group was normally fertile. They found no difference among the various groups on autonomic reactivity. The experiment had two flaws, one, sample was very small, second, women were married to partners with abnormal sperm production. All groups were patients of infertility clinic hence all had some degree of emotional arousal, hence no difference was detected between the three groups.

Premenstrual Syndrome and Personality

Some researchers have tried to assess whether personality profile of women complaining of premenstrual syndrome (PMS) differs from those who do not complain.

Forest, *et. al.* (1981) developed a personality profile of women in the eighth month of pregnancy. The reason for choosing this sample was based on the belief that pregnancy places a load on both body and personality and that the characteristics related to PMS would be more apparent in this group. The general profile associated with PMS was tension, reflection of sex role, anxiety, depression, reduced parental aptitude. The overall rate of PMS was 82% with the highest percentage occurring in group with the most extreme scores on these personality variables.

Thomas Plante and Douglas Deoney took several psychological measures related to autonomic arousal while women were engaged in stressful laboratory tests. Two groups of women were compared, Those who reported premenstrual stress and those who had no such complaints. The measures were taken at three different phases in the menstrual life cycle, the first related to early growth (follicular), the second related to ovulation (luteal) and third the menstrual phase. Outcome was that women's stress reactivity did not change during the three phases of the cycle.

There was no difference in recovery from stress. An interesting aspect of this study was that women who complained of premenstrual stress tended to endorse personality items that reflected anxiety and depression even though they were not different from non complainers physiologically.

Personality, Smoking, Stress Link

Smoking reduces tension for many people, although it is high risk, self defeating behavior. Because it is harmful, many programs have been designed to help people quit smoking and also to prevent adolescents from starting smoking.

There are many views about why smoking is maintained. These include physiological and psychological addiction. Next, smoking reduces tension of anxious people. As stress increases smoking increases while it reduces as stress reduces. What motivated people to smoke ? Theories point at peer pressure, peer reinforcement, fashionable personality, parents as models, some personal traits or combination of all these.

Personality traits linked to smokers are extroverted, somewhat neurotic, tense. Anxiety leads to smoking more in females than in males. These findings relate to factors causing people to begin smoking. Researchers have found that people with higher levels of tensions and anxiety may be more vulnerable to pressure to start smoking. Such people can easily be tempted to smoke. On the other hand strong parental models, other preferred outlets for stress, proper guidance for proper emotional release, educational programs may prevent adolescents, youngsters from starting smoking.

Making people give up smoking is highly complex. Personality factors related to maintaining smoking are hardly any except that there is desire to relax through smoking. Smoking is physically addictive. Once a person starts smoking he finds it difficult to give up. Others also accept his smoking and feel helpless in removing the smoker's addiction. One view about smokers is their confidence that they can give up smoking whenever they want. With this type of thinking they continue to smoke.

9.5 PERSONALITY OF AN ALCOHOLIC

Alcoholics generally have higher risks for illness, more rapid mental and physical deterioration and a higher death rate than non alcoholics. The personal and social costs of drinking are devastating. Alcohol related auto accidents are common sights on roads hence society should control this brutal killer. Under stress, when coping strategies are not very effective then drinking is adopted as a method of stress reduction and escape behavior. Just like smoking, as stress increases, drinking increases and as stress decreases drinking decreases.

Factors that contribute to alcoholism are as follows : -

Genetic factor make persons more vulnerable to the addictive properties of alcohol. Next alcoholics marry alcoholics, hence their children face the risk of alcoholism. There are certain intervening factors in persons development which determine whether the person will take up alcohol or not.

The diathesis–stress model is the best theoretical model that describes the overall mix of factors contributing to alcoholism. This model states that predisposing risk factors will be expressed only if a precipitating (stress) event of sufficient intensity is encountered. Predisposing factors include genetically passed down psychological vulnerability, like conduct, disorder in childhood, hyperactivity, attentional problem. The stress factors include aspects like disordered family. Disturbed family interactions, ethnic background, deprived environment.

Alcoholic is chronically distressed which is externally controlled, together with weak, ineffective psychosocial skills. One feels personally inadequate, high fear, lack of concentration. These traits are observed in the alcoholic's conflict with authority, high hostility rate and aggression. All these factors reduce the effectiveness of the person in the job and in various interpersonal relationships. Alcoholics on the road may increase the chances of accidents.

9.6 THREE PERSONALITY TRAITS LINK WITH STRESS AND HEALTH

There are three personality traits that are linked with stress and health, they are discussed here one by one.

1. Locus of Control

Locus of Control is a concept originated from the work of Julian Rotter in 1960s. It refers to the expectancy that one's action will lead to mastery over one's environment. According to Rotter, people vary in degrees on a scale that measures between extreme external control to extreme internal control. External Locus of Control means that one perceives the events occurring in his life due to fate and that one has no control over his fate or events, all events appear to be controlled by some outside power while the internal person feels that nothing is beyond one's control. Most difficult situations are also in the realm of one's control. In short, external perceive their life events are in the hands of fate while internal feel confident that whatever is happening is because of his own action and in one's control.

Internals are better able to utilize their cognitive systems. They expand a lot of their mental energy obtaining information that will enable them to influence events of significance. They are better able to cope with their personal, social and work environments. Thus, they develop ability to cope successfully with stressful events.

A study observed that when personal weaknesses were pointed out, internal people revealed a much greater tendency to implement a specific plan of action to overcome their weaknesses. Whether, it involved action taking, confronting or mastery, internals seemed to be more disposed towards behavior that will enhance their personal efficacy and will try to overcome their inadequacies.

Locus of control has been linked with coping with stress and dealing with family problems in three typologies. These are behavioral control which involves some direct action, cognitive control, which involves personal interpretation of events and decisional control, which means that the person has a choice among many courses of action. The manner in which a person controls stress is the function of the meaning which individual attaches to that stressful situation. For example, a study on tuberculosis patients showed that internally controlled patients had much more knowledge about their disease than externally controlled patients. This is consistent with the idea that internals are knowledge seekers.

Difficult problems facing health service givers are the facts that people (1) are not highly motivated to engaged in effective preventive health care, (2) they do not follow prescribed medical programs carefully when sick.

One significant view about locus of control is that it is fixed at an early age and thus difficult to change. On the contrary, it appears one's locus of control can be changed if there is desire for doing so.

Psychological Strength

Some people are not moved much by stressful occurrences in the lives. Stress does not put any mark on their lives. Suzzanne Kabasa conducted research during 1970s that put forward the view that personality can play a significant role in helping people fight with illnesses related with stress. Those who can fight illnesses are perceived as Psychologically strong or hardy. According to her there are three major traits which if present in a person can lead to person's psychological strength, they include control commitment and challenge.

Control means locus of control. Commitment is a sense of self and purpose.

Challenge reflects the degree to which safety, stability and predictability are important. Those high on psychological strength will have well integrated sense of self and purpose, change will provide them with opportunity to grow.

Kabasa performed a study on 137 male business executives to assess if hardiness and exercise acted as buffer against illness. They found that stressful life events increased illness. The positive buffering effect was also observed among a sample of lawyers. It was observed that those who showed reduced hardiness and exercised least had the highest rate of illness. On the contrary, those who were high on hardiness and exercised most had lowest rate of illness.

Positive Self–Regard

Positive self regard or self esteem is another personality trait significantly linked with stress and health. Self esteem means feeling good about oneself. Self esteem is a part of self concept which includes ways in which people compare and evaluate themselves (physically, mentally and socially) with others. Positive self is made up of two physical components *i.e.*, appearance and ability and three psychosocial factors *i.e.*, self–regard, social confidence and learning ability.

A complex relationship exists between self esteem and coping. If previous experiences of coping revealed successful outcomes, then people feel good about themselves, hence they are less likely to respond to an event in a stressful manner. Because they cope better it increases their self esteem.

On the other hand when low esteem people are put in a threatening situation they reveal poor coping ability. This difficulty with coping with low esteem people can be because of two negative self perceptions. First, low esteem persons have higher fear level under threat as compared to high esteem persons. Second, low esteem persons perceive themselves as being incapable of dealing with threat. They are governed by external locus of control, have a fatalistic orientation and don't take any preventive measures.

A number of programs have been developed to improve self esteem of high school students. One program showed a positive result of increasing interpersonal coping skills. This is only possible if people learn that stress can be controlled and they can do something about it. It increases their positive self regard.

In brief, this chapter discusses the role of personality in stress occurrence and coping. It has covered a number of theories, biotypes plus the significant traits which are linked with stress and health.

References

Alexender, F. (1939). Emotional factors in essential hypertension. Psychosomatic; medicines. 1. 173-179.

Allport, G. W (1961) : Pattern and Growth in Personality. New York : Holt. Rinehart & Winston, p. 28.

Apao, W.K. & Damon, A.M. (1982). Locus of control and the quantity-frequency inı ex of alcohol use. Journal of studies on alcohol. 43, 233-239.

Barofsky, I. (1981). Issues and approaches to the psychological assessment of the cancer patients. In C. K. Prokop & L.A. Bradley, Medical Psychology, Contributions to behavioral medicines. New York : Academic Press, pp. 57-58.

Brand, H.J., Roos, S.S. & Van der Merwe, A.B. (982). Psychological Stress and infertility. Part II Psychophysiological reaction patterns. British journal of Medical Psychology. 55, 379-384.

Dattore, P.J. Shontz, F.C. & Coy, L. (1980). Premorbid personality differentiation of cancer and non-cancer groups : A test of the hypothesis of cancer proneness. Journal of Consulting and Clinical Psychology. 48. 388-394.

Donovan, et.al (1983) Drinking behavior. p. 416.

Ferguson, W.E. (1981). Gifted adolescents, stress and life changes. Adolescence 16, 973-985.

Fleming, J.S. & Courtney, B.E. (1984). The dimensionality of self esteem : II Hierarchical facet model for revised measurement scales. Journal of Personality and Social Psychology, 46, 404-421.

Forest, G. et.al (1981) Premenstural syndrome and personality traits. A study of 110 pregnant patients. Psychosomatics. 36. 37-42.

Friedman, M. & Rosenman, R. H. (1974). Type A behavior and your heart. New York : Knopf. pp. 82-85.

Garron, D. C. & Leavitt, R. (1983). Chronic low back pain and depression. Journal of clinical Psychology. 39, 486-493.

Goldband, S. (1980). Stimulus specificity of physiological response to stress and the Type A coronary prone behavior pattern. Journal of Personality and Social Psychology, 39, 670-679.

Irvine, J. Lyle, R. C. & Allon, R. (1982). Type A Personality as Psychopathology : Personality correlates and an abbreviated scoring system. Journal of Psychosomatic Research, 26, 183-189.

Katz, J. et.al, (1970) Psycho-endocrine aspects of cancer of the breast. Psychosomatic medicine. 32. 1-18.

Kobasa, S.C. (1979) Personality and resistance to illness. American Journal of Community Psychology. 7, 413-423.

Liebert, R. M. & Spiegler, M. D. (1982). Personality : Strategies & issues. Homewood. IL : Dorsey Press.

Millon, T. (1982). On the nature of clinical health Psychology. In T. Millon, C. Green, & R. Meeghar (eds.). Handbook of clinical health Psychology (pp. 1-27). New York : Plenum Press. p. 11.

Pharses, Locus of control in personality, p. 122.

Plante, T.G. & Denney D.R. (1984). Stress responsivity among dyamenorrheic women at different phases of their menstrual cycle. More ado about nothing. Behavior research and therapy, 22, 249-258.

Rosemnan, R.H. et.al (1964) A predictive study of coronary heart disease The Western Collaborative. Group Study. Journal of the American Medical Association, 189, 15-22.

Rosenhan, D. L. & Seligman, M. E. P. (1984). Abnormal Psychology. New York. Norton. p. 317.

Rosenman, R. H. & Friedman, M. (1961). Association of specific behavior pattern in women with blood and cardiovascular findings. Circulation, 24, 1173-1184.

Rosenman, R.H. & Friedman, M. (1961). Association of specific behavior pattern in women with blood and cardiovascular findings. Circulation, 24, 1173-1184.

Spielberger, C. D. (1966). Theory and research on anxiety. In C. D. Spielberger (Ed.) Anxiety and behavior (pp. 1-22). New York. Academic Press.

Stabeneau, J.R. & Hesselbrock, V.M. (1983). Family predigree of alcoholic and control patients. The International Journal of the addictions, 18, 351-363.

Sword, R. O. (1977). The depression prone personality : Almost too good to be true. Dental survey. 53, 12.

United States Department of Commerce, Bureau of the census. (1979, September). Statistical abstract of the United States Washington, DC : U.S. Govt. Printing Office.

CHAPTER 10

ENVIRONMENTAL STRESSORS

Natural catastrophies, technological disasters, unexpected occurrences produce tremendous harm for living beings and gives lot of pain and suffering all around. Still greater stress is produced by anticipating upcoming disasters. They fear the future outcomes, and how extremely stressed they feel depends on how safe they feel in their homes and environments. Some examples of such occurences are disasters in mines, firebreak down in public places like movie hall, gas disasters like one that occurred in Bhopal on 2nd Dec 1984.

Anticipatory disasters are upcoming wars, drought floods, earthquakes etc. An interesting element in all these occurrences are the ways in which human beings have been held responsible for causing the various disasters, they have played with the environment through scientific inventions, discoveries and technological innovations. They have altered, exploited their environment, have destroyed various elements of the environment like cutting trees, nuclear explosions. The aim of all these alterations are progress, better welfare of people, but they have also resulted in disasters and destruction, people have to bear with air pollution, noise pollution, water pollutions, food pollutions, chemical hazards, nuclear risks, urban over crowding etc.

Environmental stress studies deal with both natural and human created problems and it hopes to answer some coming up questions. It reveals how physical illness, emotional distress, mental disturbance is caused through environmental stress. It also teaches some self control procedures so that people will be less wasteful of natural resources. This will help reduce psychological stress due to environmental occurrences.

The environment influences us through calamities like droughts, floods, earthquakes, volcanic eruptions etc. Human beings try to fight these natural disasters and forces by drilling wells, draining swamps, building dams, making earthquake proof buildings. People have also started farming the ocean, exploiting space and has tried to master nature.

By bringing changes in environment, there are changes in links between organisms, peoples, etc. e.g. the Aswan dam built to control floods along the Nile and to provide hydroelectric power, caused great harm to fishing business along the rivers course. Other examples are acid rains, human encroachment on natural habitats, extinguishing several species of animals. These reveal the impact of disturbing the ecological balance.

10.1 THEORIES OF ENVIRONMENTAL STRESS

A number of theories advanced to explain the basis of environmental stress include arousal theories, learning theories, behavior constraint theories, ecological theories and environmental stress theories.

Arousal Theories

These arousal theories are based on the impact of stimulation from environment on human behavior. Very intense stimulation such as loud speaker yelling at your door step will lead to too much arousal, leading to feeling of stress. On the other hand, very low levels of stimulation, *i.e.*, stimulus deprivation, like living alone with no contact with outside world, can cause so little arousal that a person feels bored, causing tension (Mehrabian & Russal).

Enviornment stimulation in the form of information may also influence human behavior. When too much information is provided the person may feel overloaded (as found in executives), attention may become selective and this may cause strain. When too little information is provided the person may not be able to make wise and appropriate decision. This may make him anxious and unsure.

Another approach is the adaptation level theory of Wohlwill. According to him each person has a preferred and optimal level of stimulation. The optimal level of information which a person can manage varies, it may also vary within a person from time to time. The current level of preferred stimulation occurs due to adaptation, for example, if someone had a tiring day at the office he may find himself fit to solve problems at home or if he had watched a highly amusing movie, then he may find his trip to the amusement park boring.

Learning Theories

Byrne & Clore (1970) studied role for conditioning of attitudes leading to environmental stress, e.g., a child gets an injection at the doctor's clinic, various elements present at the clinic were nurses, odour etc. Later on, whenever he smells that odour or sees a nurse he develops negative emotional response. This gets converted into cognitive attitude of dislike. Injection was the unconditioned stimulus (UCS), fear, avoidance were the unconditioned response (UCR). The odour, nurse were conditioned stimulus (CS) which were neutral prior to the injection, but later became as powerful as UCS and produced fear (CR).

Behavior Constraint Theories

Sometimes environment produce such effects which cannot be controlled e.g. summer heat wave, winter cold waves, earthquakes. One can only take precautions to minimize the damage due to these uncontrollable circumstances.

Work situations may also take up some characteristic found in nature e.g. Mr. Sharma was the Deputy General Manager in a flourishing factory. He did his work with sincerity, he did well for fifteen years but due to losses the factory closed down and Mr. Sharma could not do anything. His hard and sincere efforts did not provide him the job security. Many computer companies offer excellent products but closed down because of lack of finance for promoting their products, and they could not compete with hi-fi companies. Their employees suffered because of no fault on their part. Persons feel helpless, their behaviors are controlled by fate of these companies. Sometimes the limits imposed on behaviors are imaginary rather than real. If the situation is uncontrollable, behavior will be constrained. Baum and Rodins have given three steps to behavior constraint, (1) Loss of control (specified above) (2) Psychological reactance (3) Learned helplessness.

Reactance is a concept used often in consumer areas. Salesmen come with tempting products but the way in which they influence one feels cheated, this makes him react and refuse to buy the product even if he like it.

Learned helplessness is a condition in which due to previous failures person do not exert influence on the situation. In emergency situations people often give up trying because they feel helplessness, but if they do not give up sometimes, they may succeed in saving themselves. An example to prove this is the crash of Japan Air lines plane on Aug 12, 1985. The four survivours refused to give up, they tried to hold whatever control they could however desperate the situation was.

Ecological Theories

Here emphasis is on group behavior standards and behavior expected in various types of environmental settings like schools, churches, institutions etc. for example in a temple a specific behavior is expected like joining hands, removing shoes, covering head, etc. Restaurant is another example where behavior patterns are predetermined, e.g. Hot Stuff is a self service point where waiters are not available. One has to be alert to what is expected, do accordingly and then only he will be served. In large classes some students may perceive themselves as insignificant uninvolved and unknown. Barker studied some of the stress process operating in various organizations and has also suggested ways to manipulate the environment to reduce stress.

Environmental Stress Theories

This theory includes elements of Han Selye's General Adaption Syndrome theory and Richard Lazarus's cognitive transactional theory. Baum and his team analysed a variety of environmental stressors and indicated that the cognitive processes (Lazarus) and physiologoical processes (Selye) are always observed in a number of environmental stress situations like noise, crowding, sudden unexpected events.

10.2 MAJOR STRESSORS

Several major stressors have a short tenure and usually influence few people. Their impact is usually severe like natural, technological, social disasters. Next are the chronic stressors that influence more people, occur more frequently and are usually less severe. They are also termed as background stressors, like noise pollution, air pollution, chemical pollution, crowding etc. Some significant environment stressors are :

Natural Disasters : Natural disasters threaten people with physical destruction, psychological truma, family disorganization. The impact is very severe. e.g. are tornades, floods, volcanic eruptions, earthquakes etc.

The emergent impact is a temporary panic until everything appears okay. The fulsome impact is disruption of lifestyle. There is severe deprivation, discomfort, physical fatigue.

There are periods when cleaning process is followed and recovering process from devastation is pursued, attempt to restart, care for sick and injured family members. All these activities are very taxing and consume a lot of physical and psychological energy. Such calamities demand lot of coping on the part of sufferers. Both long term and short term common characteristics of natural disasters are (a) they are unpredictable, one can only be warned, however advanced the weather reporting it can never reveal when it will occur. (b) It is uncontrollable. How much harm the disaster will do, cannot be controlled, people feel they are in the hands of natural forces. (c) These disasters require short term and long term coping.

Three stages of responding to natural disasters are (a) shock stage, person feels shocked, dazed, and unresponsive to enviormnent (b) suggestibility stage where the victim takes suggestions from other and gets influenced by them (c) recovery stage, here individuals try to grasp the severity of the situation, are frightened, psychological symptoms occurring in the victims are panic, anxiety, phobic fear, guilt, withdrawl etc. They may also feel unsecure, frustrated. Other symptoms are sleep and eating disturbances. People dream about the disasters again and again. The severity of the impact will depend upon amount of loss faced by a person.

Physical symptoms include headache, colds, other illness, fatigue, weight loss etc. Physical impact is not very high, this may be because the short term acute nature of disaster stress activates the body's natural self defense mechanisms, as stress is over, very fast lowered resistance and exhaustion do not occur.

Technological Disasters : Technological disasters like natural disasters are also unpredictable and uncontrollable. They produce intense physical, psychological stress and social chaos. Examples are bombing at Hiroshima and Nagasaki, Bhopal Tragedy. Technological disasters are usually short lived, and they cause acute stress. The Bhopal tragedy cannot be forgotten by the residents of Bhopal. Technological disasters are different from natural disasters because they occur due to human fault, wrong calculations or carelessness. They could be prevented, the feeling is found in people about who is to be blamed, and what has occurred appears unforgivable.

Bhopal Tragedy : India Today (Aug 18, 2003) has referred to it as cloud of Death on 3rd Dec 1984. The sleepy capital of Madhya Pradesh got linked with one of the world's worst man made catastrophes. A poisonous grey cloud spread out from the Union Carbide Plant in Bhopal, suffocating more than three lakhs of its unsuspecting residents. More than 2, 000 people died instantly.

10.3 COPING WITH OUTCOMES OF DISASTER

A team of investigators headed by Andrew Baurn studied coping strategies used by victims of various natural and technological disasters. They came up with two strategies, *i.e.*, emotionally focused coping and problem focused coping.

Their suggestions were that in disaster situations first, attempt should be made to remove negative feelings of the sufferers. Bad feelings should not be preserved, or should not be avoided, with regards to the second strategy people should not try to control the problem as it is not predictable or controllable. Such attempts causes greater stress. Problem solving approach may be useful in other types of stress situations like interactional stress or conflict situations Another strategy suggested is information seeking. Uncertainity causes greater amount of stress, hence obtaining useful and concrete information about stress situations may reduce uncertainity but wrong information may cause greater harm than uncertainity, people may receive, inaccurate, unclear, confused information. Hence it should only be the officials holding responsibility and expertise on various types of pollutions who should be contacted for information.

Noise Pollution : Impact of noise are unpleasant. This is clear from the fact that people try to avoid noise, minimize volume or fight to control noise. Noise is the source of stress for millions of people each day.

Noise is usually defined in terms of the effect it has on people. Noise which causes pollution is an unwanted offensive element. Three dimensions of sound determine whether the sound is perceived as noise or not. They are intensity, predictability and control ability. The intensity of sound is recorded in decibel (db), normal conversation is about 60 db, auditory pain appears at about 100 db, permanent damage occurs with sustained exposure to sounds above 100 db as found in many factories. OS/A (United States Occupational Safety and Health Administration) has set a 90 db ceiling for industries.

Predictable noise is less disturbing than unpredictable noise, e.g. people living near the railway crossing are not bothered by trains noise but if suddenly they hear a bang or horrible noise they may feel the strain.

Finally, when one can control the noise it is less aversive than when one cannot control it e.g. if someone is tunning various relay stations on the radio and the noise is caused, he will not be bothered but if someone else does this then he will surely bothered.

Noise harms in many ways like it reduced production efficiency, causes deafness in factory workers, impairs performance in children. Noise may also cause illness like weak gastro intestinal disturbances (ulcers), higher blood pressure etc.

Noise may also lead to social harms like changing perception about others, may affect liking and disliking towards others, may increase aggression.

Noise control techniques can be divided into two broad areas. (1) Control noise at the source, *i.e.*, use stricter laws with regards to noise reduction in trucks, automobiles, generators, etc. Silencers are being fitted on various equipments, vehicles (2) Engage in better environmental design for work and living space that minimizes the chances of noise intruding inside. Walls thickness may be increased, sound proof walls, ceiling may be constructed. Thick carpets, curtains, plants may be used to spread the sound. Masking may be used to drown one sound under another, e.g. music played to prevent road noise.

Air Pollution : Taj Mahal is loosing it's charm, it is slowly being eaten away by corrosives, pollutants from a nearby power plant.

Air pollution causes four harmful effects.

1. It is a direct threat of health.
2. It brings many atmospheric and climatic changes like depletion of ozone, acid rain.
3. Air pollution harms buildings through corrosive effects.
4. Air pollution does not cause psychological distress like disasters, crowding and noise.

Often air pollution is not detectable by the senses. Smoke is one way of spreading air pollution. Many air pollutants are smelt by people, e.g. gases from automobiles, smokes from processing plants, tobacco odour, etc., but many gases like carbon monoxide, radon gas are undetectable to eyes or nose as observed in some stuffy houses which contain more pollution than outside environment. Air pollution syndrome have been detected by many doctors. Symptoms included are headache, fatigue, depression, insomnia, irritability, eye itching, etc. Other health hazards identified by fishes include carbon monoxide, poisoning gas to long term air pollution exposure. This can result in headaches, memory disturbances, auditory, visual impairment, etc. Particles from smokestacks, exhausts include mercury, asbestors. These pollutants cause cancer, anemia, neural or breath problems.

Other effects are human performance reduction, defective reaction time, low attention, perceptual, motor coordination, etc. They may lead to accidents, especially in highly populated cities.

Density, Crowding leads to Stress

Mismanagement of space is related to stress. Two terms used for overcrowding are density and overcrowding. In relationship to overcrowding, density is the physical condition of overpopulation, and crowding is the psychological state characterized by stress.

The effects of over crowding on human behavior can be summated as follows :

(1) Negative emotions are related to high density, this applies more to men, while women feel unhappy in low density surrounding.

(2) Physiological changes like higher blood pressure, increased sweating occur in crowding. This is also

influenced by the degree of control that people have in being in a crowd.

(3) Sickness, illness increases in high density, as observed among college students, naval crews etc.

(4) Overcrowding may cause withdrawl, *i.e.*, trying to maintain greater interpersonal distance. It may also lead to increase in aggressions.

(5) Baun and Rodins noted that overcrowding led to increased unwanted interactions, causing irritation and feeling of helplessness. Loss of control may increase physiological effects, activate the sympathetic nervous system and increase the illness risk.

Coping with crowding includes two means :

(1) Focus is on environmental design, aim at reducing the feeling of overcrowding, like higher ceilings, bright colors, rectangular rooms etc.

(2) The second approach focuses on the feelings of anxiety felt by people in overcrowding situations. Three techniques for reducing anxiety are relaxation approach, cognitive reappraisal and imagery.

Summary

This chapter pinpoints various natural technological disasters, and other environmental hazards which are faced by people and how they cope with them.

References

Baum, A. & Rodins, J. (1978). Crowding and helplessness : Potential Consequences of Density and Loss of Control. I. A.

Baum & Y. Epstein (Eds) Human response to crowding. Hillsdale, NJ, Eribaum.

Byrne, D. & Clore, G. L. (1970). A reinforcement model of evaluative responses. Personality : An International Journal, I, 103-128.

Mehrabian, A. & Russell, J. A. (1974). An approach to environmental Psychology. Cambridge, MA. M. I. T. Press.

Wohlwill, J. F. (1974). Human Adaptation to Levels of Environmental Stimulation. Human Ecology, 2, 127-147.

CHAPTER 11

STRESS VICTIMS

Ram was an alcoholic, everyday he came late at night in a drunken state. After reaching his home, he used to abuse his wife and not a single day passed when he did not beat her before he went to sleep. His wife could not speak anything about her condition to anyone for the fear that if Ram came to know about it he will torture her more.

Mrs. Khanna was a very strict lady, her husband used to live in another city. No one could say anything to her. If her children went against her she use to lock them in a room and did not give food to them. If they argued with her she used to take the children to the kitchen and burn their fingers on the gas stove. Imagine the helplessness of her children.

Tina, a twelve-year old girl was sexually abused by her uncle living in her house. He threatened her that if she opened her mouth in front of anyone he would beat her and torture her more. She was so frightened that she shut her mouth and continued to be the victim of her uncle's misbehavior.

Everyday, in the newspaper, a lot of news are about some murders, some thefts, some rapes, some kidnappings, some tortures. In the television and radio news channel a lot of cases of victimization, fears, tortures, murders, etc. are overflooded. Situation round is so bad that the metaphor 'might is right' seems to be prevailing everywhere.

Crime creates literally millions of victims in our society every year. An estimated 6, 50, 000 aggravated assaults occur each year. About 21, 000 persons are murdered each year. One rape is committed every seven minutes (United States Federal Bureau of Investigation). Material loss from robbery is estimated to approach $ 9. 5 billion annually. Corporate and white collar crime runs into millions through coercion, extortion and fraud (Meyer 1981). Apart from immediate physical losses, material losses, the after effects of crime produces more mental havoc. The memories of all painful sights pervade the mind from time to time which becomes a source of recurrent stress. The psychological scar from being victimized range from tension, insecurity to disillusionment, anger, loss of self-esteem. One feels futile, helpless. One reacts through frustration against police, verbal attacks against terrorizer.

11.1 FEAR : A MENTAL PRISON

Fear, an emotion does not wait for some event to occur. It just comes in the mind of the person at the anticipation of some crime. For example, on 3rd July, 2006 I was returning from my institution through the road which I cross everyday. It crosses the University Campus. Near the campus a group of people were standing and seeing what was happening near the University gate. As I crossed these viewers they called at me and said that a terrible fight was taking place at the

University gate and urged me to take another path. This warning in itself caused fear in me that what would have happened if I would have continued my driving without listening to them. This incident was described next day in the local newspaper. Many cars and jeeps had been broken down. So, in my case it was mere anticipation of being victimized that created fear and propelled me to take another route.

William Berg and Robert Johnson (1979) wrote about 'fear of crime' and of 'self defined prisoners'. Fear of what might have occurred, fear of what crime may occur, block our freedom, shut our access to the outside world. It tempts to move out, but one feel too frightened to move out. The impact of fear is too horrifying, cuts across many thought and feeling processes. Personal freedom is hampered because the victim is forced to change his pattern of social, market and work behavior. Constant alertness, care is necessary to ensure that personal injury or loss does not occur again.

Society appears to be useless does not provide protection, especially the courts appear useless and one's mind is always engrossed in trying to live through fear victimization rather than indulging in creative activities. Fear changes the complete personality of a person.

11.2 FACTORS OF VICTIMIZATION

Victimologists are trying to discover the factors that contribute to becoming victims. These issues have been considered. One issue is risk : what factors predispose some individuals to be more likely to be the targets of crime. Second issue relates to prevention : How can people be educated to avoid taking risk ? Third issue targets at coping : How can victims be made to live normal lives again.

Risk : Persons more vulnerable to crime exist in every society. People with certain demographic or personal characteristics are more inclined to becoming victim because of no fault of their own.

Michael J. Hindelang with his team collected data from eight cities and identified four major demographic characteristics that are observed in victims. These are age, marital status, employment status and sex. They are discussed below : -

Age : Younger persons have a higher chance of becoming victims as compared to older persons. This is because younger persons are more active, more mobile than older persons. Younger persons act on impulse and are emotional, more adventurous, hence the chances of arguments. Fights are high among younger people. On the other hand, elderly experience more anticipatory fear and are more likely to feel victimized because of their reduction in power, especially physical power. They lose sense of active mastery, *i.e.*, they feel that they cannot control their fate.

Marital Status : Unmarried persons face greater risk of becoming victims as compared to married people. As they are more mobile, indulge in such activities like seeking companionship, socialization, go to discos, hot spots for enjoyments. On the other hand married people lead a more stable life, spend more time at home.

Employment Status : Unemployed people have a higher risk of becoming victims than employed people. They are frustrated, feel alone, are easily tempted by victimizers because of the promise of jobs, e.g. a few months back about one thousand unemployed girls and boys had been tempted by corrupt people. They were asked to give four to five lakh of rupees for getting job in railway department. Poor victims, they arranged for money from various sources, gave the money, still they are without jobs, the victimizers are gone with their money and the victims are suffering. Employed people may suffer because of their employers.

Sex : Females run high risk of being victimized in offices. They are forced into sexual harassment by their employers and are victimized (Hinderland, *et. al.* 1978). But males especially unmarried, unemployed are most vulnerable, especially if they are in the wrong situation.

The offender is usually a stranger (Hinderland, *et. al.* 1975) in 80% of cases, but where the offenders is related, injuries tend to be much more serious and may lead to circumstances which opens way to suicides, homicides (Schafer 1977). There is also an observation that just like accident prone personality there is also a victimization prone personality. This observation is based on seeing some persons becoming victims of crime again and again.

11.3 VICTIMIZATION AVOIDANCE

Modern living involves risk. Girls and boys after gaining primary education move to various professions, institutions spread all over the country and outside. Parents vigilance is not possible over there. It is up to the youth to become optimistic or pessimistic about their future. If the parents teaching are imbibed in the youth and they feel more strong, more confident then they will spread their wings and fly all over the world and may reach height in various areas without facing victimization. There are two reasons for being optimistic. First, that fear of personal injury due to crime may be less than that from driving a car. Second there are simple steps that can be taken to reduce the risks of becoming a victim. These steps basically deal with bringing changes in behavioral policies (Michel Hindelang). Life styles play a significant role in personal crime, because they lead us to places and situations with high opportunities for criminal victimization. Life style refers to routine daily activities, both vocational activities (work, school, housekeeping, etc.) and leisure activities. It involves what one likes to do, where he wants to be, with whom he wants to interact.

11.4 LIFE-STYLE EVALUATION

Life–style evaluation involves interpretation of one's personal behavior and how it is linked with environmental risk, dangers. There should be a balance between feelings of personal security and a healthy caution. One should avoid extremes of obsessive fear and one should avoid feeling invulnerable.

Obsessive fear limits one's capability of reasoning, takes away the joy of daily living. The feeling of nothing can happen to me, I am very strong, I don't have any fears prevents persons from developing common sense of a normal person and may place them in dangers. Healthy caution includes being realistic, appraising the points from where dangers can come, taking steps to avoid getting entangled in those dangers and thereby eliminating the necessity of undue worry or disabling fear. For example, a few months back there was caution given in newspaper regarding metro city to young ladies of not going out alone in the night, if urgent go out only with male escorts, they were also warned not to go to restaurants in the night alone. If ladies follow these cautions then they don't have to be afraid.

A positive approach to personal security involves controlling these basic behavioral patterns that tend to place people in risky situations. The first step is to identifying daily habits of shopping, socializing, movements in living area. Habits are automatically carried out and one does not pay much attention to them. Some habits could be dangerous if one doesn't notice it.

11.5 PROPER SELECTION OF TIME

Never choose habits which have to be performed at night, unless it is very essential and you can perform it in a group. Night time carries the highest risk.

In the eight cities study, the time period between mid–night and 6 a.m. yielded a higher rate of injury than any other time. 91% of the victims said that they felt safe being out during the day. Night appears unsafe because of the following reasons : -

1. Bystanders who can notice or intervene are fewer in the night than at day time.
2. More drunkards move around at night and they often indulge in criminal activities.
3. Alcohol affects decision making, their cognitive processes are dulled and lowers inhibitions. This provokes criminal activities, which in turn lead to injury and harm to others.

The lifestyle adjustment suggests (a) avoid late night jogging, (b) be cautious about going near points where alcohol is consumed, (c) don't indulge in arguments, fights which may lead to serious impacts on others.

11.6 AWARENESS OF HIGH RISK PLACES

Three joints are high risk places, home, street, working place. However, the crimes occurring in these joints are very different from one another. Assaults at home are often started by life partners, friends, lovers, due to some domestic fights. Criminal assaults at the street are crimes for profit, power precipitated by strangers, usually who are frustrated. At employment points risk may be from employers, colleagues. Causes may be unethical behaviors, work methods, favoritism, incompetence, isolation, restriction, threats of disciplinary action (Jean Lannane 1994). Street assaults can be avoided by planning time schedules and using transportation means which would prevent them from being on street for long period. Next, try to move with others (friends, family members) rather than alone. Don't move on path which are lonely.

Employment related victimization can be avoided if a person keeps cool, does his work smoothly and does not interfere in other people's matters.

11.7 SELECT SELF DEFEATING MEASURES CAREFULLY

After the crime has occurred victims think of other ways in which they should have reacted. If I would have attacked from back may be I would have not encountered the effect which I was suffering. If I would have shouted the outcome would have been different. They thus replay the situation with alternative reactions 'ifs' and 'if only'. Hindelang's study revealed that in four cases, out of five the victims allowed the thief to carry away the loot. Thus, they did not suffer any injury.

More often (29% to 21%) as reported by Hindelang's study the most successful measure was verbal resistance in which the victim threatens the thief or attacker of exposing him or talking in such a manner that the offender leaves the look or does not cause much harm (20% were injured and 80% were not), evade the situation (16% were injured and 84% were not), if one yelled then (36% were injured and 64% were not injured). The rate of injury was twice more when the victim tried to physically counter attack (53% versus 25% who did not use physical counter attack). Use of weapon for self protection also increased the chances of injury (30% injured who had weapons, 24/5 were injured although they did not have weapons). When acquaintances, are involved in attacks and counter attacks then injuries occur more frequently. Homicides are more likely to involve family friends and acquaintances rather than strangers. Reasons for this is that acquaintances will resist the assaults and will use more violent counter attacks which leads to more severe injury or harm. These findings suggest that physical counter attack should be avoided, the means used should be verbal actions or evasion. If fight is likely to occur, as may be understood by emotional charging from both sides then one should go and stay somewhere else until the emotions have cooled down and both parties are ready to rationalize. Now a days, physical attack is not the best way to counter attack. Other methods like taking help from social groups or legal help may be perceived as a more intelligent approach.

11.8 BEHAVIORAL ADJUSTMENTS

Small adjustments in routine behaviors may prevent victimization, e.g., changing timings of daily marketing so that attacker may not be able to assess one's pattern of behavior and may thus be prevented from planning his moves.

Try shopping during day time or in early evenings, avoid night time. Job related behavior may require adjustments in terms of modes of transportation time so that you do not face lonely situations. If you have to take entertainment or go to restaurants do so in groups rather than alone. In many institutions if night movements can not be avoided then late night service escorts are provided, try to use them for safety purposes. Studies conducted by Hindelang revealed that if people made minor adjustments in their daily routine behaviors then they may not be victimized.

Psychological Processes as Barriers to Effective Prevention : The above given slight adjustments may reveal uncomplicated methods of prevention from victimization. But there are three psychological processes that can influence both the risks we take and the stress reactions we experience from victimization. They include cognitive appraisals, beliefs and emotional reactions. According to Hindelang cognitive appraisals are evaluations of the importance of various encounters with people, places, things in our environment. These encounters may be real, anticipated or imagined. Appraisals involves assessing the risk in these encounters, they influence thinking, emotions and behavior in the present which in turn influences future anticipation. With regards to past, attribution are made about the extent and causes of crimes. With respect of present, inferences are made about imminent threat, with regards to future, projections are made in terms of safety. Beliefs determine readiness to behave in a manner that will be beneficial. Problem erupt when appraisals and beliefs lead away from alertness and healthy caution. Fear alerts to something that could possibly be harmful. Fear is heightened in the victims after criminal assault. They may have a restless sleep, difficulty in concentrating or loss of appetite. This is often frustrating because of fear as unrealistic but remain hampered by it.

11.9 ERRORS OF ATTRIBUTIONS

There are three errors which play a significant role in adaptive behavior to crime. These are attributions about place of crime, who is to be blamed and who is responsible.

Attribution–1 : Place of Crime. People usually perceive themselves safe where they are and perceive that problem is more somewhere else. This is often the case even if the person is sitting in the bed of crimes.

People living in most notorious places, where crimes usually occur more feel safe over there. Their own community is perceived to be less threatening than other communities. This was proved by survey in areas having high crime rates. The people questioned thought that crime had increased in other areas. This misattribution is because of mass media that narrates about crimes from around the nation instead of news about neighborhood crime. The appraisal process helps in collecting information from outside crimes. Then, the crimes are attributed to occur at any place but here. A comparison is drawn between neighborhood crime and outside crime and that latter will be perceived as more unsafe, hence one's safety feeling is increased.

Attribution–2 : Who is the assaulter ? Usually, it is perceived that assaulters are from outside of their neighborhood. In the eight cities study, the actual finding was that there was no difference in residents overestimation or underestimation about outside involvement, the belief still prevailed in them was that outsiders were responsible for crime in their community. Schafer and Florida's finding was that this view was misattribution error, contrary to what people believe, victims are more likely to be assaulted by neighbors. 61. 5% of the crimes were committed by offenders who lived near the victims.

Attribution-3 : Who is to blame ? Much research has been done on this line of thinking. Two lines of observation are there, one on how others assign blame to a victim, second, how the victim cognitively appraises himself. Lenner worked on the first approach and suggested that people maintain their belief in a "just world". They believe that people get what they observe and deserve what they get. If something is happening to a person then Elaine Walster (1966) assessed the second motive which has to do with perception of control over the environment. It was suggested that most people blame the victim in order to reassure themselves that such assaults will not occur to them because they are different from the victim. The basis of the reasoning is that if the happening is because of unpredictable reasons, thus it could happen to anyone at any time, but it is something in the victim's behavior, mannerism which is the cause of attack. Whether, the person will accept blame or not will depend upon whether the events are viewed as under one's personal control. If the victim feels that he has voluntary control then he is ready to accept the blame, but if other people are present at the time of attack then the victim will not accept the blame easily. Another observed outcome has a positive orientation that God must be testing me or that there must be a silver lining in what has occurred to me.

The first attribution error of crime occurring at other places rather than here may reduce alertness, hence may increase victimization risk. People should be made aware of local problems, risks available and steps which should be taken to reduce the risk.

The second attribution error tht outsiders are instigators of crime may be offset by making people accept local involvements and also participating in community programs that may lead to positive corrective actions. Personally, this step may lead to enhanced self esteem, self efficacy and more internal locus of control.

The third attribution error of whom to blame requires a careful and objective assessment of various subsequent events leading to the incident. This may make them realize where the blame lies, self or others. If blame falls on self then coping becomes difficult. Blame may be denied as a defense immediately after the assault. But continued denial may prevent person from making a realistic assessment of the situation and adjusting to it by bringing changes in lifestyles which have been the cause of risk.

There are strong social elements in blaming the victim. For example, if rape occurs one talks about males perverted-ness, sexual aggressiveness but ultimately blame the women by saying that her manners are the cause or her dressing or her facial expression. This forces the women to accept the blame as a whole.

11.10 THE VICTIM'S PROFILE

According to William Berg and Robert Johnson, the effect of victimization lead to acquiring the profile of a victim. According to their model there are certain groups in societies who perceive themselves as low in position and power. They are moulded from childhood in such a way that they develop victims traits. They include confusion, anger against society, shame, vulnerability, dependence (e.g. women, elderly, unemployed group). The victims accept what is happening to them as part of their fate, whether it is unpleasant or unjust.

11.11 BELIEFS ABOUT CRIME

Beliefs are predispositions to act in certain ways that are based on positive and negative evaluations of people, places and things. As a person develops from childhood to adulthood his beliefs may become stronger. Car driving is risky but still people drive. Two wheelers cause many accidents but people use them and feel their utility as significant.

But people do not believe that they will be attacked by someone, will be robbed. All are aware and believe that strangers should be avoided or that one should not go out at night.

Thus, belief influence our cognitions of what is safe and what is unsafe. They form our views about various types of crimes, how they affect people's feelings of vulnerability. Beliefs can guide us in the right directions and prevent us from engaging in risky ways. Beliefs help in coping if attacks have already occurred. They can reduce our anxiety or increase it. Two beliefs are significant in this regard, belief in personal invulnerability and belief about crimes severity.

11.12 BELIEF IN PERSONAL INVULNERABILITY

Depending upon one's upbringing a person may develop vulnerability or invulnerability. If a person believes that he is vulnerable then he may experience high fear and prevent him from acting rightly. Under extreme condition, undesirable mental condition may develop like depression, disorientation, which in turn may curtail one's freedom. On the other hand, person who perceives himself as invulnerable may take undue risks, may hold positive view about neighborhood safety and may not like to be warned by others and won't take any preventive measures suggested by others.

11.13 SEVERITY OF CRIMES

There are three elements regarding belief in severity of crime.

1. Belief that crime in neighborhood is of a lighter nature, while away from neighborhood is given more severe perception.

2. Local crime although can harm the person more is perceived as less threatening than crime occurring elsewhere (Hindelang *et. al.*).

3. Crime is believed to have a negative effect on others rather than themselves. There is denial regarding crime happening to them.

After Effects of Criminal Attack

After effects of criminal attack may be in the form of physical or psychological disturbances. Sleep disturbances, anxiety attacks, change in appetite may occur. Repetitive checking of lock, not going out of house, being terror stricken for days. Hepborn and Monti (1979) observed that fear of crime was the most significant variable leading to giving up autonomy and avoiding moving about. Fear has a legitimate function since it alerts us to something that could possibly be harmful. Our fear interferes with activities of daily living. Fear leads to frustration which in turn hampers one's normal living.

11.14 SUGGESTED STEPS FOR MANAGING FEAR FROM VICTIMIZATION

The most successful technique used for treating fear in the past few years is systematic desensitization. Three separate steps make up this technique. First, learning deep muscular relaxation. Second, developing a fear scale ordering imaginary events from low to high fear and third, combining the events with relaxation a step–by–step fashion until no fear is felt when imagining the most feared events.

Another technique that may help fight fear is rational emotive therapy developed by Albert Ellis. In this, it is assumed that there are some irrational thoughts which aggravate the fear and reduces self freedom. The therapist tries to develop the link between the person's emotions and thought processes. The aim is to reduce irrational thinking which prevents healthy behavior. This requires an external observer as one himself does not realize that he has rational thoughts.

Next technique involves stress inoculation. It attempts to get the individual to deal with small fears one at a time. As successes build up, one acquires resistance and is thus able to tackle larger fears.

One of the behavioral manifestation of fear is the avoidance of people, lace and things that are still associated with the original event. This be termed as anticipatory fear. Behavior that reduces anticipatory fear will be repeated. Avoidance of various sources associated with original trauma helps to reduce fear. This leads to reduced personal freedom. By positive assertion one may gradually regain his freedom, increase his social encounters and may be used to deal with behavioral avoidance.

11.15 SOCIAL ACTIONS TO COPING WITH VICTIMIZATION

In this final section those social actions which increases one's sense of active mastery over the environment and which may bring changes in the localities are discussed.

One aspect in an attempt to move in a safe, secure surrounding is to focus on internal cognitions, attitudes and beliefs. This includes getting clear in your mind about what it is that you are afraid of. Try to avoid unsafe surroundings. The second aspect is to be assess the structural elements of the environment that may contribute to crime occurrence. This may not eradicate crime but if seriously planned the chances of crime being a success may reduce. Persons may inherit traits of criminal and may behave in that manner in any environment, but some people may be provoked by the environment to become criminal.

Crime Prevention Through Environmental Design (CPTED) concept has been developed by Pesce (1981). This concept comprises of three types of crime prevention, viz., punitive, mechanical and corrective types.

Punitive Measures

Design environment that makes it easy to detect and catch criminal through use of alarm and video system. Such mechanisms are now available in market. People working in their offices can also be alerted if a robber touches their house.

Mechanical Methods design safe street designs and place proper lights, they act as barriers to unwanted entries.

Corrective Measures involve eliminating criminal motives, such as, through social programming divert the criminals towards other types of activities, related to work and enjoyments.

Problems with program implementation are 1) because of money spending people resist such program except that all accept emergency assistance number 100. 2) The installed environmental design are not supported by public because they find it inconvenient. So, awareness of long term project plans should be preferred to short term profit program which turns costly in long run. Proposed projects are declined easily. But one should think and act intellectually. Assess the soundness of the program and then associate with it and finally be alert to consequences if safety measures are not adopted.

Obtain Recovery from Damages

Try seeking information from local agencies about how one can obtain assistance to recover damages. People can also get their properties insured through insurance firms, they can get medical claims if hurt badly if they have medical insurance. Such sources are of great help during emergencies where one becomes victimized.

Seeking Human Services

Take help from social organizations, NGOs, Welfare Institutions, etc., which help cope immediately following the victimizing incident. They can provide counseling, education, which help them to recover and reduce future risks. Those who refuse to take help face long term problems, they are not able to prevent crimes from occurring.

In brief, this chapter focuses on problems of stress caused by being victimized. It discussed identification of risk factor, prevention of risk and coping strategies for dealing with after effects. Risk factors point out young, unmarried, unemployed person who make as possible victims.

Prevention involves life styles evaluation to assess if habits are wrong and should be changed. Attribution of causes of crime and victimization must be inspected, faulty beliefs must be assessed and attempt to reduce them must be made.

In the end, coping strategies for dealing with fear like desensitization and rational emotive therapy, stress inoculation may be used to reduce degree of stress felt. Positive assertion, socialization are helpful in eliminating the effects of fear. Last element taken up was gaining knowledge about your environment through personal and social action and thus reducing risk of victimization.

References

Berg, W. E., & Johnson, R. (1979). Assessing the Impact of Victimization : Acquisition of the Victim Role Among Elderly and Female Victims. In W. H. Personage Perspectives on Victimology (pp. 58-71). pp. 58-59.

Hepturn, J. R. & Monti, D. J. (1979). Victimization, Fear of Crime and Adaptive Responses Among High School Students. In Personage, Perspectives on Victimology (pp. 121-132) p. 129.

Hindelang, M. J., Gottfredson, M. R, & Garofalo, J. (1978). Victims of Personal Crime : An Empirical Foundation for a Theory of Personal Victimization. Cambridge. MA : Ballinger. This project was supported by the Law Enforcement Assistance Administration (LEAA).

Meyer, P. B. (1981). Communities as Victims of Corporate Crimes. In B. Galvedy & J Hudson (Eds). Perspective on Crime Victims. (pp. 33-44). St. Louis, Mosby.

Peace, E. J. (1981). Crime prevention through environmental design : In Galaway & Hudson, Perspectives on Crime Victims (pp. 347-348).

Walster, E. (1966). Assignment of Responsibility for an accident. Journal of Personality and Social Psychology : 3, 73-79.

Chapter 12

JOB STRESS

Bhopal tragedy occurred in India, but the impact was felt by Warner Anderson, Chairman, Union Carbide. He was not directly responsible for the spilling of toxic gases, but ultimately he had to accept the final responsibility for it as he was the Chief Officer of the company. Anderson and his wife faced so much stress that they felt that they were in a private jail all the time.

Three important aspects related to job stress are as follows:

(1) Work stress involves both the organization and its employees. Often job stress affects family life and family problems often are transported to the job. Work stress usually produces negative effects for both the organization and the personnel.

(2) Organisation becomes disorganized normal working in disrupted, productivity is reduced and profits suffer. Employees face increased health problems, psychological distress and behavioral changes, job satisfaction is reduced.

(3) Work stress can only be reduced when both organizational and personal problems are solved. Without this personal coping strategies will fail.

12.1 DEFINITION OF JOB STRESS

Job Stress results from characteristics of the job environment which pose a threat to the individual. Threat may come from many sources, like insufficient supply or excessive demand.

The costs of work stress are economic loss suffered because of job stress and unsafe conditions at work. Work stress effects personal, family, business and the society.

Estimates given by government reveal that 100, 000 workers die each year from job related diseases, while another 390, 000 workers develop many job related illness.

About 14,000 workers die due to accidents on the job. Another 3 million suffer from disabilities.

Teny Beehr and Newman observed that there are three types of negative personal outcomes due to work stress, *i.e.*, psychological health symptoms, physical health symptoms, and behavioral symptoms.

The list of psychological symptoms of work stress include anxiety, tension, inevitability, frustration, anger, resentment, emotional hypersensitivity, suppression of feelings, poor communication, depression, insolation and loneliness, boredom, mental fatigue, lack of concentration, lowered self-esteem. The most predictable psychological consequences is job dissatisfaction. This leads to demotivation.

Physical health symptoms of work stress include increased heart rate and blood pressure, cardiovascular disease, gestro intestinal disorders, respiratory problems, increased sweating, skin disorders, headaches, cancer, muscular tension, sleep disordered death etc.

Often employees bring some physical health problems to the job, work conditions may intensify health problems. Job conditions may also cause problems like poor lighting, unclear work areas, high noise levels.

Behavioral symptoms of work stress include the following : avoidance of work, lowered overall performance, increased alcohol and drug use, overeating, undereating, withdrawl, depression, increased risk taking behavior, deteriorating relationships. Behavioral symptons affecting the organization include quantitative and qualitative low performance, low job involvement, loss of sense of responsibility to the job, absenteeism, accident proneness.

12.2 STRESS SOURCES

Causes of work stress may be classified into two sechoms, *viz.* : (1) Organisational stressors (2) Individual stressors

Organisational stressors include the various aspects present in the work place that can cause stress. The various organizational stressors are :

(i) **Task Demand** : Task demands are stressors linked with specific jobs performed by a person. This implies nature of occupation. Some occupations involve more risk, like surgeon, air traffic, controllers as compared to others like teacher, clerk, airplane, baggage loaders. Another aspect of job involves unhealthy working conditions such as working in coal mines, or slake lime factory. Another aspect in a task is sense of security felt, a pilot may feel less secure than a teacher, hence may feel more stress. Other aspects may be periods of lay offs or when organizations are merged.

(ii) **Role Demand** : Some aspects present in roles may make them stressful, like role ambiguity role conflict, etc. Role ambiguity means one is not clear about how he has to perform his job, he is not clear about his objectives, expectations from colleagues regarding scope and responsibilities of job. Role conflict occurs when a person has to choose between conflicting job demands, or is forced to do task which he does not want to do. Responsibility towards people is highly stressful as compared to responsibility towards things like equipments, material etc. Other role stressors may be lack of participation in decision making, lack of managerial comforts, aiming to retain high standards of performance.

(iii) **Communication, Relationship at work** : On the job a person has to communicate with his seniors, juniors and colleagues. The type of relationship one maintains with these people may be a source of stress. Poor communication may prevent maintaining good relations, there will be lack of trust low supportiveness, low interest in listening to and dealing with organizational problems of the members. Another source of stress comes from boss who lack consideration. Task oriented masters cause more stress than people oriented managers.

Stress may also aggravate due to lack of social support from colleagues during problematic situations.

(iv) **Organisational Structures and Culture** : When organizational culture is not facilitative then stress may occur. When organization is a threat to one's freedom, autonomy, identity, then stress may arise. Other stressors may be low participation in decision making, lack of belongingness, lack of effective consultation, poor communication, restrictions in behaviors and organizational politics. Autocratic structure may also lead to tension in employees.

(v) **Organisational Leadership** : Types of leaderships may cause stress. If employees need social support from leaders, but leader don't show any concern for them then stress will be felt by them. On the other hand if employees like to participate in decision making, then autocratic leader who refuses to consult them may become a pain in the neck.

(vi) **Group Pressures** : Groups pressurize their member in many ways like they restrict output, force them to confirm to group ways. Individuals who disobey the group leader is pressurized to maintain the group norm. Person who wants group acceptance plus also wants to please his boss feels the strains.

12.3 INDIVIDUAL STRESSORS

Individuals have two segments to their lives, *i.e.*, home and organization. Stressors may occur in either organizational life or personal life, like career development, personality type life changes and life trauma.

Career Development : Stressors relating to career development are (1) fear of redundancy, obsolescence or early retirement, (2) status incongruity *i.e.*, under or over promotion and frustration stemming from reaching career ceiling.

Personality Type : Mayer Friedman and Ray Rosenmen observed during their observations as cardiologists that some patients sat at the their chairs while others sat very comfortably, and thus concluded that people differed in their personality, they labelled these personality types as Type A and Type B. The extreme Type A personality is made up of the following aspects like chronic sense of time urgency, excessive competitive drive, desire to do more in less time. The characteristic of Type A personality are :

(1) Always moving, walking, talking, eating rapidly.

(2) Feeling impatient about rate at which events move.

(3) Trying to do two or more things simultaneously.

(4) Aggressive and competitive attitude.

(5) Always feel time pressure.

Type B personality is just the opposite. They possesses the following characteristics.

(1) Are not impatient and do not have sense of time urgency.

(2) Do not discuss their achievements unless such exposure is demanded by a situation.

(3) Can relax without guilt.

(4) Play for fun rather than to show superiority.

(5) Have no pressing deadlines.

(6) Are never in a hurry.

Difference between Type A and Type B persons does not mean that one may succeed at the cost of others, Type A are usually in such a hurry to succeed that they may miss opportunities of learning. While Type B may have better interpersonal reputation and may learn a wide array of skills.

Life Change : Holmes and Rahe observed that major changes in a person's life can lead to stress which may lead to illness. Such events relate to work, like being fired from work, retirement. Value attached to each event reflects upon the events impact on the individual, e.g. spouse's death is assumed to have the most devastating effect, while fight with a colleague may have a moderate effect, burning the food may be valued as having minor affect. If the number of stress producing life changes increase then a person experience a decline in health. A score of 150 to 300 life change events a year may lead to 50% of illnesses.

Life Traumas : An Upheavel : A traumatic incident in an individual's life may other ones attitudes, emotions or behaviors, e.g. divorce may create health problems, especially in the beginning when a person is taken by shock of it but the actual process of divorce may be less traumatic as the person gets used to the idea. Such traumatic incidents in the life of the person will surely influence his work life. Major life traumas causing stress include family difficulties and health problems etc.

Outcomes of Stress

Individual Level Outcomes : No person can be free from stress. Stress is the part and parcel of one's life. Stress causes distress when one starts feeling insecure, in adequate. Outcomes may be physical, psychological and behavioral.

Physical Outcomes : The physical consequences of stress are heart disease, stroke. They affect a persons physical well being, other common medical problems are headaches, backaches, ulcers, stomach disorders.

Behavioral Outcomes : The behavioral outcomes of person under stress are indulgence in smoking alcohol, drug abuse. People under stress indulge in these behaviors more other possible consequences are accident proneness, violence and appetite disorder.

Psychological Outcomes : People who experience much stress may feel depressed, sleep more or less, have family problems, sexual difficulties etc. Their mental health and well being is negatively influenced.

Job Burnout : The End of Work Stress : Robert Veninga and James Spradley defined burnout as 'a deliberating psychological condition brought about by unrelieved work stress which results in depleted energy reserves, lowered resistance to illness, increased dissatifaction and pessimism, increased absenteeism and inefficiency at work. Five stages leading to burnout have been analysed by Veninga and Spradley—

(1) **Honeymoon stage** : When the new employee feels motivated to give his best, is full of energy and enthusiasm. He is satisfied with his job.

(2) **Fuel shortage stage** : It reveals the first sign of burnout, and gradually increases.

(3) **Chronic stage** : Here symptoms of exhaustion, illness, anger, depression appear on a continuous basis.

(4) **Crisis stage** : Where the symptoms become so severe that the person feels that his life is falling apart.

(5) **Hitting the way** : It is the final stage when the person can no longer functions, and signs of deterioration become obvious.

12.4 OUTCOMES FOR THE ORGANIZATION

When individuals are stressed, the organization they work in will severely experience stress. The organizations are influenced in the following areas :

(1) As individuals performance is declining, the overall productivity of the organization, goes down, losses start occurring.

(2) There is increase of absenteeism and labour turnover. A person may also withdraw psychologically from the organization

(3) Another area in which organization experience the outcomes of stress is attitudes like job satisfaction, morale, organizational commitment. They may also be adversely affected.

(4) Decision making takes a longer time, and decisions may also be of poor quality.

(5) Communication will be hampered, human relationships will deteriorate.

12.5 COPING STRATEGIES FOR STRESS

Stress occurs in everyone's life, hence one should be prepared to cope with it. Two strategies that work are copying strategies from individuals point of view and strategies from organizational point of view.

Individual's Coping Strategies

(1) **Relaxation** : One must relax so that one becomes fresh enough to think of creative, fulfilling ways to cope with stress. Either one may take long vacation or may take regular rest breaks during their normal workday. Relaxation may be in the form of sitting quietly with closed eyes for 10 minutes every afternoon.

(2) **Time Management** : Daily pressures can be reduced by being prepared for them and one way of doing so is by managing and planning ones daily routine. One way prescribed is making a list of what one has to do that day. All the things should be sequenced according to their importance and urgency. This helps people in doing more significant things first, and insignificant things later, or may also think of delegating them to others.

(3) **Role Management** : Roles stresses include role overload, role conflict and ambiguity. One should get these problems sorted out with the help of his boss.

(4) **Meditation** : Meditation involves quiet, concentrated inner thought in order to rest the body

physically and emotionally. Yogic exercises are often performed regularly by people to relax themselves.

(5) **Social Support** : One should be within family and friends with whom one can share his problems, may ooze out his fears, strains they may act as safety valves for him. Daily problems can easily be solved with the help of various social groups in which one belongs.

Organizational Coping Strategies

Strategies used by organizations to manage stress include the following.

(1) **Organizational Role Clarity** : Usually stress in organisations occur due to role ambiguity and role conflict. Such situations can be remedied by analyzing each role specifically and pinpointing what is expected from each role. If the job of a person is segmented, each duty specified, then it will solve the problem of role ambiguity and role conflict.

(2) **Job Redesign** : If jobs are designed in a manner which makes working comfortable, time schedules are properly fixed, then stress may be reduced.

(3) **Stress Reduction Programmes** : These programmes aim at identifying the causes of stress in organizations and reducing their ill effects by redesign, reallocating work load, improving supervisory skills, providing autonomy and variety in job, etc. Stress management techniques help persons and work groups to manage stress effectively.

(4) **Facilitative Organisational Culture** : Usually organizational policies and practices are defective, and unfavourable. These can be controlled by creating a facilitative environment in the organization. The culture created in organization depends upon managerial leadership type of power used and money used to control behavior. Participation and involvement of employees in decision making must be encouraged. This climate leads to feelings of close ties which help in reducing tensions.

(5) **Counselling** : Counselling is one of the personal wellness programmes. It seeks to improve employees mental health by the release of emotional tension building in them Counselling involves a discussion between the counsellor and the employees about the problem.

(6) **Wellness Programme** : Various stress management programmes have been created in organizations to overcome stress, like health promotion programmes through gyms, insurance policies, career development programmes through growth, advancement schemes, etc. and other programmes.

12.6 SPECIAL GROUPS FACING WORK STRESS

Certain groups of people and certain professional groups are more subjected to work stress than others. Description of few groups is elaborated upon

Working Women and Job Stress

Women face a lot of open discrimination in work places. They are given less pay in works, less respectable work, given more boring work than their male counter parts. Another day to day problem for women is that they often have to take up double career, one at home as housewife, the other as jobholder. This type of overloading on women is because of our social and economic values. The stress they carry cannot be reduced until this discriminatory practice is changed.

Sexual Harassment : In the offices women face exploitations, oppressions, feelings of disgust and add to their stress. According to Barbara Pletcher, sexual harassement is a weapon used against women in the pervasive power game. It is an insult to women. Active efforts are required to weed out the sexual harassers from the work place. Lot of courage is required on the part of the women to file a legal suit against their boss. Women should have knowledge about various agencies working for helping out women in problems so that they can approach them. If their job would not get affected many women may open up about harassament at work places. Often men may also agree to help women in problems. These men realize that harassers are an insult to men community, and they should be taught lesson to free them from this dirty habit. There are men who value the women and feel that they should not be exploited just because they are physically weak.

Stress in Professionals

Persons often take up professions which are very risky like police and army service, CBI, air traffic controllers. People in these professions often experience stress effects like hypertensions, peptic ulcers, diabetes, indigestion, chest pain etc. These symptoms start appearing as a person crosses a few years on the job, they do not appear instantly.

A research work by Frank revealed that as a person passes through stressful event for a number of years, a blunting of emotions occurs and a person gradually stops feelings tensed up even during stressful circumstances. Based on this finding a conclusion can be made that persons on risky jobs don't feel the tensions, but of course as fear is hidden somewhere in their systems they develop the physiological effects described above.

Summary

Stress has been a major concern of the modern times, it causes harm to employees health and performance. It causes both physiological as well as psychological effects. Some coping strategies for both individuals and organizations are suggested.

References

Beehr, T. A. & Newman, J. E. (1978). Job Stress, Employees Health and Organizational Effectiveness. A Facet Analysis Model, and Literature Review. Personnel Psychology, 31, 665-699.

Friedman, J. L. (1986) Television violence and aggression, A rejoinder, Psychological Bulletin, 100, 372-378.

Pletcher, B. A. (1978). Saleswoman : A guide to career success. Homewood. I. L. Dow Jones-Irwin.

Veninga, R. L. & Spradley, J. P. (1981). The Work stress connection. Boston : Little Brown, p. 10.

Chapter 13

NUTRITION, EXERCISE, HEALTH AND STRESS

As stress has an arousal effect on the person there is substantive change in both energy expenditure and energy intake. Stress increases the rate of metabolism, the rate at which the body changes food supplies into energy. This leads to increased levels of sugar, free fatty acids and lactic acid

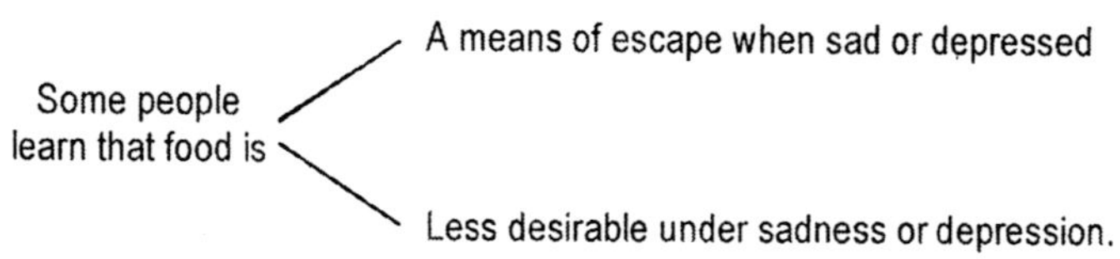

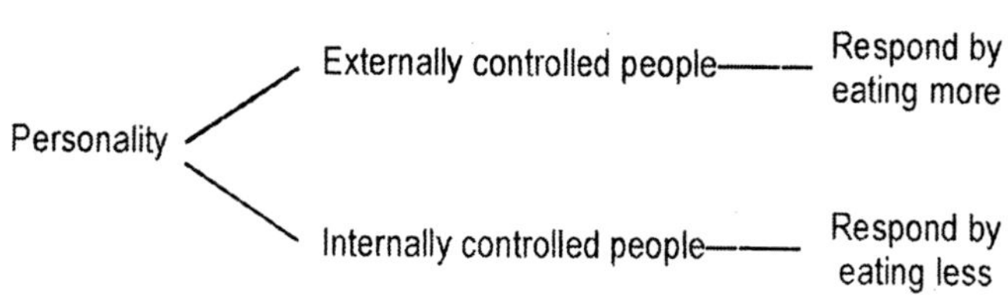

in the blood. The pituitary gland also indirectly affects the rate of metabolism. These effects include changes in water balance, suppression of immune system and increased carbohydrate and protein metabolism. The net effect of stress is that the body uses energy at a faster rate. On the intake side, pattern of eating depends on a variety of factors such as learning, emotionality and personality.

When pattern of responding to stress is to eat more and eat more frequently, a cycle may be established that leads to difficulty in controlling weight, or obesity, when the pattern is to eat less, or going without food for substantial periods, the body may be depleted of energy reserves at an even faster rate.

When there is any dramatic change in eating patterns, look carefully at what is the reason, what unresolved conflict prevails at work, at school, or in the family.

13.1 ROLE OF DIET ON STRESS

Just as arousal can change metabolism and eating behavior, diet practices can change sensitivity to arousing stimulation and environmental stressors, thus eating right may help in managing stress. Poor diet increases vulnerability to poor diet.

There are two ways for eating right.

1. Excess sugar intake can deplete vitamins and minerals. Since, vitamins and minerals are essential for working of many body parts like nervous system, they will be adversely affected hence excess sugar intake must be prevented.

2. A number of foods commonly taken in large amounts have the potential to increase stress sensitivity. For example,

Coffee, Cola, Chocolates contain caffeine, hence are abused beverages and food products in our society.

1 cup coffee contains 250 mg of caffeine which causes headaches, insomnia, nervousness.

Now it is well known that caffeine acts as a stimulant to the central nervous system, has a tendency to change up the autonomic systems and lowers the threshold for stress reactions, *i.e.*, if someone is on a diet, loaded with caffeine he will respond to tense situation more quickly and strongly than if someone had taken less caffeine. Before moving further into the effects of nutrition on stress it will be desirable on individual part to fill out the nutrition and diet scales given in self study exercise. (13.1)

Self study Exercise 13.1 Health Behavior Profile for Nutrition and Diet

The following scale will help in comparing dietary practice to what is considered good practice. Instructions for scoring are provided at the end.

Circle the answer that most accurately describes one's eating habits.

DAILY= Once or more per day

FREQUENTLY = Every week but not once per day

OCCASIONALLY =A few times each month but once per week

SELDOM= No more than once per month

	How Often Do You	*Seldom*	*Occa- sionally*	*Freque- ntly*	*Daily*
1.	Eat, fruits, vegetables, fiber ?	1	2	3	4
2.	Drink five or more cups of coffee in a day?	4	3	2	1
3.	Eat fats, red meats, and dairy products?	4	3	2	1
4.	Drink five or more soft drinks (diet or regular)	4	3	2	1
5.	Eat candies, sugars, pastries?	4	3	2	1
6.	Take vitamins' supplements ?	4	3	2	1
7.	Overeat at meals?	4	3	2	1
8.	Eat between meals ?	4	3	2	1
9.	Eat while watching TV, reading and so on?	4	3	2	1
10.	Skip breakfast	4	3	2	1
11.	Skip Lunch	4	3	2	1
12.	Skip Dinner	4	3	2	1
13.	Use crash diets to lose weight?	4	3	2	1
14.	Take diet pills?	4	3	2	1
15.	Use amphetamines to lose weight	4	3	2	1

After completing the scale, go back and sum the values listed in the boxes, circled. Then circle the point on the scale below that correspondence to the total score. A high score suggests that the eating habits is fairly good and on the other hand a low score indicates there is some risk in the eating habits. If the score is in the high risk region, look back at the items checked that have values of 1 or 2. These items provides clues to some areas where a change in diet and nutrition habit may be warranted

Score Sum ..... 42..... 45..... 47......48.... 49.... 51..... 52..... 53......54

High Risk Normal Nutrition Excellent

Percentile ..... 10...20..... 30......40.... 50..... 60.... 70..... 80. 90

The average score on this scale is 49. 2 and the median is 49. 5. The median indicates that 50% of the respondent scored higher than 49. 5 and 50% scored below this. The scale has a reliability of .695, which is acceptable for this type of scale. This scale is not intended to be comprehensive nutrition assessment and is provided for instructional purpose only.

Right Diet

If one eats right food in balanced amount one gets proper nutrients. Research on nutrition has shown that the adult human being must have 46 nutrients in order to be healthy and remain healthy. To maintain a constant weight the average women needs about 1, 600-2, 400 calories, the average man needs 2, 300-3, 100 calories. Table 13.1. gives the Recommended Daily Energy Intake for Children and adults.

To obtain the 46 nutrients, the normal adult needs a minimum of 1, 300 calories per day (Mirkin, 1983). Any diet that reduces to an extreme either the type or the quantity of food is dangerous in the long run, and should be avoided. Rules provided above are for normal adults, and not for children, adults above 55-60 years, for pregnant and nursing women, for ill persons, for larger persons, for persons doing strenuous job. Their requirements will differ due to different demands made on their bodies.

Distribution of 46 nutrients

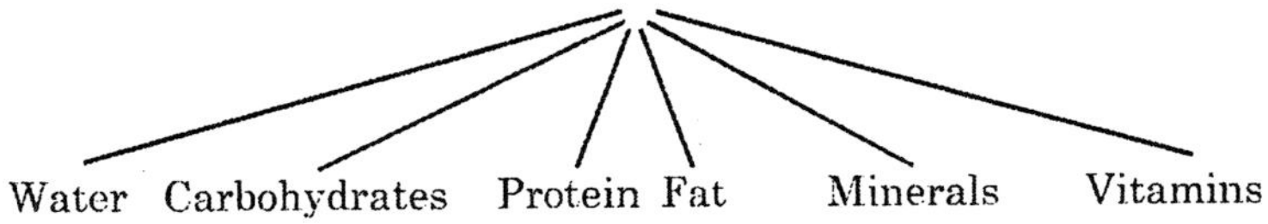

The body's requirement of 46 nutrients is distributed into 6 categories, *i.e.*, water, carbohydrates, 9 proteins, fat, 13 vitamins, and 21 minerals. In these categories only carbohydrates, protein and fats contain calories. Calories provide body with energy for internal processes and for muscular and brain work. If consumed in excess may add body weight. Fats cause greatest harm while carbohydrates cause least harm. Water, vitamins, minerals are essential for proper body function but they do not add calories. Most of these nutritional needs are met by natural food supplies. The aim is to obtain the proper balance of foods so that all nutrients are maintained and sufficient calories are provided to maintain right weight.

Carbohydrates are complex food molecules made up of carbon, oxygen, hydrogen and sugar. One simple sugar is glucose, the high energy fuel in your blood stream. Fruits and honey contains pure glucose which can pass directly into the blood streams for fast energy. Foods such as bananas and oranges also contain simple sugar, but they must be converted into glucose in order to be used by the body. Common table sugar and milk are sources of double sugar, while corn, beans and potatoes are sources of complex sugars.

Carbohydrates provide the primary fuel for exercise, labour, brain work. The brain depends on continuous supply of glucose to work properly. It cannot reserve or hold back fuel for later use. Hence, breakfast is important for starting the day, in the morning if food is not eaten the brain does not get immediate energy to work properly. Apart from providing quick source of energy, carbohydrates fill you up more quickly with fewer calories than any other food, hence when you eat carbohydrate you stop eating quickly. Carbohydrates that are high in fibre are most beneficial. These are called complex carbohydrates. Two characteristics of high fibre foods make them valuable to a healthy diet

1. High fibre food do not break down in the digestive system as readily as other foods.

The upper intestine cannot break down fibre at all. Since they cannot be broken down, they cannot be absorbed into the body, hence one does not have to worry as much about adding weight when eating high fibre food.

2. Fats bind to fibre. If there is some fibre in the stomach, when fat is added, some of the fat will stick on the fibre and pass out of your system as part of the body waste.

Common foods containing carbohydrates are vegetables, fruits and whole grains. If you feel hungry between meals eat an apple or carrot. This will reduce hunger, provide energy and add fibres to the digestive tract.

The Proteins : A wrong stereotype is that protein is the source of strength and that the best source of protein is meat, hence vegetarians are weaker than meat eaters. While there are calories in protein, it seems to be the last foodstuff converted to energy after the carbohydrates and the fat. The body uses protein only during periods of severe starvation or dieting.

Proteins are the basic building blocks for all the tissues in your body. Hair, skin, eyes, muscles, and organs are all built with protein in combination with other materials. Even enzymes that regulate body functions are proteins. In the human body, proteins are made of 21 different amino acids, the body is capable of manufacturing 12 of the 21 amino acids by itself, but the other 9 have to come from the diet.

Protein can be obtained from various sources. Most common sources is animal sources such as poultry, eggs, fish, lean meat, cheese, milk. It is also available from many plant sources such as cereals, nuts, beans, and leafy vegetables.

Gabe Mirkins points that you can get virtually all the proteins you need in two large glasses of milk or in 12 ounces of corn and bean per day.

During periods of intense stress, infections and injury, the body may increases its demand for protein by as much as 100%. During body building or intense exercises also one requires more protein.

Fats : Good and Bad

Fats are the most over used food. It is associated with obesity and coronary difficulties. Normal diet should contain not more than 30% fat to the maximum. The average male should carry no more than 15% body fat and the average female should carry no more than 25% body fat.

A male of 45 years of age carrying 25 pounds of excess fat has a life expectancy reduced by 25%.

But it cannot be denied that fat are essential to a healthy body, and to survival. Fat is a storehouse of energy and fluids for the body to draw on whenever need arises. Fats get converted into energy faster than protein. It is essential for transport of vitamin, the immune system's ability to protect the body against viruses and bacteria is also dependent on the presence of fat. Fat also protects body against cold.

Maximum danger from fat comes from cholesterol in the blood stream and the buildup of yellow fat on the body. Excess calories may be converted by the liver to a type of blood fat called cholesterol.

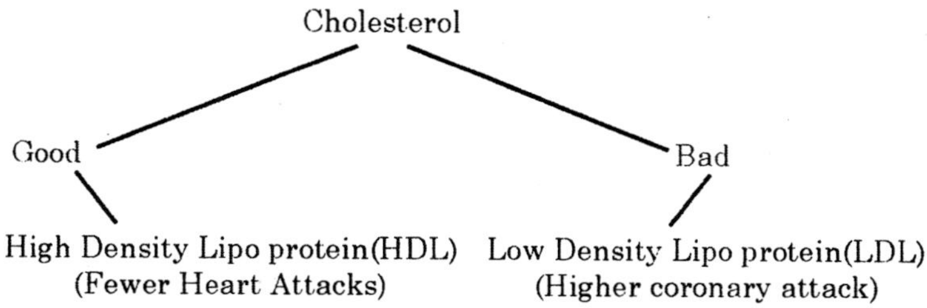

Cholesterols are of two kinds, one is good type of fat, which is called high density lipoprotein, (HDL), the bad cholesterol is called low density lipo protein (LDL). Coronary attacks are associated with a high concentration of LDL, persons with HDL tend to have fewer attacks.

HDL keeps the arteries clean and elastic. While LDL embeds itself in the arterial walls, beginning to narrow and harden the artery so that blood can only pass with much greater efforts for the heart and much higher pressure in the arteries. Regular exercises carry more of HDL as cholesterol while sedentary people carry more of LDL as cholesterol.

Fat is consumed in bitter oil, salad dressings, ice cream, fatty meat.

By reducing intake of diet with fat and by maintaining regular exercise program one can prevent many bodily problems.

Vitamins : A balanced diet is able to supply most of the vitamins one need at all the levels. If one supplement his diet with common vitamins providing 100% of the daily requirement, he may be taking twice of what he require. Very little attention is paid to the overdose of vitamins and their dangers. Charles Marshall noted that the practice of taking vitamin supplement has turned into a pattern of abuse based on the mistaken notion that more is better. This is often combined with a false security that translates to "I take so many vitamins I don't have to worry about the rest of my diet." Some vitamins are also addicting. Some dangers of taking vitamins are pointed by Marshall. Of vitamin A, negative effects of over dose may include loss of appetites, weight loss, loss of hair, anemia, blurred vision, extreme drying and thickening of skin, dry and cracking lips, uncreated brain and spinal fluid pressure with headaches, irritability in children, and birth defects in children born to mothers who took mega dosages during pregnancy.

B complex may cause toxic effects. Vitamin C overdose may cause diarrheas, complication in pregnancy (spontaneous abortion), lowered sperm count, increased uric acid excretion, decreased tolerance for low oxygen levels, decreased resistance to bacteria infections and tumours and damage to tooth enamel, (Mirkins 1983). Overdose of Vitamin D causes loss of appetite, nausea, headaches, depressions. Long term use may result in calcification of soft tissues and kidney failure. Excessive urination, diarrhea or constipation may also occur. Mega dose of Vitamin E may result in elevated blood triglyceride levels in women and a reduction in thyroid hormones in both sexes. Apart from dangers from megadose of vitamins physiologically also the body is not prepared for excesses. Body can hold only limited amount of vitamin before overflowing. Body cannot use the huge amount of vitamins which are pumping into their bodies.

Eating Light

Any diet program should focus not only on what goes in but also on what goes out (energy expenditure through exercise)

Gabe Mirkin suggested that the diet should never go below 1, 000 calories, if someone is not exercising, and then the intake should stay above 1,300 calories.

Another risk is dieting without exercising. Dieting takes off muscle tissue, not fat, while by exercising one can remove fat but tone muscles. You get rid of what you need to get rid off and keep what is more important.

Proper exercise is one of the most effective methods for obtaining weight loss, especially by getting rid of yellow fat.

The final difficulty is that restricting your diet may actually go against weight loss. The body reads reductions in food as an extreme starvation event. It responds by slowing everything down, a conservation strategy that retains fat instead of discarding it. Under very low calories' diet condition your body draws out of the protein and fat reserves so that weight loss occurs. Following guidelines must be observed if you must diet.

1. Keep calories intake above the minimum so that you obtain all the essential food groups

2. Combine dieting with exercises that burns off more calories than you consume.

3. Keep food intake balanced in the proportion of 50% carbohydrates, 20% proteins, and 30% fats if you cut anything further, cut fat.

4. Avoid diets that require a dangerously low calories intake for any period.

5. Avoid diets that eliminate all of one types of food or suggest excessive amounts of a particular food.

6. Do not assume that vitamin supplements can take the place of carbohydrates, proteins or fats. Vitamins contain no calories.

Table 13.2. Recommended Daily Energy in take for children and adults

Age (Years)	*Weight (pounds)*	*Height (inches)*	*Energy Needs (calories)*	
Youths	1-3	29	35	1, 300 (900-1, 800)
	4-6	44	44	1, 700 (1300-2, 300)
	7-10	62	52	2, 400 (1, 650-3, 300)
Males	11-14	99	62	2, 700 (2, 000-3, 700)
	15-18	145	69	2, 800 (2, 100-3, 900)

	19-22	154	70	2, 900 (2, 500-3, 300)
	23-50	154	70	2, 700 (2, 300-3, 100)
	51-75	154	70	2, 400 (2, 000-2, 800)
	76 +	154	70	2, 050 (1, 650-2, 450)
Females	11-14	101	62	2, 200 (1, 500-3, 000)
	15-18	120	64	2, 100 (1, 200-3, 000)
	19-22	120	64	2, 100 (1, 700-2, 500)
	23-50	120	64	2, 300 (1, 600-2, 400)
	51-75	120	64	1, 800 (1, 400-2, 200)
	76 +	120	64	1, 600 (1, 200-2, 000)
Pregnancy				+300
Nursing				+500

Note : Adapted from Mayo Clinic Diet Manual (p. 270) by Mayo Clinic, Committee on Dietetics (Eds.) 1981, Philadelphia : Saunders.

13.2 EXERCISE–HEALTH AND STRESS

Why has exercise become a necessity? Reasons lie in science and technological developments. Before their inventions daily life was taken up with the continuous struggle for existence and survival. Now, however, virtually every work that once demanded physical activity has been mechanized or streamlined to reduce effort. Even for viewing television one need not get up. In this climate, people are continuously dieting and exercising. Even a very low calories diet will probably put weight on because the balance between input of calories and output of energy is not balanced.

Self study 13.2 : Health Behavior Profile for exercise

Physical benefits of exercises

Physical exercises have a wide range of positive effects for the body. These include the following—

1. Increased respiratory capacity.
2. Increased muscle tone.
3. Increased strength in bodies, ligaments and tendons.
4. Inproved cardiovascular functioning.
5. Reduced risk of heart disease.
6. Improved circulation.
7. Reduced cholesterol and triglyceride levels.
8. Increased energy.
9. Improved sleep and reduced need for sleep.
10. Increased rate of metabolism.
11. Reduced body weight and improved fat metabolism.
12. Reduced risk of injury from slips, falls and so forth.
13. Slowed down aging process.

Mental Benefits of Exercise

Mental benefits of exercising can be best explained by the euphoria experienced by many athletes. The experienced feeling of elation, spiritual ecstasy is so powerful that

Self-Study Exercise 13.3. Health behavior Profile for Exercise

This profile is intended to help in determining the adequacy of your current physical activities and exercise program. Read the instructions carefully before completing the profile. Instructions for scoring are given at the end along with the necessary information on how to interpret your own score.

Indicate the level of your participation in any of the listed activities by circling the appropriatenumber given below.

AEROBIC =Four or more times per week.

FREQUENTLY =Two or three times per week.

WEEKLY = About once per week.

MONTHLY = About once a month.

NEVER = Almost never

S. No	*How often do you Participate in :*	*Never*	*Monthly*	*Weekly*	*Fre-quently*	*Aerobic*
1.	Swimming	0	1	2	3	4
2.	Walking one mile per day	0	1	2	3	4
3.	Hiking or backpacking	0	1	2	3	4
4.	Gardening	0	1	2	3	4
5.	Bicycling	0	1	2	3	4
6.	Calisthenics, aerobics, dance exercise	0	1	2	3	4
7.	Racquetball, tennis	0	1	2	3	4
8.	Canoeing or boating	0	1	2	3	4
9.	Water or snow sking	0	1	2	3	4
10.	Hunting or fishing	0	1	2	3	4
11.	Golfing	0	1	2	3	4
12.	Team sports	0	1	2	3	4
13.	Running (five or more miles per week	0	1	2	3	4
14.	Other physical exercise	0	1	2	3	4

After answering all 14 questions, sum the values in all the circled numbers. Then, count all the circled numbers with the value of 1 or more. Divide the sum by the count. This is aerobic index. Finally, locate your aerobic index on the scale below. A low aerobic index suggests that you are not getting enough exercise. A high aerobic index suggests that your pattern of exercise is fairly good. If you have score at the high risk end of the scale, you should think about how to begin a consistent exercise program that will place you in the normal, if not excellent, range.

Aerobic Index 1. 00. . 1. 25. . 1. 50. . 1. 75. . 2. 00. . 3. 00. . 3. 50. . 4. 00		
→ High Risk ←	→ Normal Exercise ←	→ Excellent ←
Percentile..... 20 ... 30 .... 40 .... 50. . . 60.... 70 .... . 80 .... 90 100		

Achieving the same state again becomes a goal in its own right. It, thus serves as a powerful incentive to continue the activity.

Some other mental benefits include

1. Increased feelings of self control, independence, and self sufficiency
2. Increased self confidence
3. Improved body image and self esteem
4. Mental changes of pace from the pressure of work, even when the work is physical
5. Improved mental functioning alertness and efficiency.

6. Emotional cleaning out of tensions from interpersonal conflict and job stress

7. Reduced overall levels of stress

8. Relief from mild depression.

Warm Up Phase for Exercise

Each exercise session is divided into three distinct periods, warm up, exercise and cool down. Before any sport 10-20 minutes should be scheduled for warming up prior to the exercising phase. During this period do some stretching and limbering routines, goal is to bring your body temperature up slowly and get your muscles ready for more demanding exercise next. Whether cycling or running never go full speed from the start. After completing the exercises, allow 10-20 minutes for cooling off. The longer and harder the work out, the longer you will probably need for cooling down. Just take a brisk walk or do light calisthenics. If you do not cool down properly, the muscles may become congested, with increased blood flow. Kelones or poisons may build up in your blood producing pain and discomfort, such as cramps.

Another significant point to make is that if you are just beginning an exercise program than it must pass through a session of developmental stages. Start off with light exercises in relatively short sessions. As your fitness improves to a degree that is adequate for your sex and age, you can increase the intensity and the length of the sessions. Don't try to progress to higher levels than is adequate. Just maintain the right level of exercising.

There are some rules to guide an adequate exercise program. The exercise program must aim at Aerobic fitness which means the ability to take in, transport and utilize oxygen. To achieve aerobic improvement, four factors may be considered, *viz.* frequency, type, duration, and intensity of exercise. How effective your exercise program is over the short run and long run depends on the interaction of these four factors.

When to Exercise

One should exercise at least three times each week, preferably four, in order to obtain aerobic improvement. Anything more than this may wear down your body, leading to increasing fatigue which may reduce motivation for exercise. Usually schedule major workouts on every other day basis. Schedule light workout on the off days. You may also use different variety of exercise to provide some change and motivation.

Calorie Burnt in Various Exercises

One way of rating different types of exercises is to calculate the number of calories burned in the course of one hour of exercise. Table 13.4 contains information about calories consumed in various exercises. For example walking briskly burns more calories than even swimming or running. One need not indulge in strenuous exercises to achieve aerobic fitness. Any activity that burns 200-300 calories per hour is sufficient if one do it consistently three to four times per week.

Table 13.4 Energy expenditure per hour during different types pf activity.

Form of activities	*Calories per hour*
Sleeping	65
Awake, lying still	77
Sitting at rest	100
Standing relaxed	105
Dressing & undressing	118
Tailoring	135
Typewriting rapidly	140
Light exercise	170
Walking slowly (2.6 miles per hour	200
Carpentary, metal working, industrial painting	240
Active exercise	290
Severe exercises	450
Sawing wood	480
Swimming	500
Runing (5. 3 miles per hour)	570
Very severe exercises	600
Walking very fast (5. 3 miles per hour)	650
Walking up stairs	1, 100

Note : Adapted from Basic Human Physiology : Normal Functions and Mechanisms of Disease (p. 737) by A. C. Guyton, 1977. Philadelphea : Saunders.

Activities like running, bicycling, swimming, or aerobic exercises are most beneficial. Home treadmills and exercise machines provide adequate exercise. Skipping rope is also a simple form of aerobic exercise. Another exercise good for health is step up. Climb 2-3 steps and come down. Practice this for 15 minutes continuously and it is equivalent to walking 3 miles. Given all the benefits of exercise, it is surprising the many people do not establish exercise programs. Reasons are many attitude and perceptions that prevent people from taking up exercise programs. Two attitudes which prevent people from exercise programs are society's obsession with competition. They feel that exercises should only be performed if you are in any competing sports. Another attitude is the perception of lack of need. People feel they are slim hence they do not exercise. These two attitudes are no excuse for preventing people from developing exercise programs for themselves. If your physical activity does not meet the criteria for aerobic fitness as specified earlier, you need exercise no matter how fit you feel.

Excuses are also made regarding costs of exercising. This is also ruled out as there are several exercises that cost virtually nothing yet provide all physical conditioning needed. Another excuse is that exercise takes too much time or you are busy in other more significant activities. The reply is that three to four hours per week given to physical activity is not compared to the results it gives.

Some people feel embarrassed about attending exercise classes, than don't feel so, remember all are there for learning to be fit, and you are one of them hence why feel embarrassed. All you do is take up an exercise program and practice it.

References

Frank, J. D. (1973). Persuasion and healing. Baltimore, Johns Hopkins University Press.

Friedman, M. & Rosenman, R. H. (1974) TypeA behavior and your heart. New York. Knoof. ining : A psychological approach to psychotherapy, New York, Grune & Stratton.

Marshal, C. W. (1983). Vitamins and Monerals : Hep or Harm. Philadelphia, Stickley, pp. 122-132.

Mirkin, G. (1983). Getting thin. Boston : Little Brown, p. 3.

CHAPTER 14

STRESS MANAGEMENT EXERCISES

The preceding chapters have elaborated on the various sources of stress in family, social and work environment. Various theories and concepts about stress have also been elaborated. These topics have specified the attitudes, beliefs, behavioral patterns and risky behaviors which add a person stress. Effects of stress, both psychological and behavioral have also been discussed.

This chapter and further chapters elaborates on various stress management program. This chapter is focussed on some stress management skills.

14.1 RELAXATION TECHNIQUES

The relaxation techniques includes progressive muscle relaxation. A number of techniques that make up progressive muscle relaxation includes cue-controlled behavior differential relaxation and desensitization. Relaxation can relieve a person from various tensions. The advantage of relaxation are that it can be practiced anywhere, whether it be sleeping room or office room, or on the road, or on the top of a mountain. In various matches like table-tennis, cricket fields, skiing, relaxation has been used to smooth down tense muscles. In many cases this method is used for treatment, like migraine, hypertension, insomnia, headaches, performance anxiety etc.

Progressive relaxation or deep muscular relaxation is becoming very popular day by day. It was discovered by Edmund Jacobson. It is being used extensively by clinicians, who have also refined it. Step by step instructions are used to apply this technique. The technique does not require a face to face encounter, once it is mastered also it is not a costly affair. Once one learns the steps, he can practice them at his own convenience.

Several varieties of relaxation procedures have become popular among people for stress management. These include relaxation response, transcendental meditation, autogenic training and hypnosis. The relaxation response is the westernized version of Yoga, developed by Herbert Benston. Autogenic training is more imagery based and was developed by Johannes Schultz in Germany. It is the most popular relaxation procedure in Europe, hypnosis is a relaxation technique. All these variants are equally effective. One should master only one of them for high level of proficiency.

Another aspect regarding these skills is that a coping technique effective for one person may not be effective for another person. If one person is skilled in one technique stick to it, and not try to change to another skill just because another person finds it, ineffective.

Elements of Relaxation Techniques

Tension and relaxation are two body states which correspond to two very important parts of our nervous systems, the sympathetic and the parasympathetic. When one is in charged up state, as when afraid, angry, excited, the sympathetic nervous system takes the control. It is the emergency system. Blood is pulled out from the digestive tract and delivered to the important muscle groups like arms and legs. During the changed stage, the body burns up energy at a tremendous rate. Muscle tension increases automatically. Depending upon the type of stress only certain muscle groups will tense up, which group will tense up varies from person to person, some feel the tension at the back, some in the forehead, some in the neck etc. Depending upon the degree of stress, muscle tension varies upon the degree of stress, muscle tension varies from mild to extreme tension.

On the other hand, when one is in a quiet contemplative mood, happy, contended, or asleep, the parasympathetic system is in control. Blood flows in the normal direction, muscles tensions are decreased, one feels relaxed. It works as the constructive force of the body heart rates, blood flow which had increased dramatically when sympathetic system was operating slows down to normal rate, breathing also slow down and is easy.

The establish scientific theory described autonomic nervous system as the involuntary system. Virtually all like support systems of the body are involuntarily controlled. However, studies and researches have now accepted that these systems can be voluntarily controlled. Examples have come from Indian Yogis who got themselves buried alive for days and survived through respiratory and heart control inspite of freezing cold weather. They were able to control their temperature. The various internal processes perceived to be internally controlled were found to be voluntarily controlled. Now, Jacobson defined relaxation as a voluntary behavioral method of controlling the alternating relationship between the excited and calm sides of autonomic nervous system. If one is tense, then by getting the parasympathic nervous system back in control one can induce relaxation.

Four steps to start deep Muscular Relaxation

Four items must be considered to start practicing deep muscular relaxation *i.e.*, setting, mood, preparation and medical precautions.

Setting : The place in which one practices relaxation is of great significance. First, one should select a room which is comfortable, properly ventilated and one which can be closed while practicing relaxation. In summer it should be comfortably cool and in winter it should be properly heated. One should not sweat or shiver, because then one will not feel comfortable enough to practice relaxation. One will get engrossed in considering the body condition rather than relaxation practice. At least in the beginning one has to concentrate on learning to concentrate on relaxation rather than discomfort.

Use a comfortable reclining chair for relaxation. It should of course not be so comfortable that one may fall asleep.

The room should be quiet and free from distractions as possible. Telephone should be disconnected or someone else should be made to attend it. If Children distract you then appeal to them to be quiet while practicing relaxation. If children are too small to obey and one may be distracted then relaxation should be done while the baby is asleep.

A very important aspect about relaxation is consistency, if one starts practicing relaxation, one should do so twice a day for half an hour each. Try to fix a time every day and practice at that time every day and practice at that time only whatever the situation. This is easy to say but difficult to practice. The background music may also be played to foster a sense of tranquility and facilitate relaxation. Type of music may be light, classical, something which may not distract you towards it. Usually, natural music which comes from winds, animals birds may be preferable for practicing relaxation.

Mood : In order to practice muscular relaxation one must be in a proper frame of mind. Some important tips to help in practice of relaxation are :

Unstrained attention : One obvious requirement is a quiet place. Another significant requirement is ability to apply skill successfully to ooze out the tension from ones muscles. Muscular tension reveals that one is tense. In the beginning one has to learn the instructions stepwise, *i.e.*, it is the education phase, this requires unstrained attention. If one is strained one will feel more strained than feel able to remove strain. Slightest cramping of neck, stomach, laboured breathing means that one is experiencing muscular tension.

Do not force relaxation to happen : The relaxation techniques are not like other learned skills like typing, skating. It cannot be learned by force and it can not come naturally, it can only be acquired quietly, gently. One gradually finds himself capable of enjoying and feeling relaxation.

One cannot hurry : Time is of great importance. It cannot be rushed. One has to be patient, should not be in a hurry to practice relaxation. Relaxation takes time. One has to practice it for sometime to feel the full impact of relaxation.

Addiction should not be used : Usually relaxing and tranquilizing drugs serve more as depressant of normal brain functions. They block the normal link between brain and signals coming to it, some signals may also be missed by the brain. It will be difficult to discriminate between signals from body tension and problems created due to drugs. Drugs usually interfere with primary aim of relaxation training. Drugs will only provide temporary relief but may prevent a person from getting relief from life stresses in a permanent manner.

Train before application : Usually while we learn relaxation techniques we apply them also for solving our tensions, forgetting that first we should learn the techniques and than apply it, because if we are novice in these techniques and we want to solve our problem than may be we may not succeed and then we may feel frustrated, hence the mantra is, first learn the techniques thoroughly so that when we apply it for problem solving we may succeed.

The sequence of exercises for muscle relaxation must be learnt to the required level and then one will feel confident in solving major stress problems.

Experiencing different feelings : A person who has learnt the relaxation technique, may feel a sensation of loosing control when he is in trance. If he feels afraid about how to control this freeness state, then he may feel uncomfortable, this may be a momentary feeling but it may occur.

Another fear in the exerciser is a fear of not being able to come out from the trance state. A person finds himself in a hypnotic trance, and in isolation, hence he may be unsure of how to come out of it. The coming out from relaxation may be perceived as risky. Sometimes, a person may feel as if he has taken a nap. Hence advice is, not to feel afraid because later one will start appreciating the relaxation and will welcome it.

Getting Ready : Steps involved in preparing for relaxations are (1) Go over the steps of what one have to do just before each relaxation session. (2) Review the instructions about sequence of relaxing the muscle groups. (3) Make final arrangement about phone, music, light etc. Music should be switched on, volume controlled. Gradually, as one become a master in relaxation techniques he will learn all these preparations and they will become habitual for him.

Caution : Persons with certain physical conditions should be cautious about practicing relaxation.

1. If one had back injuries, muscle strains, or fractures he should consult physician and take their permission about practicing relaxation. In cases of severe back problems, alternate procedures for stress control may be prescribed.

2. Persons with heart problems should also consult their physician before starting relaxation practices. Under acute heart problem, the cause of problem

may be severe cold which may congest the chest and create breathing problems, which may cause anxiety and lead to greater problems.

3. If one has just come out from some medical problem, like malaria, jaundice, etc. then one must wait for enough time to cure completely, to be out of medication before he starts the relaxation practices.

Starting up phase

The instructions of relaxation should be read thoroughly before trying to relax. These instructions are self directive. After reading go over it in your mind. You may also bring changes in the instructions as desired by you, you may tape it in your own voice so that you can be sure of what will come next, hence feel comfortable, as it is an essential condition for relaxation.

Instructions

By following the instructions given for relaxation one can experience the difference between tension and relaxation.

First, one should remove all the tight clothes, shoes, and ornaments one is wearing, Sit down in chair in a relaxed manner, *i.e.*, place arms on the arms of the chair, with palms and hands open over the end of the chair's arms. Sit back and let head fall gently over the chest. Close the eyes. Put the legs on a stool or foot rest.

Now take a few deep breaths, hold each breath for a few seconds and then breath out fully and completely. As one breathe in, tension is felt in chest and diaphragm, as one breathe out, one feels relaxed, you feel completely limp. One feels relaxed, comfortable and feel nice. Again, when one breathes in he feel tensed, especially while holding breathe, then breathingout makes him relaxed.

Next one should start relaxing the various muscles. First he should start with right hand, and flex biceps as if protruding muscles, by spreading his elbow on the arm of the chair. Flexing as tight as possible and holding it for about 10 seconds, make him feel tensed. Now let it go all at once, feel the limpness. Now there is feeling of relaxed state. Same sequence will be repeated for several other muscle groups. Steps followed are tense, hold, observe, relax and observe. The cycles will be about 10-15 seconds for tension and 15-20 seconds for relaxation, together a bit more time to relaxation then to getting tensed up. In the early stage it is better to make about three repetitions for each muscular group, later, when learnt it may be as many times as desired, but being strict about time limits and repetition in the beginning is must.

Next set of muscles will be the other arm. While arms may not be frequently involved in tension patterns, but fingers and palms may reveal tension by sweating or fidgeting. Athletes often try to relieve their hands of tension to perform better on the sports field. One may relax his fingers and palms also.

Next set of muscle is the shoulder muscle group. Shoulders may feel the tensions. The shoulder muscles may form knot and ache. For this purpose, taking a deep breath and, holding it for a moment, makes to study the tension. Saying to yourself relax as one let the air out of lungs completely, feeling the tension oozing out. Repeating this cycle two or three times, then moving to the other shoulder and performing the same steps on it allows to. See that the parts which have been relaxed remain so, or not and if not, repeating the steps for them again for moving further, otherwise the purpose of relaxation for the whole body may not be served. Next, relaxing the neck muscles is must as they get tensed up under high mental pressure. They may also be linked with severe types of headaches. Flexing the head backward, until one feel the pain and tightness, feels the tense sensation. Holding it for about 10 seconds, then releasing tension by letting head fall back onto the chest and enjoying the relaxed sensation. Repeating for two more times have a good effect.

Concentrating on forehead muscle, or frontalis muscles is. One solution is to relax these muscles. Biofeedback is used to relax the frontalis muscles. It helps people learn how to relax and how to read body signals of tensions through visual pictures that electronic feedback provides. PMR can also be used. Procedure involves the following steps :

1. Wrinkle the forehead, 2. Squint eyes if possible, scalp gets tightened up, 3. Gold the tension, feel it, 4. Let it go, 5. Feel relaxed, 6. Repeat atleast two times, feel the difference.

Next moving the jaws and tongues, which includes the similar procedures. For jaws, clenching them by biting down as if chewing a stick, lightness, occurs upto the ears. Cheeks swell out, and letting it go, makes one feels relaxed. For tongue, rolling it up to the middle of the roof of the mouth and pushing again the roof of the mouth feels tightness, than relaxed.

Next area to be relaxed is the stomach. Pulling stomach in, shrink it by pulling in the muscles around it, and feeling the knot is uncomfortable, but holding it tightly, next letting it go, makes one to feel the relaxation.

Next comes the lower back, when it pains it is highly distressful but one should not practice relaxation if he has had back surgery or back disorders. Procedure for relaxing the back is bend forward, pull in the shoulders make the back stick out. Holding the tension for sometime and then releasing the arch in the back makes one feel relaxed. Repeat once or more times.

Next come the legs, starting with thighs right, next left. Tightening the large muscles on the back of the leg, thinking as if climbing the mountain and pulling upper leg muscles tightly without influencing calves, feet and toes. Holding it for a few seconds and then let it go.

Next come the calves, and feet, right then left. First, pull foot towards the body, tighten calf muscle and holding for a moment, then let it go.

Thus every part of the body becomes relaxed. Breathing become easier and one feels good and relaxed.

An exercise may be performed by the practioner of relaxation technique, after one week of relaxation technique, note down various signs of muscular tensions occurring during the week. The most frequently occurring signs may be tension in neck, cramping, knotting of shoulder muscles, lower back muscles tightening etc.

The objective is to identify these signals in the normal course of working life and doing appropriate relaxation exercise to overcome them before one become physically sick.

Table 14. 1 : Sequence and timing for Engaging in Self-directed Progressive Muscular Relaxation

Sequence guide for relaxation practice

1. Preferred arm
2. Alternate arm
3. Preferred hand
4. Alternate hand
5. Shoulder muscles

a. Preferred hand side

b. Alternate side

6. Neck muscles
7. Forehead, eyes, scalp
8. Jaws and mouth (tongue optional as extra steps)
9. Breathing-chest & trunk
10. Stomach.
11. Lower back
12. Buttock
13. Preferred thigh
14. Alternate thigh
15. Preferred foot & thigh
16. Alternate foot & thigh

Additional Reminders

Two sessions per day same time same place

Three repetitions with each muscle set

10-15 seconds for tension sets

45-75 minutes for first few sessions.

Sessions will be greatly reduced in length after the first few sessions.

Methods of presenting instructions

There are four ways of preparing instructions :

1. Recall the gist of the instructions and think of learning it in one's own style without any external prompting. This helps to relax wherever one is present.

2. One can get the instructions read out, a number of times. This helps in relaxing and concentrating only on it. Gradually one will learn the steps and do it himself without any prompting.

3. Tape the instructions in one's own voice. once you have put the instructions on tape you can concentrate on relaxation exercises without undue worry about the sequence.

4. Buying a commercially prepared tape that gives all instructions in a sequence.

In brief this chapter has stated about stress management techniques and has emphasized muscular relaxation techniques, it describes about muscular relaxation techniques, its preparation, relaxation instructions for various muscles groups of the body.

References

Benston, H. (1975). The Relaxation Response. New York. Avon Books.

Jacobson, E. (1938). Progressive Relaxation (2nd ed.) Chicago : University of Chicago Press.

CHAPTER 15

STRESS AND TIME MANAGEMENT

Time is a fixed commodity. It is not how much time one has and how one uses it, that matters. Until school days start, time passes without being thought about. It is only parents who bother about time, when children have to take bath, when they have to be fed and when they have to sleep. It is only when school starts that children are gradually made to realize about time for everything, which includes time for going to school, time allotted for various subjects taught, lunch time, game time, closing time, homework time, sleeping time. As time passes, a child passes through all levels in school and gradually a time comes when he adopts some profession and start his adult life. Then, also time has to be managed like getting up in time, getting ready in time for office, punctuality in organization, time for various tasks, meetings, conferences, etc. First, when a child moves from class to class time hangs. One keeps on waiting for time to move on. But as one becomes an adult and starts his job, time appear to be in a hurry and there never seems to be sufficient time for all activities.

15.1 NEED FOR TIME-MANAGEMENT STUDY

Ferner defined time management as "efficient use of our resources including time, in such a way that we are effective in achieving important personal goals." There are many reasons why time management is significant in relation to stress and health.

1. Time management technique can enhance one's personal productivity, it also leaves time for social pursuits, exercise, recreation and hobbies. By proper time management one can gain time for every personal pursuits without feeling stressed. One may also get sufficient time for one's family and also for oneself.

2. Modern society's movements reveal that time is the driving force behind all activities. Whether wrong or right time is perceived as valuable. Value is calculated in terms of money, power and position, which requires high productivity for attainment. For productivity attainment one has to work for hours and that also very hard. How to balance time and work in such a way that time urgency, a Type A personality trait does not lead to stress ?

But emphasis is on using time management technique only when an unbalance is felt, stress is encountered just to reset priorities and remove inefficient habits, otherwise time management need not be pursued in a regular manner, as then it will itself become stressful. It is bad to let time management manage one's own style.

15.2 ATTITUDE TOWARDS TIME

How seriously time is viewed ? Perception about time has changed from past till present. Attitude towards time varies from culture to culture. Let's look at some of the common attitudes towards time.

Historical Perspective : In ancient culture, time was not given much significance. Exact timing was not demanded, like come in evening, noon, morning, night. But as clock came into existence in Medieval Europe, keeping an eye on time, became an important activity. Later, with the advent of Industrial Revolution, everything including monetary value of goods, products, people were valued in terms of exact time. Another significant figure Sir Isaac Newton viewed each time interval as unique but equal. He gave emphasis to time bound short term activities. He felt not a single moment should pass without any change or occurrence. In modern society time is highly valued, especially by people who are high on need for achievement. For them time keeping watch was a necessity and they could not survive without it.

Versions of Time : In the present era, there are a number of versions about time, like (1) time is money, (2) time is a resource, (3) wasting time is sinful, (4) an idle mind is a devil's playground, (5) I have all the time in the world. Metaphors for time reflect the implicit, often untested values that focus efforts and guide behavior. The first metaphor is accepted by all and practiced to a great extent. The second focuses to time as a means for utility. The third focuses on time study by Taylor which focuses on minimum time expenditure on every work. Fourth attitude aims at using time wisely and not wasting it in sleeping and gossiping. Fifth attitude is the reverse of perceiving time as precious. They are never in a hurry.

Time is Money : Time is precious like money. One economises spending money, in the same way one should economise on using time in the most profitable manner. Time should be planned in such a way that one has time for his home as well as for his work. Both are significant in one's life. Persons who get engrossed in their work in a very hectic way and forget that their family also needs some of their time, very often face counseling.

As far as profession is concerned, some professions like, brokers, property dealers face the impact of time. Within minutes or seconds they have to take decisions about buying or selling. For other professions creativity and quality are as important as speed.

Time is a resource : Like land, time also cannot be increased. Time is 24 hours per day, 8, 736 hours per year. If time is perceived as a resource, then to get most out of it one should manage it with alacrity. One can't buy, sell or save time, it can only be monitored in such a way to get maximum advantage.

Idle Mind : Day dreaming, mental idling may sometimes develop sudden insights, plus it may provide a means of emotional outlet. This state is a passive mind set. On the contrary active mental set occurs when a person's mind is filled with purposeful thought. He concentrate on work.

Time Wasting is Sinful : If a person's car tyre gets punctured, he has two options in front of him, one of replacing it by oneself or getting a tyre repairer to do it. In the first option he is spending more time on tyre repairs, although it may be spent on some other work like taking children for an outing. In the second option one is spending money. Both have some loss, in the first it is the time loss, whereas in the second it is money loss. One has to assess the value that he attaches to both options. If one feel that some work or outing is wasting time it reveals the value for that work. If one has to prepare for examination or class, and he spends that previous time in seeing a movie or cricket game then at that point time wasting may be perceived as sinful.

Lot of time : Youngsters often feel that they have just started living, hence there is lot of time to plan up their various activities. This thinking prevents them from time management. They waste a lot of time in aimless actions. One should not be time obsessed, but one should not take time lightly and miss out an important activities. For example, many people feel that there is lot of time for preparation of examination and waste the meaningful time in useless activities. Often people don't have time of marrying and they don't give it considerable thought and later feel frustrated and repent this decision. The goal of effective time management is to find the balance between work, life and personal need fulfillment.

15.3 TIME MANAGEMENT : IT'S IMPACT

Time Management is an omission which leads to helpless repentance later because one cannot reverse the clock. The various acts of omission that lead to time mismanagement are confusion, indecision, diffusion, procrastination, avoidance, interruptions and perfectionism.

Confusion : Many people are not sure about how to spend their time meaningfully. Many housewives spend most of their idle time seeing T. V. serials as they don't know what to do with their time. Many people have wrong perception about time spending, they are not clear about which time spending is meaningful and which is waste, e.g. people viewing T. V. serials feel that they get ideas about deceptive behavior and how they should cope with it, hence they perceive it as meaningful. They should assess the degree of productivity they get from specific time spending. This will help them resolve the confusion about time. According to time specialist Rutherford (1978), time management does not make sense unless one knows where he wants to go.

Indecision : Failing to make a decision on choosing between two or more alternatives is another omission of time management. One should be confident enough to choose a decision, because there is no way out. Indecision is the enemy of time management. If one cannot decide intelligently then one may face tackling many decisions instead of one. This creates confusion, tension. This indecision may also irritate or harm others, who are part of one's group (team, family). There is lingering of final decision making. It is always in the mind and prevents one from concentrating on other tasks, and relaxation. It may also create other problems such as procrastination, avoiding other duties, drinking, smoking, etc.

Cause of indecision may be many psychological factors, like lack of interest in the task, fear of making the wrong decision or ignorance. In this case indecision may be acceptable and a right move.

Jim Davidson suggested that one should find out why one does not like to do some tasks. Then, instead of delaying it one may delegate it to others or if this is not possible one may break up the task into small pieces or change the style of doing that task to make it more easier.

Diffusion : The overload : Mental and Physical : Trying to do far more than is possible. It may result due to unawareness of one's own capabilities and taking too much on oneself. Often persons are not able to say no to others, this may be because they are their friends and relatives and they don't know how to say no to them. Another reason for taking too much upon oneself is their inability to assess their limits. Mental diffusion leads to other ailments like ineffective problem solving, lack of concentration and poor motivation for doing various tasks.

Charles Kozell has studied the battered mind syndrome which basically describes diffusion and it's impact on a person. This syndrome is observed among educators, administrators. The major characteristics of this syndrome include (1) Many thoughts at the same time, (2) Continuous anxiety about what is left to be completed, (3) As too many tasks are on a person, he losses focus on what is most significant and what is less significant, (4) Because there are too many interruptions while working one is not able to concentrate thoroughly on various tasks which he is performing. His interest is lacking.

Procrastination : Delaying the Work

Procrastination is defined as putting off to the next day what one should do today. Merrill and Douglas have identified three types of procrastination : delaying in doing unpleasant things, delaying in doing difficult things and putting off things that involve difficult decisions. Procrastination is a cardinal sin of time mismanagement.

According to Rutherford people usually make two types of excuses for delaying work. 'I wish' and 'I just can't get started'. 'I wish' excuse is often used by people to avoid the task at hand or feel that somehow the work may get completed without their putting any effort in it. 'I just can't get started' is a self defeating prophecy. One should try to give up this habit of procrastination. Some steps should be taken to remedy it. First step involves making notes of tasks which one don't feel like doing hence always keep putting off. Next, observe what are the common elements in these tasks which one hate to do.

Another approach for handling procrastination is to do the disliked tasks first and then do the pleasant tasks. Once the disliked tasks are over, concentration on pleasant tasks will be better and have accumulated stress and will thus concentrate better on tasks which are left. One may self motivate, by saying, for e.g. that if half of the unpleasant task will be completed, there will be a short tea break or will buy something from gain from the task. This may make one work alertly on the task.

Avoidance : People often avoid doing work. They do so by writing useless letters again and again in the name of perfectionism or may just catch hold of someone and chat or may get so engrossed in reading some magazine or they may indulge in daydreaming. Often heads of departments avoid the work they dislike and do what they can delegate to juniors.

Interruptions to normal flow of work : Phone calls, boss calling, colleagues coming to discuss something, emergencies, all represent disruptions in normal flow of activities. These aspects are not planned for but they come up causing great time loss which could have been utilized in productive activities. Sometimes, these interruptions may not be so uncontrollable, if strict actions may be taken on these matters. According to Davidson (1978), the average manager is interrupted once in eight minute. Sometimes, these interruptions occur on demand by manager.

When work is complex and requires lot of time and concentration then interruption is highly damaging, for example, thinking and putting together a project proposal as one needs time to get into proper frame for working on it and then only can work smoothly.

Hence, frequent interruptions break the chain of concentration and cause damage to creativity, productivity. If interruption occurs due to emergency for which one is not prepared then tussle occurs regarding whether important matter should be attended to or emergent matter should be attended to. Usually, crisis diverts attention away from significant matters. There seems to be no option. But it delays the important activities. Thus, interruption leads to time mismanagement.

Perfectionism : Compulsive overdoing : When one indulges in doing the same task again and again until one reaches perfection, then he may be using this behavior to delay doing other more significant activities. If because of a very small error a task is done again then it may be termed as compulsive overdoing. One should access where perfection will lead to better result and where it will go unnoticed. It is like diminished return. One should make extra effort until it is worthwhile, but after that point he should not repeat activities as it may lead to lot of time wastage.

15.4 READY FOR TIME MANAGEMENT

Confusion, interruption, perfectionism, etc., are seldom perceived in the light of time mismanagement. If one thousand people were asked if they waste their time or do they need time management, they will deny that they are wasting time. If they are watching a serial on a television, they rationalize it as a means for entertainment in mundane life, if they are gossiping with neighbors they rationalize it as gaining local news which according to them is essential. None of them feel that they should plan their time properly. None are prepared to assess how their valuable time is being spent. If this need is not felt, why will they indulge in time management. Only when the need for time management is felt, one spends sometime of his day in time management although, it should not be perceived as time obsession or should not make a person continuously worried about spending time and creating guilt in him when doing some light activities.

To begin time management programs one needs to know what needs to be changed. This can be done through time inventory, which gives details about how and where one spends one's time. One can also do this by jotting down what one does through out the day or one can buy books on time management.

A daily log to assess time spent : -

A simple way to get information about daily time spending is to find answer to questions like what do you do? When do you do ? How much time does it take ? The list may be made in the following way : -

Days Time Period	Mon	Tue	Wed	Thurs	Fri	Sat	Sunday
15 Min	Work	Work	Work	Work	Work	Work	Work
30 Min	Work	Work	Work	Work	Work	Work	Work
40 Min	Work	Work	Work	Work	Work	Work	Work
50 Min	Work	Work	Work	Work	Work	Work	Work
60 Min	Work	Work	Work	Work	Work	Work	Work

This type of table may also be prepared for classifying personal and professional activities of a whole week's activity schedule. After one week's information is collected one should observe the type of pattern which is formed of daily activities. Separate job related activities, meaningful activities and useless activities, next access the people involved in each of them. Add up uncontrolled activities, like transportation to job and back, office hours, boss interactions and add up controlled activities. As observed by Peter Drucker manager have only about 25% controllable time, while the remaining 75% of their time is uncontrollable. Uncontrolled time cannot be altered, but time under control can be modified and attempt may be made to see where wastes can be removed and some time curtailing may occur. But never try to curtail uncontrolled activities as it will mean shirking from responsibilities. Think of simple plans of actions to remove interruptions and to bring corrections in time management.

15.5 TIME MANAGEMENT SOLUTIONS

After assessing the error in time management the next step involves tackling with these errors and trying to do away with them.

Priorities

The best solution for confusion is to set goals and reevaluate those goals periodically. A few guidelines for setting these goals are mentioned.

(1) Establish clear and achievable goals.

(2) Assign priorities to each of your goals.

(3) Assess all the tasks for reaching the each goal, breaking them into small simple tasks which may not appear tedious.

(4) Set target time for each small piece of task.

(5) Make revaluation of your short term goals so that the final goal may be achieved without any difficulty e.g. five year plan has to be reevaluated yearly. Goals should be clear and achievable and not a dream which is unachievable.

Goals should be set in short term, medium range and long term frame. Long term goals are very far off, they can only be reached if medium term and short terms goals are in alignment. For this alignment long term planning with intermittent plans and monthly goals should be made, moreover weekly, daily break ups of the tasks is also essential. Short term goals should have weekly conclude-able objectives leading to medium to long term goals. Even day to day tasks should have a list of do's and don'ts, this will help in organizing meaningful life spending. In the morning 'to do list' should be assessed and day should be spent in doing the various activities and before closing for the night check should be made of the do's accomplished and unaccomplished. According to Lakein (1974) top managers are well versed in making 'to do list' and seeing that they are following.

Pareto Principle

Vilfredo Pareto, a sociologist and economist of the 19th and early 20th centuries, came up with the view summarized in the phrase 'the vital few and trivial many'. This is based on the list prepared, which puts priority-wise the various things a person wishes to accomplish in the long term, medium and short term basis. Give most attention to the first 20% of the desired activities because they have 80% value for you, and the remaining 80% activities will have

20% value hence can be achieved gradually or may also be skipped. This principle is also highlighted by Peter Drucker who said that do the right things rather than do the things right, *i.e.*, do valuable activities first and less valuable things later. One should work for goals which have value for you rather than wasting time on less valuable activities.

Goals should not be set for one major achievement and then one may feel as if there is nothing to do as it may lead to loss of interest in life and one may reach a dead end, which has often lead to death or other severe problems, for example, executives who devote a lifetime to the company, collect some medals, trophies for themselves, then retire, within two years they die, reason pointed by Douglas and Douglas (1980) is that they did not set any further goal in their lives, goals completion lead to psychological death which later lead to physical death for example, Buzz Aldrin, one of the first astronauts to set foot on the moon, suffered a nervous breakdown shortly after his return to earth, *i.e.*, his aim in life had been fulfilled and he no longer had any other aim in life.

Solution to diffusion

When too much work is lying to be attended to it is essential that one should go through the time work schedule and try to prune out useless activities like reading memos again and again, filing them and then going on file clearing activity. Think long term and prevent this filing up. Attend to memos demands, finish up and put them in dustbins. One will save time and unnecessary tasks will not pile up.

Next step is to weed out impossible tasks. One should not try to get involved in all activities put forth by all people around. It is better to give time to 20% of important.

meaningful, attainable tasks rather than 80% of unimportant, meaningless, unattainable tasks. Also an attempt to say no when one feel that a specific activity is beyond, one's level because of scarcity of time. If hesitation in say no is there, then giving the confidence to say so should be developed.

Break Procrastination Habit

If the job appears to be very big like writing a book then preplan the whole work in such a way that the job is divided into parts and sub-parts, if sub-parts are long, break them into simple tasks so that one may get started and the reluctance in embarking on the job is highly reduced.

For example in book writing there are several parts, like background work, library work, reading, organizing, drafting, writing, editing, rewriting. One should measure the amount of time required in each task based on realistic assessment. Then chalk out time for each sub-part, and move gradually according to the plan formulated. Once one get started he will gradually get more and more interested in the job and will try to achieve the goal in the right time. This example shows that structuring of work situation will give cues for moving to the various steps and will prevent the mind set from losing interest and becoming lazy.

Sticking to the Job

Once a person start working on a job he have to continue on it until it is achieved. For this purpose he require two psychological elements, one is concentration and the other is interest. Concentration can maintain the interest or interest can lead to concentration. Both have to be there until the job is complete. This requires that you prevent interruptions from distracting you from your work. Two other elements should also have to be considered. First, people cannot stick to a task for a long time. If this is a recurrent problem then keeping a clock is best idea. After working the normal time period, start the practice of promising oneself, a break only after working for 10 minutes more, if the goal is achieved, then delay this period before taking break, and then may be one is able to concentrate on that task for longer period. Another linked element is building up of tiredness, reduced mental efficiency, etc. The way to overcome this problem is to distribute work sessions and alternate tasks. For example, after spending one hour at work, one may take break for 10–15 minutes, in which he may do something light like conversing with someone or closing eyes or shift to a different type of task for a short time to get out of monotony.

A major problem in normal work environment is unscheduled interruptions. One way of warding of interruption is to close the door while concentrating on work, and communicating the information to others that he is busy and don't come when the door is closed. Next, prevent mental interruptions which hinder concentration at work by training oneself to create such blocks when busy. If still interruptions occur then one may need sometime for oneself to develop stronger will power to say no to interruptions. If chronic drop–in can be a problem then there is a solution for that also. When they come, it is better not to indulge one's self in any pleasant talk rather keep doing work and let him/her feel as misfit in the environment. Gradually that person may stop bothering. One can also say that he/she is busy or to come at break time. Phone interruptions can be dealt easily. One can easily tell the person that he have only two or five minutes, say what he wants to say or by saying that he is busy and will talk later. You may call back at break time. This may prevent the caller from calling in busy hours. One can also set apart some time for checking and replying mail.

Check the Progress

Tangibly check the steps completed on a chart showing the whole project break ups with 'dos' of specific days. Tick mark the work completed.

15.6 SUGGESTIONS FOR EFFECTIVE TIME MANAGEMENT

There are various ideas which may be useful for the problems of Time Management.

Using Transit Period Meaningfully

In big cities like Delhi, Mumbai, people travel large distances between homes and office, say about 1–2 hours. How to use this time effectively ? One way is to relax in the journey so that you are in full form at the office. If work is too much in the offices and 'dos' of each day has to be planned everyday then this work can easily be done while commuting. Scheduling, planning, inductive, deductive reasoning, all can be practiced at this time, or one may listen to some meaningful tapes which may help in developing some skills.

Delegating Work

If one delegate work of junior to them then he can concentrate on more meaningful work fit for them. Thus, one can achieve twin goals of completing the task as well as doing higher level planning, creativity work. Thus, helping juniors to develop their skills.

Thus, all round achievement of the organization is achieved.

Assessing Prime Time

Everyone has his own prime time based on his internal clock which may differ from person to person. Prime time is the period of day when a person can work the best ; structure work in such a way that he can do the most demanding work at his prime time.

One should also assess one's sleeping habits. Many people sleep more than they need to. The norm is 8 hours per night, this may vary from 6–9 hours. Some feel fresh only after 6 hours sleep, while some sleep 9 hours or more. Sleeping over 9 hours can have three bad effects.

(1) Overall metabolic rate may be lowered leading to difficulty in maintaining a desirable weight.

(2) Muscle tone may drop, leading to increased effort in carrying out normal tasks and also will reduce ability to exercise.

(3) Performance of mental system may drop due to lethargy.

If a person sleeps for 10 hours or more then he should try to change his sleeping habit.

For this purpose one may try getting up half an hour early the next morning. Next assess in the night whether he is more tired than previous day, if he feels the same, then it means that he is sleeping half an hour more. This experimental method may be repeated until a balance is maintained between required time for sleep and amount of time one should sleep. If a person is taking 6–7 hours of sleep then he should not try this method, because minimum essential time for sleep should always be kept for it, otherwise a person's performance level will drop down.

Habit of Reading

Often people read word by word, whether it is a technical book or newspaper or journal article. One should assess how significant the matter is for his further development and growth. Newspaper matter, no matter how much matter a person read, he will forget everything excepting the main headlines and gist. Hence, develop the ability to scan material and pick out basic details from an article without having to read the whole article. Fear of missing some important facts may propel people to read word by word, here one should be aware of the great power of mind, of its ability to fill in gaps. The main message will come through even if one can not read all the word. Another way of reducing the time for reading is to adopt the author's style of providing the main idea at the beginning of a paragraph, elaborate in the middle and summarize or provide transition at the end.

Read Information Once

Never read notices, memos, more than once, pick it up, read it, take action on it's basis and remove it from present to past. If one read and revise again and again he will waste at least 25% of time. Taking work to home should also be avoided as home also requires some time for itself.

Don't be too busy

If one have not have time for morning walks, going to gyms, relaxation, socializing, then he is very busy. Resting, exercising is equally important if one have to do work better, *i.e.*, one have to concentrate and want no disruption, interruption, etc. Edwin Bliss suggested that being in good physical condition, one should increases one's working hours which are usually one's prime hours.

But working without relaxation, exercising reduces one's performance level. This matches with the saying 'More work and no play make Johny a dull boy'. All have their significance, exercise, enjoyment, work, all should be included in time schedule of a person.

15.7 THE ACTION PRIORITY MATRIX

Making the very most of the opportunities

The Action Priority Matrix is a simple diagramming technique that helps to choose which activities to prioritize (and which ones to drop). If a person want to make the most of his time and opportunities.

It is useful because most of the people have many more activities on "wish list"–whether these are bright ideas to pursue, exciting opportunities or interesting possibilities–that they have time available. By choosing activities intelligently, one can make the very most of his time and opportunities.

However, by choosing badly, one can quickly bog oneself down in low–yield, time–consuming projects that close down opportunities and stop moving forward.

How to Use the Tool

Figure 15.1 below shows the basic form of the Action Priority Matrix :

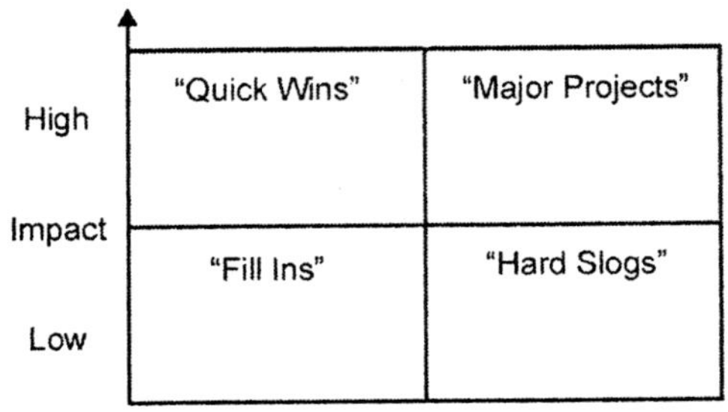

Fig. 15.1 : Action Priority Matrix

The principle behind using the tool is that one score each activity one want to complete on two scales–firstly on the impact the activity will have and secondly on the effort involved.

By pointing each activity on the Action Priority Matrix using these scores, one can quickly see the projects that give the greatest returns on efforts; and adopt the most appropriate approach for that type of activity :

Quick Wins (High Impact, Low Effort)

These are the most attractive projects, giving a good return.

For relatively little effort. Focus on these as much as one can.

Major Projects (High Impact, High Effort)

While these give good returns, they take a long time to complete-Meaning that one "Major Project" can crowd out many "Quick Wins". If one is engaged in these, make sure that he will complete them quickly and efficiently and that he will disengage his effort as soon as he can.

Fill Ins (Low Impact, Low Effort)

Don't worry too much about doing these–if a person got spare time, do them, but drop them if something better comes along.

Hard Slogs (Low Impact, High Effort)

Avoid these. Not only do they give low returns, they crowd out

Time which would be better used elsewhere.

Conclusion

This chapter includes seven time traps like confusion, indecision, diffusion, procrastination, avoidance, interruptions and perfectionism. Causes of these traps are revealed. Next, major means for dealing with these traps have been discussed.

References

Davidson, J. (1978). Effective Time Management. New York : Human Sciences Press, pp. 75-77.

Douglass, M.R. & Douglas, D.N. (1980). Manage Your Time, Manage Your Work, Manage Yourself. New York : AMOCOM, p. 235.

Ferner, J.D. (1980). Successful Time Management, New York: Wiley. p. 12.

Lakein, A. (1974). How to Get Control of Your Time and Your Life. New York : New American Library/Signet. p. 64.

Rutherford, R.D. (1978). Administrative Time Power : Meeting the time challenge of the busy secretary/staff assistant/ manager team. Austin, TX : Learning Concepts, p. 89.

CHAPTER 16

ALTERNATE DE-STRESSING TECHNIQUES

Often one faces a number of anxieties, fears and panic situations which require some thing more than relaxation. They require some new ways to grip the irrational thoughts and attitudes that prompt self-defeating and self-restricted behaviors. Take an example of Rajesh. At the age of 37 he was suffering from diabetes plus blood pressure. Hence, he had to start his day with medicines and end it with medicines, he felt highly tensed most of the times that he may have increased diabetes or blood pressure. Even, when he got headaches or backaches he got panic that may be his problems were getting aggravated. He was afraid of attending social gatherings where he felt he would be forced to drink and have delicacies which would cause excess in diabetes or blood pressure. He often had difficulty in sleeping thinking about his problems. He did not feel relaxed at all. Because of scarcity of sleep and relaxation he could not concentrate on his work and was afraid about making mistakes at work and this made him feel that he would have problems with his boss.

In order to overcome such cases some other techniques apart from relaxation have been elaborated in this chapter. They include autogenics, desensitization and finally stress inoculation principles will be described further.

16.1 MENTAL PICTURE : IMAGERY

There are some internal thinking, internal activities going on in the mind of a person trying to relax. They were using some mental pictures or images which were used to relax e.g. one person heard church bells in a distance which gave relaxation to him, while another person get a picture of a jungle with deers running, which calmed him. This method is highly popular in eastern meditators, it uses imagery techniques to gain control over one's mind and body. An in between state lying between alert working state and first stage of sleep is created during meditation, this state produce a brain wave called alpha wave form. Joe Kamiya a researcher in bio-feedback, showed that people can learn to control their alpha waves through the use of bio-feedback. He noted that many subjects used some usual imagery to keep alpha tuned on. Runners, athletes also report that visualization helps in both training and competition.

16.2 AUTOGENICS THERAPY

Autogenic means self produced imagery or suggestion used as a relaxation techniques. A German psychiatrist J. Schultz introduced this therapy in Europe in 1932. According to Schultz, autogenic is a means of maintaining the internal psychological balance of the body. It is a simple technique for beginners who want to learn a basic tension reducing method, although advanced autogenic may require professional guidance for effective impact.

The training procedure for autogenics bears a certain resemblance to the procedure of deep muscular relaxation but there are certain points of difference observed both in practice and in application. Relaxation training involves active muscle exercise procedure for teaching the difference between tension and relief. In autogenics, the goal is to develop an association between verbal (thoughts) cues and the desired body state of calm. There is no active physical exercises, the body is in a passive state, focusing on imagery and self suggestions.

Conditions for Successful Autogenics Training

Schultz and Luthe have recommended some conditions for autogenic having to succeed. These include

1. A high willingness and motivation to follow the instructions clearly.
2. Ability to self-direct and self-control.
3. Correct body posture should be maintained.
4. Concentrate on internal physical and mental states rather than on external stimuli.
5. Use of monotonous, repetitive input to the various senses.
6. Concentrate on somatic processes in order to bring about an inward focused consciousness rather than an outward focused consciousness.

These conditions are essential for creating a passivity, an indifferent mental state that gets altered into state of consciousness. The outcomes of autogenic training are revealed in the following conditions.

1. Emergence of an overpowering reflexive psychic reorganization.

2. The occurrence of dissociative and autonomous mental processes leading to changed ego states.

They signify that the person is ready to follow the instructions that will be given next. This changed stated is strange for the person himself but he should be prepared for this state. It includes choosing the time and place for comfort and relaxation, by reducing external distractions, removing tight fitting clothes, jewellery and preparing your mood for passive attention to the exercises.

Recommendations for Body Postures

In autogenic training, three body positions are allowed *i.e.*, 1. lying down 2. seated with back support 3. seated without back support.

In the lying down situation, one lie down on the floor with pillows under the head and knees. A shallow pillow is preferred. Arms should be at sides, hands should be near the thighs, palms turned up. Legs may be slightly apart, with toes pointed away from the body.

In the second position, one require a chair with a high, straight back. Position oneself in the chair, supporting back and head. Arms may be supported on the arms of the chair or in the lap.

In the third position, one may use a stool or low backed chair. Sit forward on the stool, arms may be supported on the thighs, or hands may dangle loosely over the knees. Head may come up to the chest but may not touch the chest.

Next step involves the imagery suggested by Schultz and Luthe. They suggested that one can imagine himself as a big rag doll with a string attached to the top of your head.

This string is attached to the ceiling and are lifted up, limbs are lump hence they will hang loosely on both sides, next the string is broken and the person fall back in the chair, head, shoulders and neck collapse forward. The position which one prefer should be adopted from the very beginning, only change position for exercise which want so.

Learning autogenics consists of two different segments, each with six different exercises. The basic exercises focus on body sensation in order to establish a balance and rhythm in the autonomic system. Next are the imagery exercises which focus on the mental capacity to form, hold and manipulate mental images of external objects

Do not be in a hurry to complete exercises to move to imagery.

The Six Primary Exercises of Autogenics : These exercises are six stages that focus attention on different parts of the body or different sensations. The first and the last stages are explained.

Stage 1 : Focus on arms that are most active (right/ left). Concentrate on your arms and repeat these instructions. "My right (left) arm is heavy".

Do this about 3 to 6 times in a 30-60 second period. Close your eyes (optional). At the end of this period shake yourself out of any drowseness and lethargy. Thus, the verbal cues of autogenics may accomplish a behavioral switching of the autonomic system from sympathetic arousal to parasympathic calmness.

Stage 6 : A Cool Forehead. This involves practicing cooling of the forehead, the instruction is " My forehead is cool".

All the other exercises focus on warmth or heaviness, this stage tries to induce a feeling of coolness on the forehead. This exercise may require the prone posture. In this exercise it is advised that one should start slowly with no more than two or three repetitions over about 20-30 seconds. Later, it may be build upto four or five repetitions lasting two to four minutes.

Sometimes during the first year, most people reach a point where they can go through the entire exercises in less than five minutes. Atleast two months are required to grasp the exercises. Some exercises may feel better earlier like breathing, while others may feel better later. One should remain in the state of autogenic meditation from 30 minute to 1 hour.

Begining Autogenic Imagery

According to Schultz and Luthe, the aim of imagery practice is to be able to hold on to images for a period of time while determining their effects on consciousness itself. One can move to this stage only after he had mastered the prior rise exercises. Some persons may require assistance from autogenic therapist in the beginning of this sequence. If a person feels unsure of himself and finds progress difficult he may contact an autogenic therapist.

It is advisable to remember the cancellation exercise if one encounter any distorted, unpleasant, or disturbing images.

Ist Exercise : One has to look at his forehead. Roll eyes balls upward, and imagining that he is trying to look at a spot just above and between the eyebrows on the inside of the forehead. It enhances trance-like state.

IInd Exercise : One has to see his favourite color. He has to pick a favourite color and try to see that color.

Imagining himself in a room, with his favourite color in the room everywhere. Let his mind immerse in the color. Next moving to more complex images. Trying different colors as different colors have different effect on a person, e.g. purple, red, yellow may lead to warmth green, blue, may lead to coolness. If one find these associations between various colors and their effects, then using them to reinforce autogenic meditation is good.

Next one may visualize various shapes, like shapes of clouds, geometric forms. Let these shapes be colored in various colors and see that they fill the mental frame, next draw away to visualize them from a distance, gradually a person will be able to manipulate these colors and form in his mind.

IIIrd Exercise : One have to visualize objects as focus points. Visualizing about some object, preferably a simple one against a dark surface. Object of some significance may be considered. Training with this step may require more time. First introduce the autogenic state and then spend 40-60 minutes in object imagery practices.

Abstraction Exercises

These exercises concentrates on some abstract idea like love, freedom, justice, etc., the aim is to draw a mental picture of what these ideas are and than transforming them into concrete symbols, e.g., joined hand may remind you of unity, palms joined may remained you of respect, revearance etc. This exercise may take about two to six weeks.

Focus on Feelings

This exercise involves visualizing some mental images and seeing what emotion is evoked by that visual, e.g. imagination of a river side, with water flowing smoothly may evoke calmness in a person. Some scenes may evoke erotic feelings. When one is able to switch from reality to dream like situations and get filled with specific emotions gradually he may get into a position where he can delve into own psyche to gain insight into conflicts and tensions of life. This exercise may help to manage the stressful events most effectively.

Visualizing Others

In the final stage one may visualize some other person. First he may focus on innocuous persons, with whom he maintain distance, next he may visualize close ones, like family members, peers, etc. As one progress, he may visualize other with whom he may have some problem, try visualizing some transaction with them, the emotions one encounter in their presence may be experienced here. He may get insight into his feelings about them, help him alter his attitude, feelings towards him. Thus, changing the perception about them.

In brief, the autogenic exercises are ways of self regulation and self study. Through, the power of imagery, a balance is obtained between the arousing influence of the sympathetic system and the calming influence of the parasympathetic system. These exercises may also provide a way of bringing tension laden feelings closer to the surface, thus may reduce the strength of that emotion.

Success of Autogenic Training

Luthe studied 78 patients who had been treated in eight weekly group training sessions, clients had many complaints like anxiety, phobia, hysterical disorder. 12% of the patients showed very good progress, 26% showed not change, remaining 62% showed good improvement. This technique has achieved success over the years, specially in some specific types of disorders.

16.3 MANAGING UNIQUE KINDS OF FEARS

Some time people are surrounded by fears and anxieties which are not cured by relaxation and autogenics. They are aware that their fears are irrational, silly, but they cannot be removed from consciousness. Fear of any type may produce (1) behavioral changes (2) physical reactions and (3) altered thought processes. Behavior occurring under fear may be avoidance or escape behavior. Physical reactions occurring may be sweating, light headache, nausea, fainting, etc. Thought processes may include images of feared scene coming repeatedly, there is feeling of helplessness and being out of control.

There are three types of fear. First is simple fear, which is defined as alarm to some real a imaginary danger. The most severe fear is a phobia, the irrational, repeated fear of some object or situation. Anxiety is the feeling of impending doom, under severe anxiety a person is uncapable of coherent thought, speech etc. Panic attack anxiety reaction are more severe. Terror is created in the person, physical reactions like fainting, dizziness, shallow breathing may also occur.

A very common kind of phobia is agoraphobia, it is fear of open, person is housebond. Social phobia includes irrational fear of situations that subject the individual to embarrassment. Simple phobias are fear of animals, tunnels, height etc.

16.4 DESENSITIZATION FOR MANAGING FEARS

In recent years desensitization has proved to be a very effective method of dealing with specific kinds of fears. Desensitization was developed by Joseph Wolpe, in 1950s. He reasoned that when a feared object is presented at low levels through mental imagery then it's power to produce fear is controlled. If person relaxes while imaging objects then if gradually more intense representations of the feared object can be presented, then the person may remain relaxed while imagining the most feared object. This means desensitization is removing the sensitizing power of feared objects.

16.5 ELEMENTS TO DESENSITIZATION

Three elements compromise desensitization—

1. Training in deep muscular relaxation.
2. Construction of hierarchy of feared objects, events.
3. Imagining the feared objects while relaxing. 1st element has been discussed in the previous chapters.

The other two elements are described below : -

Constructing a stimulus hierarchy i.e., ladder of fear

This step involves building a stimulation hierarchy, a type of ladder of feared objects, in which lower steps represent less feared objects while higher levels occupy the most feared objects. Objects are placed in all steps of the ladder. (ladder of flying fig 16.1), the most feared object is placed at highest step. Real objects cannot be used, hence visualization is used. The feared objects are imagined. The images of feared objects are replayed again and again. The mental videotapes of anticipated encounters, containing fear elements, just like real objects are used. Imagining of feared object gradually reduces fear and produces positive effects. Desensitization uses a controlled voluntary replay of images to maintain psychological distance from the object and thus keep fear at a distance.

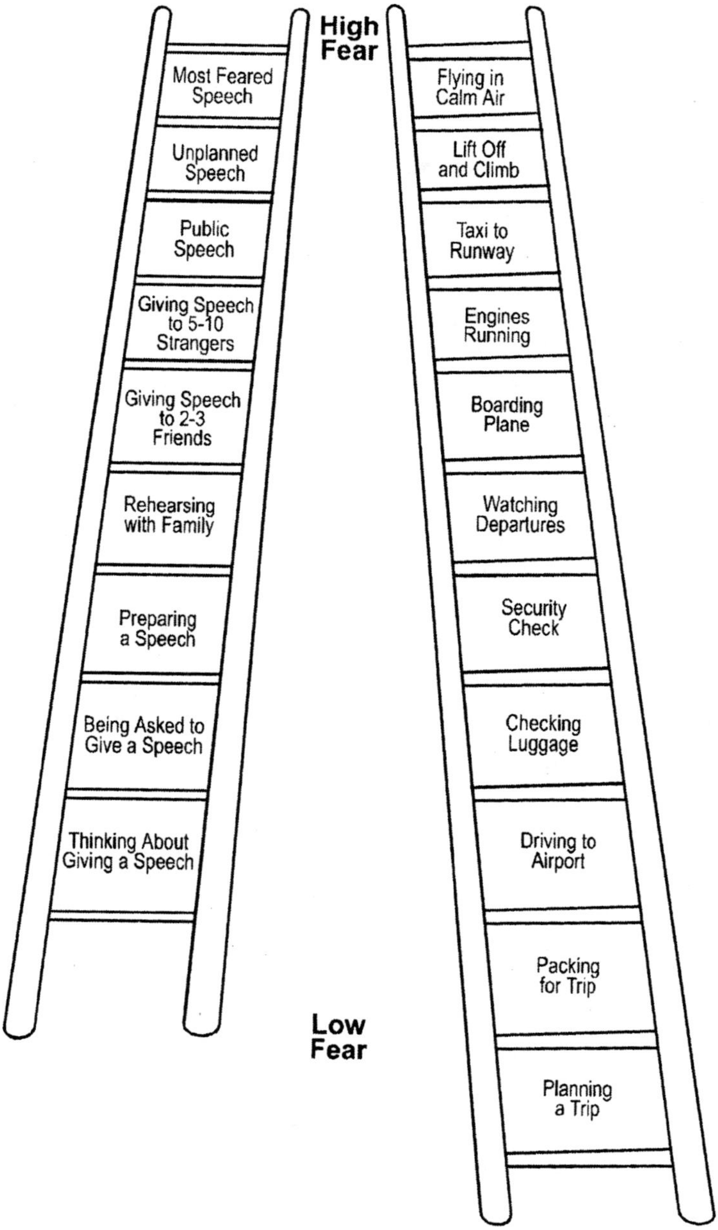

Fig. 16.1 : Ladder of Feared Objects

When one imagine the fear object at the lowest step while staying relaxed, he feel calm and does not feel afraid. Next he moves to the second step, so that object moved to the second step produces less fear than it did before. As he climb the ladder he gradually becomes able to handle more feared objects calmly, desensitization gradually spreads and finally the extremely feared object is handled calmly. Thus, fear for the object is overcomed. There are some rules about number of steps in the ladder, usually 15 steps, should be made. First select 20-25 objects of fear, next put the most feared objects at top step of the ladder, select least feared object and place it at the lowest step, next arrange the feared objects on the basis of degree of fear evoked on the various steps. One important point to be remembered about this ladder is that objects should be similar to the most feared object, e.g. is figure 16.1 the least feared object 'planning a trip' is related, linked to the most feared object flying high on the aircraft. After the objects are placed on the ladder, go through the objects from lowest to the highest step and try to visualize each object and the amount of tension created, if the placing appears wrong then bring the necessary changes.

The two methods most often used for presenting the fear ladder are emotive imagery and pictorial representation. If one is good at visual imagery, one may use emotive imagery, if one needs more concrete stimuli and feel incapable of visualization rightly than the pictorial method will be the best. Of course with the help of autogenic exercises one may learn to visualize.

Desensitization procedure

When one is comfortable and relaxed, he may imagine the first feared object. He may concentrate on the image, make it appear real, stay relaxed, see that his body does not tense up. Holding the image for about 1 minute, if no disturbance is felt, he may stop the image, relax, repeat the imagery of the first step for two more times, then go to the second step and repeat the process for the objects at all the steps. At any point, if fear is experienced, he may discontinue, relax deeply, go back to the object below that step and repeat the procedure and then come to the disturbing object. He may not get worried by these regressions. They are part of the process. Each session usually works uptill four steps. About three weeks one spends in learning desensitization. When the procedure has been learned properly one may try it in the real world. It is suggested that one may go about it slowly.

16.6 STRESS INOCULATION : VACCINE FOR STRESS

Just as vaccines are injected into the body in controlled amounts to develop immunity again severe diseases, similarly stress inoculation is based on the same formula. Problem is psychological stress, while vaccine is exposure to low levels of psychosocial threat in controlled condition. If people are exposed to low levels of psychological threat and then given ideas and skills to deal with them, they develop a resistance to the effects of stress. Later, when exposed to threat they may develop immunity against them. They are not affected by psychological stress.

This procedure has been used successfully in a variety of stress situations like surgery, painful medical tests. People with phobia, test anxiety, depression anger have also been treated.

Stress inoculation involves three distinct phases, education, rehearsal of coping skills and graded exposure stressors combined with practice of coping skills. Educational phase provides some understanding of the nature of the stress response and normal stress reactions. This information must be linked to anticipated stress. In the second phase, specific techniques for dealing with particular situations are provided. Techniques may include relaxation cognitive rehearsal, self instruction, etc. The third phase involves applying the new coping skills to a graded services of imaginary and real stress situations. Epstein emphasized self-pacing and exposure to small dose of threat while developing coping skills in men who were engaged in dangerous activities as such as parachuting, combat flying.

Stress inoculation is a type of broad based desensitization. If one find himself in trouble in some situations he may apply stress inoculation principles to manage them.

In brief this chapter presents autogenic training, deep relaxation, desensitization and stress inoculation to manage stress effectively.

References

Kamiya, J. (1969). operant control of the EEG alpha rhythm and some of it's reported effects on consciousness. In C. T. Tart (Eds.) Altered Stress of consciousness. (pp. 519-529) Garden City, NY Anchor Books.

Schultz, J. & Luthe, W. (1959). Autogenic tra.

Wolpe, J. (1958). Psychotherapy by Reciprocal Inhibition. Stanford, C. A. Stanford University Press.

CHAPTER 17

COMMON MAN DE-STRESSING TECHNIQUES

We are living in a wonderful world. Life is the greatest adventure imaginable. Although, some lives are without much interest and excitement, others are full of extraordinary experiences. It is possible to imagine that under favourable conditions (and if there is no waste of vital essence and there is proper food and right thinking) the human body could go on indefinitely but the pressures on the body are terrific. When a mouse is caught in a trap, its heartbeats starts many time faster than it does normally, and when one is unable to pay the bills, the heart does the same. Thus, worry takes its toll. And there are other kinds of stress. Police Commissioner of Chicago has demonstrated with instruments, the possibility that if noise were taken away from the cities, their residents would live ten years longer.

When the baby is born, he smells and tastes and he breathes. As time goes on the baby struggles for control over his body. Often he thrusts his hands and feet up in the air in an attempt at coordination. When the baby grows into a little child he is surrounded by the influences of the mother's and father's guiding will and the will of other relatives as well. Each one wants him to be something different, and his naughty friends want him to be still something else.

The child has a great many struggles with these conflicting pressures. Think of all the struggles, physiological and mental, one has to go through until he becomes a youth. At that time of life the senses become more active and the youth has a great inner battle with himself. The struggle with the senses is a tremendous contest. To conquer in this adventure of youth, to go victoriously through middle age, old age is a great experience.

It is wonderful to be alive, but there are many agents waiting to kill us. An adventure with wild animals in South Africa is nothing compared to the adventure of life itself. Man with his intelligence knows how to protect himself against animals, but he does not know how to protect himself against his own bad habits and evil ways. The greatest of all enemies of man is himself. More than personal or national enemies, more than germs, bombs or any other threat, a man should fear himself when he is living.

The Subtle Enemies

It is easy to picture starting off to explore some wild and unknown country. If one is going by ship he want a lifeboat with him, as if the steamer sink, he knows that he should get into the boat and save ourselves. But in so many of life's experiences there seems to be a leak in one's life boat, no matter what precaution one take. In a jungle infested with animals one can reasonably take care against them, but subtle dangers are more difficult to overcome. How to protect oneself against a barrage of germs. Millions are floating around us all the time. If one could examine his food under a microscope he will not eat it. He is swallowing the germs alive in food. The water he drink is alive with such organisms.

Prepare for Every Kind of Battle

In order to go safely through this jungle of life one must equip oneself with the proper weapons. One may have to be a well trained soldier. The layman who does not know how to protect himself is soon killed. The wise man who is armed against all forms of warfare–against disease, against destiny, karma, against all evil thoughts and habits–becomes the victor in this adventure. It requires carefulness, and, in addition, the adoption of certain methods by which one can overcome the enemies. As one progress, he learn better methods of vanquishing the causes of physical, mental, moral and spiritual disasters. When one have gone successfully through physical illnesses, accidents, various stressful experiences, inner struggles, then he can say that life was a sweet adventure. The possibilities of charm to the body are numerous.

So be equipped. The scientist says “Eat nourshing food and follow health laws to protect yourself from germs.”

The Importance of Mind Power

In this mess of life, surrounded by enemies–disease, poverty, suffering, bad habits and wrong desires–there are so many rules to be observed that life becomes intolerable when one try to keep them all in mind. One live with them because each department of life is limitless in its potential for diversity. When a person attempts to apply health rules, he becomes overwhelmed–there is no time to think about anything else. Everyone has different set of health, precepts for him to follow. According to Sri Sri Paramahansa Yogananda, mind controls the effectiveness of them all.

God has given one tremendous instrument of protection– more powerful than machine guns, electricity, poison gas or any medicine–the mind. It is the mind that must be strengthened. An important part of the adventure of life is to get hold of the mind and to keep that controlled mind constantly attuned to the Lord, this is the secret of a happy successful existence. One can finish this life adventure only when he conquer its dangers by his will power and mind power. Man is playing at life like a child, but his mind grows stronger through fighting sickness and troubles. Anything that weakens him is his greatest enemy and whatever strengthens his mind is his haven.

Self–Analysis : Key to the Mastery of Life

Million of people are mechanical products of the factory of their environment, preoccupied with breakfast, lunch and dinner, working and sleeping and going here and there to be entertained. People go on as robots, conditioned by their environment. True self–analysis is the greatest art of progress. Everyone should learn to analyse himself. Writing down one's thoughts and aspirations daily, one can find out what he is because he want to make himself what he ought to be. Most people are not able to see their faults hence they don't change.

Thought Produces Everything in the Universe

Mind is the architect of the Microcasm and the macrocasm. As water by cooling and condensation becomes ice, so thought by condensation assumes physical form. The physical and mental aspects of man are closely interrelated, it is commonly observed that a person whose liver is out of order becomes cranky. When a person doesn't feel like smiling and saying "Peace to everyone," this reflects that his thought and emotions are affected by his physical state. A weakening of the organs has a corresponding weakening effect on mental power. Those who eat great deal of meat are often surly and full of vexation. If one takes in grapevine juice diet for a week, he would feel uplifted and harmoniously disposed towards all.

Change of Mental Attitude

We should bear in mind that it is not wise to disregard the body wholly. One should eat proper foods in preference to wrong foods. And if, one must live with people who make him nervous, then once in a while he should change his surroundings. But it is better still, if one can change his mental environment, so that he won't be disturbed by other's actions. Changing oneself and one can then live anywhere in peace and happiness.

Most of the world is like a mental hospital. Some people are sick with jealousy, others with anger, hatred and passion. They are victims of their habits and emotions. But one can make his home a place of peace. All emotions are reflected in the body and mind. Envy and fear cause the face to pale, and love makes it glow. Learn to be calm and one will always be happy.

Whatever type of ego one have, whatever type of personality one have, he should make an effort to analyse his true nature and develop its best qualities. One may develop a moral ego, or a patriotic ego, or an artistic ego or a businessman's ego. If morality is one's ideal, then he should show compassion for others in their ignorant wrong doings. Those with material ego should learn self control, otherwise they will suffer a lot. They have to smoke so many times a day, they must eat certain foods, they always get a headache if they miss their lunch, they can sleep only in a particular kind of bed. It is all right to utilize creature comforts, but never be enslaved by them. If one's ego is a mixture of intellectual and materialistic ego then maintain a balance between them. It is unwise to let the materialistic ego govern one's judgment, conscience and intellect to decide.

The Conditions of Happiness : Plain Living, High Thinking

Plain living and high thinking should be one's goal. Learn to carry all the conditions of happiness within oneself by meditating and attuning consciousness to the ever existing, ever conscious, ever–new joy, which is God. One's happiness should never be subject to any outside influence. Whatever the environment is, it is suggested not allow inner peace to be touched by it. One should analyse oneself, make oneself what he should be, and what he wants to be.

They are the keys to real success and happiness (real de-stressors). One should not keep one's mind engaged in too many activities and waste time. Remember, if each day does not find anybody a better person than he was the day before, he is going backward in health, in mental peace and in soul joy. One oneself made habits and he can only change them. If one is thinking wrong, he should make up his mind to be with good company and to study and meditate. When a person go to a dance or a party his mind is restless, nervous and excited. Afterwards, if he enters a different, calmer atmosphere, he feel more peaceful again. The greatest influence in one's life, stronger even than one's will power is environment. Change it, if necessary. Until a person is mentally strong, he can never be what he want to be without a good environment to help him. Self analysis is also essential to help him better himself. If one can analyse oneself fearlessly, he will be able to stand the critical analysis of others without flinching.

Those who like to dwell on the faults of others are human vultures. There is already too much evil in the world. Becoming like a rose, wafting to all the sweet fragrance of soul goodness. One must make everyone feel that he is a friend, that he is a helper, not a destroyer. If you want to be destressed, analyse yourself and develop the virtues in you. Banishing the thought that evil has any part in one's nature, and it will drop off. Study, meditate and do good to others. Don't lead the aimless life. Meditate and read good books. Happiness will never come if one doesn't concentrate and act on the wisdom of great men. Happiness depends on meditation, on knowing great minds through their thoughts in books, and on surrounding oneself with people who are noble and kind.

Destress by following the Supreme Power 'God'

There are three types of illness, physical, mental and spiritual. Physical illness is due to different forms of toxic conditions, infectious disease and accidents. Mental sickness is caused by fear, wrong and other emotional in-harmonies. Ignorance is the supreme disease. If one banishes ignorance he also banishes the causes of all physical, mental and spiritual disease. Sri Yukteshwarji said 'Wisdom' is the greatest cleanser. Only in the unlimited power of spiritual methods many men find a permanent cure for the disease of body, mind and soul. One should never doubt God, but should constantly affirm his faith in God's omnipresent divine power.

Chemicals and medicines affect only the outer physical composition of the bodily cells and do not alter the inner atomic structure or life principle of the cells. In many cases, no cure of disease is possible until the healing power of God has corrected from within the imbalance of "life......." or intelligent life energy in the body. When the natural harmonious balance of these subtle energies is restored, the healing is perfect and often instantaneous. So, long as balanced vitality is maintained by right living, proper diet and 'pranayama' meditation (life energy control techniques), the body's own life energy "electrocutes" disease before it can develop.

Simple outdoor exercise, such as, walking, balanced diet and moderation in eating and quiet meditation are all conducive to health. These destressing activities can easily be adopted by common man and prevent them from feeling stressed at various occurrence in life.

Obey Nature's Laws

The ordinary individual should be careful to maintain physical well being by right observance of the laws of nature.

One's diet should be wisely chosen. The body requires for health certain amounts of starch, protein and fat but in excess they can be harmful. Very little starch is necessary. Too much starch causes over accumulation of mucus in the body. (A certain amount of mucus is necessary of course, to prevent the entry of harmful microbes into the mucous membranes). Eat abundantly food that contains high proportion of mineral salts, such as, fruits and vegetables to prevent constipation (a physical stressor).

Harmful microbes are ceaselessly attacking the body, good ones are ceaselessly defending it, aided sometimes by diets, herbs, medicines and other health measures. Many health authorities state that iron and vitamin rich foods, such as, eggs, cashew nuts, soya-beans, molasses, dried apricots, dried lima beans, dried peas, parsnips, spinach and parsley may successfully be substituted for liver and other organs of animals to ward off various diseases. They are the safest diet for man. In vegetables and fruits God has infused medicinal power to help in overcoming disease.

Purify the Body of Harmful Toxins

Three fourth of the body consists of water, hence the bodily demand for water is much greater than that for food. One should make it a point to drink plenty of liquids to wash away toxins in the body. It is also important to keep the bloodstream healthy. Beef and pork may release into the blood stream toxic poisons and microbes. Hence, for meat eaters fish, chicken and lamb are preferable to beef and pork, which are highly acid–producing.

The most important principle in connection with eating is to avoid any form of over indulgence. As one learns to restrain himself he becomes healthier. If he refuses to perpetuate his bad habits, he will find that he comes to dislike what is injurious and to like what is beneficial. Many persons thoughtlessly eat late at night, this is unwise as food is not properly digested. If one drinks intoxicating drinks he may be badly influenced by it, and may indulge in violence, greed, lust for money, sex, murder. Man must overcome this habit in order to realize his true nature. It is wisdom to strive to maintain only normal appetite to prevent stresses from entering his life.

Physical stresses can also be prevented by fasting, a natural method of healing. The bodily machinery gets an opportunity to obtain much–needed rest. Most diseases can be cured by judicious fasting. Another method recommended for physical healing is through suitable herbs extracts. Next instead of medicines, healing rays, the rays of sun are better able to heal. Ten minutes sunbath everyday reinforced by good health habits will keep the body supplied with sufficient life energy to destroy all harmful microbes.

Healthy persons possess a natural resistance to stress occurrence. Illness comes when the resisting power of the blood has been diminished by wrong eating or be overeating or overindulgence in sex has depleted the vital energy. By conserving the vital energy followed by a balanced diet and always smiling finds that his body is charged with electric current, life energy which is provided by God. A sincere joyfulness makes man a smile millionaire. A genuine smile distributes the cosmic current, prana, to every cell. The happy man is less subject to disease for happiness actually attracts into the body greater supply of the universal life energy.

There are many aspects about de-stressors but the main idea is that one should depend more on mind power. The rules for guiding against stressors should be self control, exercise, proper eating, drinking plenty of fruit juices, occasional fasting and smiling all the time from within.

Some Instant De–Stressors

Feeling Stressed ? Tense ? Anxious ? Even overwhelmed?

Wondering how to slow down and get control again ?

Don't have time to take a vacation, or even a nap ?

Can't even leave the room right now ?

Here are six steps to De–Stress Instantly !

1. Remember that feeling tense is a physical sensation one can learn to control. Sure, a person have thoughts that are associated with feeling stressed and tense (may be a test is coming ?) –but they are only thoughts. One can learn to feel relaxed even when one have those thoughts.

2. Closing eyes and picture a place which a person like where he feel happy and comfortable and relaxed. A warm beach ... a cool forest ... favorite ski slope ... what works for him.

3. Breathing from abdomen, and not from chest. Breathing slowly and evenly, and focusing on one's breath moving in and out. Yawn deeply to get oxygen into the system.

4. Dropping one's jaw. Then dropping one's shoulders. Gently rolling head from side to side several times. Keep picturing in that place of comfort and relaxation.

5. Standing up and stretching the body. Sitting down and stretching it. If any stretching is just too public, quietly tense-hold-release one's muscles. Doing that 3 times, holding for 10 seconds each time is good.

6. Calmly move through the activity. As one does, he must think about his toes, fingers, and tummy. Make sure they are not flexed and tight, but rather loose and light. It's hard to hold muscle tension when one's toes, fingers and tummy are relaxed.

One Can Do This Anytime, Any Place

Some other instant de-stressors are given below and one can stick to anyone of them.

De–Stressors # 1. Simple Relaxation Breathing (in three breaths.) Take a nice, long, deep breath–through nose–Longer–deeper–Now let it out through pursed lips–slow and easy...And again–take a nice, long, deep breath–through nose–Longer–bigger–deeper–Feel the diaphragm expand as one allow air to fill the lower lungs–Now let it out–slow and easy-through pursued lips– (blow kiss)–long and easy–and once again–another deep, long breath–through nose–Really deep–Now let it out slowly–slowly–through pursued lips.

De–Stressor # 2 : Breathing Helpful Thoughts : Another technique for reducing tension is to observe self breathing slowly and rhythmically. As one take a breath in through nose, think "relaxation"–and as one let the breath out slowly, through mouth, think "tension". So that one is inhaling "relaxation" and exhaling "tension." It is important to use these words as one does this : Breath in through nose, think the word "realization"–breath out through mouth, think the word "tension." One could also think of inhaling "serenity" or "peace" and exhaling "aggravation"–or "upset"–or whatever words and concepts work.

De–Stressor # 3 : The Slanted Lie [Takes 5 to 15 minutes] : Lying on back on a bed or sofa or on a mat on the floor and placing the feet slightly higher than the head. In other words, instead of resting head on a pillow, rest the feet on a pillow–or a cushion–so that feet are farther from the ground than the head. Now close eyes and do SIMPLE RELAXATION BREATHING–three long, deep breaths–slow in through nose–slow out through pursed lips. After the last breath, keep the eyes closed and just focus on the black space before eyes and as one breath out, say the word, "Nah-dahm... " (It doesn't mean anything–it's just a sound to help relax and emptying the brain ...).

Again, breath in slowly, deeply and then breath out–slowly–while one say again, "nahh-dahmm"–while one let every muscle in his body relax–let his head roll–arms rest by his side–legs fall as they may–and do nothing but listen to the sound of "nahdahm."

Lie like this for five to fifteen minutes–no more–and just think about the sound of the word "nahdahm" and nothing else–not the problems–not the crises–not all the aggravations–just "nahh-dahmm..."

De–Stressors # 4 Total Relaxation : FIRST do SIMPLE RELAXATION BREATHING Here's one way to do it. Lie on the bed–straight–on the back preferably without a pillow. So one is in a nice straight line–not rigid–very relaxed–hands resting by the side.

Then, take a good deep breath through the nose–nice and deep–and gently blow the air out the pursued lips–very slowly–long and drawn out–counting backward from ten–and do it again–take a deep long breath through the nose–deeper–feel lower abdomen swell up with oxygen–and slowly let the air out from the pursued lips–and do it one more time–a good deep breath–and let it out slowly through the lips.

Then, still lying on your back in a straight line, one's hand gently at his side, one's going to relax each muscle–one by one–in the body. Start by focusing on the muscles in left foot–first tense up and then release the muscles in left foot–then tense up, hold for a moment and release the muscles in your right foot-then tense up, hold for a moment and release the muscles in the right foot–then focus on legs–tense up the muscles in the left leg–hold for a moment–then relax–and then the right leg–tense–hold–then relax–and work the way up–to thighs–squeeze each muscle, hold it for a moment, then relax it–just let it go–and slowly, gently continue working the way up body–tensing and relaxing every group of muscles–buttocks, stomach, chest, arms, neck–chin, face–till one get to the hair on top of head!. . . .

Then reverse direction and work the way back down to the feet–muscle group by muscle group–tensing and relaxing–all the way down the body. If one do this properly, by the time one get back down to the feet.

Then, with the eyes still gently closed say statements to oneself like :

"Now it's time for me to calm down-

I am calming down now-

I'm feeling more and more calm and relaxed....

I'm getting ready to go to sleep-

I'm feeling more and more sleepy-

I'm feeling very relaxed and very sleepy-

I'm feeling very, very sleepy...."-

And now picture oneself in a most desirable, but very calm setting–nothing too exciting–perhaps a tropical isle–or some place one's in the past that has peace and calm and happy memories–and get a sense of memory of that place–and then start filling in all the details–the setting, the furniture, the cast of characters–and just put oneself there.

Allow oneself to cool-out in that lovely, calm, quiet environment–let the fantasy take you off to a peaceful, pleasurable sleep....

References

http ://www. K. –State. edu/counseling/topics/quick/destressor 'htm.

Sri Sri Paramahansa Yogananda (2003) Man's Eternal Quest. Collected Talks and Essays on realizing God in Daily Lif, vol. I. Yogoda Satsanga Society of India.

Woodford, Joyce (2001) Kansas State University Counseling Services, Manhattan, K. S. Quick Help De–Stressors.

CHAPTER 18

QUICK RELAXATION

Often people hesitate to practice relaxation for fear that they may waste a lot of time every day and may not get results very fast. Sometimes people need relaxation at odd times and when they don't have the right means to practice it like recliner, music, quietness etc., they are unable to do so. Hence, a quick approach to relaxation is being introduced.

First, one learns to relax the whole group of muscles at once, then one learns to obtain quick partial relaxation based on indication revealing where problem lies in a person. It may provide instant relief. Later, one may learn to relax specific group muscle through differential relaxation.

But before starting reduction of relaxation time one must atleast have had two weeks of practice in full term relaxation procedure, must have learnt the steps' instructions properly, so that he is clear about what step will lead to what effect. Then only he will be able to reduce relaxation time without loss.

18.1 EIGHT STEPS INSTEAD OF SIXTEEN STEPS

Table 12. 1 Guide for Reduction Steps in Relaxation Practice.

First Reduction Set	*Second Reduction Set*
1. Both arms	1. Both arms & hands
2. Both hands	2. Shoulder, neck & head
3. Shoulder & neck	
4. All head muscles	
5. Chest and stomach	3. Chest stomach, lower back and buttocks
6. Lower back & buttocks	
7. Both thighs	4. Thighs, feet & calves
8. Both feet and calves	
Additional reminders	
Two sessions per day, same time, same place	
Three repetitions for each muscle group	
10-15 seconds for tension sets	
15-20 seconds for tension sets	
25-35 minutes for first few sessions	

Sessions will be further reduced in length after the first few times.

Reduce tension about 25% after the main criterion has been reached and before going on to the second reduction set. Reduce tension about 25% more at the end of the second reduction set.

Reduce tension about another 25% and practice to criterion. Go on to cue controlled relaxation.

The overall procedure is exactly the same as before, but here one groups muscles together. Setting is the same as before, mood factors observed are similar, one's mental attitude is as before, so that one knows where one is going.

Eight steps are—

1. Relax both arms together.
2. Relax both hands together.
3. Both the shoulder and neck muscles should be relaxed.
4. The forehead, scalp, jaw and mouth should be relaxed together.
5. The chest and stomach muscles are relaxed together.
6. The lower back and buttocks are relaxed.
7. Both thighs are relaxed simultaneously.
8. Both calves and feet are relaxed together.

The 16 steps procedure has been cut in half to 8 steps.

Now one should be informed about instructional changes. For this the instructions for long term relaxation must have become a habit for him. If one is dependent on tape or a friend for instructions one must prepare an alternate tape, or a new list of instructions. The instructions for the first tension relaxation cycle are as follows.

(1) Take a few deep breaths, hold each breath for a few seconds, and then let each breath out fully and completely. When tension in breathing will be felt

in chest and diaphragm, then when breathing out one will sense relaxation. Try at least two times.

(2) Concentrate on both arms. Flex the biceps on both arms as though showing off the muscles. Flex them as highly as one can, sense the tension then let it go all at once and feel relaxed. Practice atleast twice.

The difference in instructions is that one is made to relax the muscle groups in pairs rather than singly.

(3) Concentrate on arms, by tensing them and then relaxing them together. One will feel relaxed.

(4) Concentrate on both shoulders and neck muscles in the same way as specified earlier.

(5) Concentrate on the forehead, scalp, jaw and both muscles together. Instructions are similar as given earlier.

(6) Relax the chest and stomach.

(7) Relax the lower back and buttocks.

(8) Relax the thighs together.

(9) Relax the calves and feet simultaneously using the instruction given earlier.

During the first few sessions the person may experience difficulty, he may need a few sessions until he feels tension and relaxation in both the muscle groups being relaxed, in the same way as he felt when relaxing them individually.

The whole relaxation process may require at least 5 days to grasp, but if people are able to make rapid progress, then they may require 3 days. One get a satisfying relaxation then only one may feel successful.

Once a person starts getting as much relaxation from the grouping of muscles, as when relaxing them individually, another step is required before moving to the second reduction phase, *i.e.*, try to reduce the intensity of the tension phase of the tension relaxation cycle, *i.e.*, if one have to tense biceps, one may not tighten them intensly but moderately, or when one tense his forehead muscle, tense it a little bit less than before *i.e.*, lower the amount of tension without reducing the amount of time devoted to the tension cycle itself. This process helps to sense the difference between light stress and severe stress. By reducing the tension in the muscles one will learn the skill one need to get maximum benefit for relaxation. Another reason is, that one wants to hurry the process of relaxation, hence under moderate or light tension one shift to relaxation process, gradually one will learn to go directly into relaxation as soon as one feel a bit of tension, hence one will save a lot of his time.

18.2 QUICKER RELAXATION PROCEDURE

The procedure is as used before, only instead of relaxing single or a pair of muscles, one have to relax all the muscles simultaneously. If a person has problem in relaxing any particular group of muscles, then he should relax that muscle group as before. The general idea is to make one flexible. Allowing the freedom to read one's own body and adjusting the grouping as one feel is right. The process will require another five or seven days for this reduction phase. Aim is to economise on the relaxation steps, hence additional efforts will be required. After learning this quicker tension relaxation procedure, one should learn to reduce the voluntarily produced level of tension (50%) even further, *i.e.*, from moderate level feeling it should reduce to 75% feeling of tension. This will enable to relax as quickly and as deeply with the 4 steps procedure, as one did with either the 16 or 8 step procedure.

The four steps procedure involved—

(1) Reduce from 16 muscles to 8 muscle groups over a five to seven days period when one reach the criterion, when one is able to relax as quickly and as deeply as before, move to the next step.

(2) Reduce the amount of artificially induced muscle tension. Reduction should go down at almost 75%.

(3) Reduce from 8 muscles group to 4 muscles group over five to seven days, until one start relaxing as before.

(4) Reduce the amount of artificially induced muscle tension further, and get the same level of relaxation.

Now, the stage has come when one instruct one self, the tension only goes upto 25%. This procedure takes about 3-5 days to get right, than when relaxing one should get quick and deep relief, *i.e.*, a stage may arrive when one get deep relaxation in 5-15 minutes.

Relaxation : A Rescue

There are many real life events in the life of people when they are very tensed up and they need relaxation. Some examples are given.

Event 1 : Ram had to appear for a job interview. He wanted this job desperately. Hence a night before the interview he was very nervous, and was not able to sleep, hence in desperation he tried praying to God and next he tried relaxation, and it was through relaxation that his body could relax and he got some sleep. Thus, he was able to appear in front of the interview board bravely.

Event 2 : Seema had learnt car driving. Next day was a driving test so that she could get the license, she was very nervous, because she had heard that the testers made the candidates drive in complex ways like driving and forming 8 sign while driving forward and backward. Seema's body was shaking in anticipation of what may occur in the driving test hence in order to cool down she practiced deep relaxation for half an hour before going out for the driving test, she felt quite normal while giving the driving test and succeeded in doing so successfully, she got the driving license.

Event 3 : Mr. Ramesh was facing a crisis situation in business. His last hope was getting the one crore deal finalized with a Japanese Firm. The fear of unsuccess made him very nervous, he could not eat or drink properly nor could he think of sleep. He was very restless. His neighbour came, when he saw his bad condition he prescribed deep relaxation for reducing his nervousness. Mr. Ramesh did as told by his neighbour, and he was able to get some sleep. Next day, in the morning hour before his significant meeting he did the quick relaxation procedure and this helped him in meeting the Japanese delegate with a cool, relaxed mind.

Such taxing events occur in lives of most of us, and if we practice these relaxation procedures in a regular way then we may always remain calm and quiet, and will be able to cope with all types of problematic situations.

These quick relaxation procedures may act as boon.

18.3 CUE BASED RELAXATION

Cues help in producing responses automatically. If a child is used to his mother saying yes or no for various activities, he gets used to getting these cues every times he does something, he starts waiting and depending on these cues for what ever he does. In the same way when we practice relaxation techniques we come back from tensed state to relaxed state and at that point we say 'relax', and then only feel relaxed, this is termed as cue controlled relaxation. The secret of this technique is that repeated connection between a cue and a response makes it possible for the cue to produce the response more or less automatically. For example, for a child no from a mother means that there is danger in what he was wanting to do, so every time he approaches a dangerous things he get's no warning from the parent, and later it becomes internalized. Thus, he will develop a personal control after such dangerous incidents.

Instead of relax word one can use some other word, which may alert him, but the word he chooses should only be used every time he practices relaxation.

Procedure for Cue Controlled Relaxation

This procedure is somewhat easier than the other steps taken to learn relaxation. To begin this phase, it will be assumed that you :—

1. are still relaxing twice daily.

2. have reduced the number of steps for getting relaxed.

3. are able to relax in about 5-15 minutes

The instructions that you follow are—

Breathe in deeply,

Hold the breath for about 10 seconds,

Breathe out completely as you are saying your personal cue word.

As you use the cue word let your entire body go limp.

Go immediately into deep relaxation you will be helped if you see the mental image of your body going limp

Evaluate your feeling of relaxation

Do this procedure alteast 15-20 times. If in these sessions you experience about 50-75% relaxation than this means you have succeeded. If you are not able to relax to that level, then wait for the next relaxation period to try the deep breathing-cue-word-relaxation cycle again by itself. Repeat the learnt cue word relaxation cycle for about one week. One should enjoy the relaxation state. One point to be noted in this technique is that if you achieve 50% relaxation then also you should feel a sense of success.

The decrease in tension produced by cue controlled relaxation should help prevent defensive posturing and garbled communication. It enables one to be at his best, to thinks more clearly, see alternative interpretations for the words and behaviors of the conflicting party and helps in finding solutions to problems. Complete relaxation is not constructive in interpersonal conflict. Hyper arousal is replaced through cue-controlled relaxation by moderate arousal.

Table 12. 2. Work Sheet for Home and Work Stressors

	Home	*Work*
HIGH TENSION		
LOW TENSION		

Cue Controlled Relaxation Procedure

In order to use the cue controlled relaxation, it is advisable to categorize the incidents of stress in diary on two dimensions, Homes and Work (Table 18.2). Using a paper, divide it into right and left halves, label the top protion as home for the left half and Work for the right half (if in job). Next label on the upper side high tension and for bottom half low tension. The Home and Work classification is clear and simple. The classification for level of stain, tension should be made on the basis of muscle tension, if tension is intense, label it high tension, if tension is not so intense then label it low tension. For example, select a low intensity tension from Home category, something light but occurring very often. When such tension occurs (sudden arrival of guests or sudden occurrence of test) prompt oneself to try cue-controlled relaxation. Take a deep breath, hold it for a moment, and let it go completely while one say a personal cue word. Do it quietly, one will feel a decrease in overall level of arousal. One warning is to first try low intensity tension situations, only when one succeed in them then only try on major problems.

Differential Relaxation

In variety of situations a person feels physical fatigue or is tensed up due to stress than he may practice differential relaxation. It involves finding out the muscle group under strain and then applying the relaxation techniques on that muscle only.

Mental scanning involves scanning all the body channels until one detect the tensed muscle group, then one should focus on that muscle group. This mental scanning technique is built on all the steps one have learnt about muscular relaxation, like attending to all parts of the body for practicing relaxation, making note about home and work stress situations, tensions warn about where and when stress occurs then one may practice cue based relaxation when required.

Suppose at work one diagnose a pain in back, which was there but one had ignored it till now when it has started interfering with one's work, this situation demands differential relaxation on the back muscle group. Now, one have to practice relaxation on this muscle group. For this, tense the muscle by itself and then relax. Make sure one is working on that muscle group only. When one is able to get fairly deep relaxation in that muscle, work on graduated levels of relaxation. Even if one get 50% level of relaxation then he is doing well.

Two other techniques have be given. One is to attach a cue word to the relaxation of the particular muscle group.

Second technique involves forming a visual image, like taking a bath, with warm shower falling on that particular muscles group, or imaging a massage on that muscle group. This is like autogenic.

Whatever techniques one uses the following rules should be followed.

1. Develop the mental scanning skill first.
2. Practice regulating depth.
3. Attach cue word for better control.
4. Practice first in neutral environment like home before practicing at other places.
5. Ensure that the application is situationally appropriate.

This chapter emphasis to help people understand deep relaxation in quicker time, using of cue words for controlling relaxation process and has also delved into differential muscular relaxation.

CHAPTER 19

CONCLUDING STRESS

Becker (1973) said that of all things that move man and one of the principle movers is his terror of death. According to him, threat of death haunts human mind like nothing else. It plays an important role in human activity. Human beings design their activites in such a way that they may avoid the fatality of death.

In interviews which Kubler-Ross (1969) conducted, it was found that persons who were old or severely ill often talked about living long enough to experience or see a particular event, like weddings, anniversaries etc. People feel threatened by death when it denies them the opportunity to achieve certain goals. Another source of death anxiety is the thought of psychological and economic impact of their death on dependent survivors. Choron (1964) has delineated three components of the fear of death, the fear of dying, the fear of what happens after death, and the fear of ceasing to be. These dimensions are clearly observed when a distinction is made between situations where death is a real threat in opposition to those where death is given an abstract quality. The fear of dying and ceasing involves factors like fear of pain, suffering, helplessness, dependency and loss of one's love for others at the other end. There is a feeling of sadness, the emotional suffering associated with death. The fear of unknown including the fear of punishment served as yet another source of death anxiety.

When a person's fundamental understandings are thrown into question, he is said to experience threat. Although the person is threatened to some extent by any event which poses a serious challenge to the adequacy of his construct systems, death is perhaps the paradigmatic threatening phenomenon (Kelly 1959). According to Krieger (1975) death threat occurs in those conditions in which an individual has explicitly or implicitly organized his world in such a way that it assures his immortality, or conversely, in such a way that it excludes death as a real personal eventuality.

Lazarus' Cognitive Theory of Stress

Lazarus's (1981) approach to stress coping is explicitly cognitive phenomenalism. Whereas in 1950, coping was viewed generally as a product of emotions, and an emotion viewed as a drive. He and his colleagues argued that emotions and stress are produced by cognitions *i.e.*, the way in which a person appraises or construes his or her relationship with the environment. It is only recently that emotion and motivation have been seen as clearly shaped by the way a person construes ongoing relationship with the environment, in effect by cognitive processes. The term which Lazarus uses to express this idea is "Cognitive Appraisal" which includes primary and secondary appraisal.

Primary Appraisal : Such appraisals are formed in terms of either positive transactions or stressful transactions. The stressful appraisal are further classified into three sub types : (a) Harm Loss (b) Threat (c) Challenge

Harm Loss refers to injury or damage which has already occurred as in bereavement, loss of physical function, social esteem, etc.

Threat refers to similar kinds of injuries or losses, only the term emphasizes that they have not yet occurred but are anticipated. Challenge means opportunity for growth, gain, etc.

A set of complex cognitive appraisal processes which are devoted to coping process are called secondary appraisal. As most highly stressful transactions include numerous specific encounters spread out over time, as in grieving, or bolstering damaged or threatened self, the person needs information about personal and social resources that can be drawn upon.

Determiners of Appraisal of Threat

Lazarus (1966) mentioned three groups of factors in the individual personality that provides the capacity and dispositional basis for interpreting the significance of stimulus cues when threat is encountered.

(1) Motivational characteristics of the individual.

(2) Intellectual resources, sophistication, education.

(3) Belief systems concerning transactions with environment.

Motive Strength and Pattern

Threat increases as the number of threatened motives increases. Death can mean for some, the end of all goals. Therefore, for many, death will pose a severe threat. But the degree of perceived threat in death related stimuli will depend on the way it is construed. Shniedman (1963) suggested that the motive to avoid death vary from individual, to individual. Some may regard it as the end of all experiences, while others may regard it as an entrance into a new kind of existence. According to Feifel (1959), death is a multifaceted symbol. To many death acts as a media for reaching trancedental truth which cannot be understood in life. For others death may acts as a friend who puts an end to pain by granting peaceful sleep.

Intellectual Resources, Education and Sophistication

There is some evidence that low intelligence make individuals more vulnerable to threat. Cantril (1947), analysed the panic which followed the Orsan Welles radio dramatization of an invasion from Mars in 1938. People who fled from the scene because of dramatization were of low educational level. Johnson (1945), made a similar inference in his study of historical outburst in Mattoon, Illinois. It seems that dull or uninformed individual perceives himself to be vulnerable to danger, as he lacks in capacity to interpret the cues adequately.

General Belief Systems about Transaction with the Environment

Lazarus (1966), has defined general beliefs as "a total outlook that has no connection with the specific stimuli configuration except through a broad generalization". It serves as a cognitive context within which specific events are evaluated. A mans belief in compose his understanding of himself and his environment. Beliefs have been classified into three types : First are the zero order beliefs, which are one's most fundamental primitive beliefs, which are taken for granted. Next are the first order beliefs which are based upon direct sensory experiences. Last are the primitive beliefs based on external authority such as belief in intangible like God, such beliefs are passed down from generation to generation. Existential belief systems such as faith in God, or some higher natural order helps individuals to make life a meaningful experience, inspite of suffering and unhappy experience (Folkman, Shaffers, and Lazarus 1979), such systems also help individuals to explain inexplicable events such as a traumatic accident, death of loved one's, one's own imminent death, and destructive evil, such as Nazi concentration Camp.

The work done by Shneidman (1963) on death and suicide clearly pointed out the importance of beliefs regarding death in determining threat appraisal. He held that death, a form of termination is the ubiquitous ending of all living things, but man, being able to report verbally introspective mental life, can conceptualize fear and suffer ceasation.

Sinha (1986), studied the role of cosmological beliefs in influencing threat of death. Subjects included students as well as householders with settled and unsettled families. Analysis based on both zero order correlation and multiple regression revealed that students showed more positive relation between their beliefs and perceived threat in death related stimuli as compared to householders. Among householders only those residing in low exposure areas revealed significant relationship between beliefs and perceived threat. All the relationships, contrary to the hypothesis were positive. Results revealed that data lent support to the Freudian view of the role of religious beliefs in anxiety control.

Meeting Death : Facing the End of Life

Given that death is the inevitable end of life, how do persons confronted with their impending death react ?

The most famous study on this subject was conducted in the late 1960s by Elizabeth Kubler-Ross (1969). She studied terminally ill cancer patients, and on the basis of extensive interviews with them concluded that they pass through five distinct stages.

(1) **Denial** : In this phase patients refuse to believe that the end is in sight 'No, it can't be true' they seem to say.

(2) **Anger** : Why me, dying person feels that it is not fair.

(3) **Bargaining** : They offer prayers good behavior or other changes in life styles in exchange of postponement of death.

(4) **Depression** : But because postponement of death is not possible because of medical reasons, they pass to the next stage of depression.

(5) **Acceptance** : Many people ultimately move into a final stage of acceptance. At this stage dying persons are no longer angry or depressed. Instead, they seem to accept their impending death with dignity, they concentrate on saying good-bye to

important persons in their lives and putting their affairs in good order.

These findings have not been confirmed by other researchers. Aronoff and Spilka (1985) video taped terminally ill patients at various points during their illness and examined their facial expressions. They found an increase in sad expression over time. They did not become calmer or happier as their deaths approached. Mertzger (1980) observed expression of hope through-out terminal illness. None of these views can be viewed as scientifically valid unless they are further confirmed by further researches.

Bereavement

Coming to terms with the death of loved ones :

Bereavement means grieving for the loss of persons who are dear. It is an experience most people have. Research by Norris and Murrell (1990) suggest that bereavement is a process in which individuals move through a series of discrete stages. The first is shock–a feeling of numbness and unreality. This is followed by stages of protest and yearning, in which bereaved persons resent the loss of their loved one and fantasize about this person's return. These reactions are often followed by deep despair, which can last a year or more, a period when bereaved persons feel that life is not worth living. Finally, bereaved person usually enter a state of detachment and recovery, in which they gradually separate themselves psychologically from the loved person who has died (Hart *et al*, 1995) and go on with their lives. Even during these stages however, painful bouts of grieving may recur on birthdays. anniversaries, and other occasions that remind the bereaved person of his or her loss. Bereavement is especially strong in cases of unexpected deaths, which make it a high grief experience for all. When death is expected, grief may be less pronounced. One type of death seems to leave especially deep and long lasting scars, the death of a child. Parents who go through it may never recover from it entirely. They continue experiencing shadow of grief for their entire lives (Knapp 1987). Fortunately, a large majority of grieving persons do ultimately recover from the pain of their loss and go on to resume their lives. Life goes on–as it must.

References

Becker, E. (1973). The Denial of Death, Free Press, New York.

Cantril, H. (1947) With the Assistance of H. Gandent and Herzog. The invasions from the Mars, Prineton, University Press.

Choron, J. (1964). Modern Man and Mortality : New York.

Feifel, H. (1959). Attitudes Towards Death in Some Normal and Mentally Ill Populations. In H. Fiefel (eds.) The Meaning of Death. New York. Basic Books. Inc. Publishers, pp. 114-130.

Folkman, S., Shaffer, C., Lazarus, R. S. (1979) Cognitive Processes as Mediators of Stress and Coping. In V. Hamilton & D. M. Waiburton (Eds.) Human Stress and Cognition. An Information-Processing Approach.

Hart, D., Stinson, C., Field, N., Evert, M. & Horowitz, M. (1995). A Semantic Space Approach to Representations of Self Others in Pathological Grief : A Case Study. Psychological Science, 6, 96-100.

Johnson, D. M. (1945). The Phantom Anesthetist of Mattoon : Field Study of Mass Hysteria. Journal of Abnormal and Social Psychology, 40, 175-186.

Kashyap, A. (1986). A study of Certain Determiners of Perception of Threat. Doctoral Thesis, Dept. of Psychology, University of Allahabad.

Kelly, G. A. (1959) The Psychology of Personal Constructs. New York : W. W. Norton & Company, Inc. 2 vols.

Knapp, R., (1987) When a Child Dies. Psychology today, 60-67.

Kubler-Ross, E. (1969). On Death and Dying. Tavistock, London.

Lazarus, R. S. (1981). The Stress and Coping Paradigm In C. Eisdorfer, D. Cohen, A. Klienman & P. Maxin (Eds). Conceptual Models for Psychopathology, New York, Spectrum.

Norris, F. H. & Murrel, S. A. (1990) Social Support, Life Events, and Stress as Modifiers of Adjustment to Bereavement by Adults : Psychology and Aging, 5, 429-436.

Shniedman, E. S. (1963). Orientations Towards Death, A Vital Aspect of the Study of Lives In R. W. White (Eds.) The Study of Lives. Atherson Press, 201-227.